All the King's Ladies

ACTRESSES OF THE RESTORATION

By

John Harold Wilson

THE UNIVERSITY OF CHICAGO PRESS

Library of Congress Catalog Number: 58-11962

THE UNIVERSITY OF CHICAGO PRESS, CHICAGO 37
Cambridge University Press, London, N.W. 1, England
The University of Toronto Press, Toronto 5, Canada

Midway Reprint   1974

For JAMES FITZ-JAMES FULLINGTON

Preface

Soon after the Restoration of King Charles II, two enterprising courtiers, Thomas Killigrew and Sir William Davenant, acquired patents to organize acting companies and produce plays. At first, hungry for theatrical entertainment after eighteen years of famine, the aristocratic Restoration coterie supported the new enterprises with enthusiasm. Fine theatres were built, embodying the latest developments in scenes and machines brought over from France. A new generation of playwrights, amateur and professional, provided the theatres with plays to augment their stock supply of old dramas. Plays were presented by skilled actors, some of them trained in the old acting traditions before the closing of the theatres in 1642. New actors were developed, and women replaced boys in female roles. The theatres became fashionable; all the signs pointed to a long period of prosperity, a new golden age of the theatre.

There is no need to do more here than summarize the often told subsequent history of the Restoration stage: how the audiences gradually diminished until there were not enough playgoers to support two theatres; how the King's Company succumbed to waste and mismanagement and in 1682 was swallowed up by the Duke's Company; how in 1695 Thomas Betterton and a group of dissidents seceded from the United Company to form a new company; and how the rivalry between two companies struggling to survive led to quarrels, reprisals, and amalgamation again in the theatrically turbulent early years of the eighteenth century. All these matters have been discussed in detail in a number of excellent studies. The history of the drama, too, has been well and fully written, and the works of numerous playwrights have been reprinted, edited, and criticized. Elaborate studies of stagecraft, stage business, curtains, disguises, songs, scenes, and machines have thrown light into every dusty corner of the Restoration theatre, and the male actors have received a good deal of attention from compilers and biographers.

For some reason the women of the stage, whose appearance for the first time in English theatrical history strongly affected the development of Restoration drama, have been neglected or have been dealt with only cursorily in other connections. It is the purpose of this study to gather all available information about the actresses who began their stage careers between 1660 and 1689, to consider what kind of women they were, the conditions under which they lived and worked, their behavior on stage and off, and, finally, the effect they had on late seventeenth-century drama.

I am indebted to the John Simon Guggenheim Memorial Foundation for the funds which enabled me to do the research for this book. For constant help and encouragement I am grateful to Richard D. Altick, William Charvat, Claude M. Simpson, Jr., and, as always, Louise Walker Wilson.

J. H. W.

Table of Contents

I. *Enter the Actress*

At noon on January 3, 1661, Mr. Samuel Pepys dined on a
leg of roast pork at Will's Tavern, near the Exchequer in
Old Palace Yard. Afterward he set out for the new theatre
in Vere Street, near Lincoln's Inn Fields. There was no
hurry; the play would not begin until half-past three, and
it was a fair day, hardly wintry at all. The sun shone, the
ways were dusty, and even the rose bushes still held their
autumn leaves. Mr. Pepys sauntered up King Street to Char-
ing Cross, eastward along the Strand, and thence up through
a maze of narrow streets toward Lincoln's Inn Fields. He
quickened his pace in Clare Market, turned into a passage-
way, and pulled up before the playhouse, a large, barnlike
structure with a steeply pitched roof and a row of windows
high in the wall. At the door he paid a half-crown admission
fee and entered. The shadowy theatre was already half-filled
with men, with a few ladies in the side boxes and here and
there in the pit a gaily dressed trollop flaunting a vizard, the
sign of her trade.

Although to Mr. Pepys's wondering eyes it was "the finest
playhouse that ever was in England," it was only Gibbon's
old tennis court hastily turned into a theatre by Tom Killigrew, Master of the King's Company of Comedians, who had

recently brought his troupe thither from the old Red Bull, an open air theatre in St. Johns Street, Clerkenwell. Here for three long years the players were to work in cramped, inadequate quarters while Killigrew was building a fine new theatre in Bridges Street, near Drury Lane.[1]

Gibbon's tennis court—the first Theatre Royal—had a level pit with rows of backless benches, galleries running around three sides, and a platform stage hung with rusty tapestries. There were no scenes and very few machines. The wooden seats were far from friendly. The light, especially on a dark day, was poor, even with the help of candles in sconces about the walls and in chandeliers over the stage; and, of course, there was no heat. The spectators sat with their cloaks wrapped tightly about them until the animal warmth of the noisy, restless audience tempered the chill a trifle. At the same time the animal effluvia, overlaid with the odors of musky foreign perfumes (handy substitutes for soap and water), produced an atmosphere thick enough to shovel. There were no toilet facilities, no bars, and no refreshments except the China oranges and seasonal fruits sold by the orange girls, who stood in the pit with their backs to the stage and cried their wares between the acts. To Mr. Pepys all this was splendor. He settled down on a bench and prepared to enjoy his half-holiday.

There was music, a prologue, and the play began—Fletcher's sunny, romantic comedy, *The Beggars Bush*. Pepys lost himself in the action, savoring the play to the fullest. From earlier visits to the theatre he had become acquainted with the names and abilities of a few of the leading actors in the King's Company: Nicholas Burt, excellent as Othello; Major Michael Mohun, "said to be the best actor in the world"; and Edward Kynaston, "a boy" who acted women's parts and made a very lovely lady. When a woman shortly appeared on the stage, Pepys had to look twice to make sure it was not Kynaston in disguise. But there was no doubt about it; it was truly a woman, a lusty young wench, very handsome in flowing gown and laced petticoats, with her

[1] Pepys, November 20, 1660, January 3, 22, 1661, July 2, 1661; Hotson, chaps. i, v, vi. (Full citations are given in "References," pp. 195–96.)

bosom and shoulders gleaming in the candlelight. One by one three more women appeared. The roles they played were small, and they were far from being polished performers, but they were women and their physical allure was undeniable. That night Pepys wrote in his diary that January 3, 1661, was "the first time that ever I saw women come upon the stage."[2]

This was Mr. Pepys's first glimpse into a brave new world. As a lover of beauty, and especially of beautiful women, he found thenceforth a double joy in playgoing. Except in his periods of self-discipline, when he bound himself by strict oaths to attend to his business and avoid all forms of pleasure, he was lured to the theatres by an almost compulsive ardor, delighting in music and spectacle, costume and dance —and the opportunity to rub elbows with the great. Everything about the theatre interested him, especially the tiring rooms. In time he came to know some of the players intimately, and one pretty actress, Mary Knep, became, if not his mistress, at least his *bonne amie*, refusing him only the ultimate favor.

But January 3, 1661, was not the date of women's first appearance on the stage. Pepys had been too busy with his duties as Clerk of the Acts of the Navy to attend the theatre regularly; he was more than a little behind the times. We can be sure that women had been appearing sporadically at either the Theatre Royal or the Duke's Theatre in Salisbury Court for at least a month, and probably much longer. On December 15, 1660, a courtier, Andrew Newport, had written to a friend in the country, "Upon our stages we have women actors, as beyond seas."[3] His phrasing suggests that while the situation was new, it was not immediately so, and that women had been on the boards for some time.

Now there were theatres in operation as early as June, 1660 —almost immediately after the return of King Charles II— and during that summer there were probably three independent companies acting in London. Rhodes's "young" actors were playing at the Cockpit in Drury Lane; Mohun's "old"

[2] Pepys, August 18, October 11, November 20, 1660, January 3, 1661.
[3] *HMC, Fifth Report,* p. 158.

actors at the Red Bull in St. Johns Street; and perhaps a mis-
cellaneous troupe at Beeston's Salisbury Court Theatre. In
this period of theatrical anarchy, Thomas Killigrew and Sir
William Davenant, backed by the King's warrant for a
monopoly, fought to gain control over all the players in London. There was a brief period in October when the two courtiers managed jointly a single company, made up of the best
players from all the troupes. Then, early in November, two
permanent companies were formed: the King's (the "old"
actors who had played before the Civil War) under Killigrew and the Duke's (the "young" actors) under Davenant.

In the months from June to December, 1660, any one of
these shifting groups could have been the first to employ
women. The King's warrant to Davenant and Killigrew
(dated August 21, 1660) ordered that thenceforth only wom-
en should play women's parts, to the end that plays might
be "esteemed not only harmless delights but useful and in-
structive representations of human life."[4]

These were brave words indeed. The employment of actresses was an innovation long overdue; the time was ripe;
and there was the King's order. It would seem that women
should have almost immediately blossomed forth upon the
stage. But the problem was not so simple. The women had
to be found, introduced to theatrical ways and customs, and
given at least some slight training. Moreover, as with all
theatrical novelties, there was the question of audience re-
sponse. The managers moved with caution.

Probably we shall never know for certain the name of that
bold adventuress, the first English actress. We cannot even
be certain which company did the pioneering. In a "Prologue
to the Tempest" (ca. 1674), the Duke's Company, sneering
at their rivals, the King's Company, took the credit for all
stage improvements, including the introduction of actresses,

> Without the good old Playes we did advance,
> And all ye Stages ornament enhance:
> To splendid things they follow us, but late:
> They ne're invent, but they can imitate:
> Had we not, for yr pleasure found new wayes,

[4] Hotson, pp. 197–218; Nicoll, pp. 70–71.

We still had rusty Arras had, & thredbare playes;
Nor scenes, nor weomen, had they had their will,
But some, with grizl'd Beards, had acted Weomen still.[5]

But this is a prejudiced claim, a wild shot in the never-ending war of the theatres. In fact, when we consider that the Duke's Company of young actors started out with half a dozen youthful female impersonators, including Angel, Mosely, Floid, James Nokes, William Betterton, and Edward Kynaston (who later transferred to the opposition company), while the old actors of the King's Company had no young impersonators at all and therefore badly needed women, the claim sounds like impudent effrontery.[6]

The chances are that the King's Company made the first experiment. In Thomas Jordan's *A Royal Arbour of Loyal Poesie* (1664) appears "A Prologue, to introduce the first Woman that came to act on the Stage, in the tragedy called The Moor of Venice." Jordan was closely associated with the Red Bull company of "old" actors, and it is very likely that he wrote the prologue for that troupe after it became the King's Company in the autumn of 1660.[7] The prologue begins,

> I come, unknown to any of the rest
> To tell you news, I saw the lady drest;
> The woman playes today, mistake me not,
> No man in gown, or page in petticoat;
> A woman to my knowledge; yet I cann't,
> (If I should dye) make affidavit on't.
> Do you not twitter, gentlemen? I know
> You will be censuring, do't fairly though;
> 'Tis possible a vertuous woman may
> Abhor all sorts of looseness, and yet play;
> Play on the stage, where all eyes are upon her,
> Shall we count that a crime France counts an honour?

[5] British Museum, Egerton MS. 2623, p. 54.

[6] Downes, p. 18.

[7] See Jordan's references to the Red Bull, pp. 18 and 22. Herbert lists *Othello* among the "Red Bull Plays" and mentions a performance of the play by the King's Company (ex-Red Bull players) on "Saterday the 8. Dec.," 1660 (*Dramatic Records of Sir Henry Herbert*, ed. J. Q. Adams [1917], pp. 82, 117).

After this appeal to gallantry, Jordan offered a very practical reason why "the woman" should be received with favor: the boys who had been trained as female impersonators had all grown up, and the company, in sheer desperation, had been forced to "civilize the stage,"

> Our women are defective, and so siz'd,
> You'd think they were some of the guard disguis'd;
> For to speak truth, men act that are between
> Forty and Fifty, wenches of fifteen;
> With bone so large and nerve so incompliant,
> When you call *Desdemona*, enter *Giant*.

Mr. Jordan was quite properly apologetic and anxious. There was always the chance that the audience—particularly the ladies, steeped in conventional morality—might be shocked. In the epilogue to the play Jordan addressed himself earnestly to the feminine members of the audience:

> But Ladies what think you, for if you tax
> Her freedom with dishonour to your Sex,
> She means to act no more, and this shall be
> No other Play but her own tragedy;
> She will submit to none but your Commands,
> And take Commission onely from your hands.

We can only hope that the chief character in this noble experiment was received with courtesy and approval. She should have been. Many of the twittering gentry in the pit had seen plays in France with women in their proper roles. A few of the older men could remember, before the bitter Civil War, French troupes acting in London with women players. Some had seen private theatricals at Court, with titled ladies acting, much to the wrath of that old Puritan, William Prynne. Some had only recently seen Mrs. Coleman as Ianthe in Davenant's "opera," *The Siege of Rhodes* (1656) —no actress, but a forerunner singing in the wilderness. Certainly the male playgoers were ready enough for the change, and no doubt they welcomed it with delight.

The probability is, then, that the first English actress played Desdemona in *Othello* for the King's Company in November or December, 1660. Who was she? Anne Marshall,

Mary Saunderson, Margaret Hughes, and Mrs. Norton have all been nominated for the honor, and the first two are distinct possibilities.[8] But we have one actress who claimed to be the first, and her pretense deserves consideration.

On March 11, 1689, in a "humble petition" to the Lord Chamberlain, Mrs. Katherine Corey said of herself that "she was the first and is the last of all the actresses that were constituted by King Charles the Second at His Restauration." She said further that she had served the Killigrew family (Thomas and his successor, Charles) faithfully for twenty-seven years. This, of course, is probably an approximate figure, but if she counted the years carefully and made allowance for the theatrical interruption caused by the Plague and Fire (June 5, 1665, to November 29, 1666) she must have started serving the Killigrews about November, 1660, shortly after Thomas Killigrew got control of the original Red Bull Company.[9]

At first thought one is tempted to reject Mrs. Corey as a most unlikely Desdemona. She was best known as a comedienne; Pepys, who called her "Doll Common" because of her excellence in Jonson's *The Alchemist*, rejoiced in her performances. In her maturity she was a large woman ("robust" and a "strapper"[10]) and most successful in secondary roles: governesses, nurses, mothers, maidservants, and bawds. Yet she was versatile enough to play equally well in comedy and tragedy, and during her thirty-two years on the stage she was often assigned to major roles, among them Octavia in Dryden's *All for Love*. Probably as a young girl she was slender enough and attractive with the charm of youth. At any rate, here is a lady who claims to be the first actress, and if we cannot dispute her claim we may gallantly accept it.

Of course Mrs. Corey may merely have meant that she was

---

[8] Malone, Part II, p. 110; Downes, pp. 93–95. The argument that Margaret Hughes was the the first actress is disproved by the facts of her career. See J. H. Wilson, "Pepys and Peg Hughes," *Notes and Queries*, N.S. III (October, 1956), 428–29.

[9] A. S. Borgman, "The Killigrews and Mrs. Corey," *Times Literary Supplement*, December 27, 1934.

[10] Wycherley, *The Country Wife*, Act III, scene 2.

the first of a group of women sworn in as His Majesty's servants. In that case her priority over her fellows was only a matter of minutes, and any one of the group could still be the proto-actress. We can never be certain of the names of all the other early actresses at the two theatres, but we can be sure of a few. In 1708 John Downes, prompter at the Duke's Theatre from June, 1662, to October, 1706, published his *Roscius Anglicanus; or, An Historical Review of the Stage.* He himself was responsible for the account of the Duke's Company, and, although his memory often betrayed him, on the whole his information is extremely valuable. For the King's Company he depended on the more erratic memory of "Mr. Charles Booth sometimes Book-keeper [i.e., librarian] there." From Downes's records, corrected by other sources of information, we can be reasonably sure that among the earliest actresses at the King's Theatre were Katherine Corey, Anne Marshall (later Mrs. Quin), Elizabeth Farley (alias Mrs. Weaver), Margaret Rutter, and perhaps Mrs. Eastland. At the Duke's Theatre they were Hester Davenport, Mary Saunderson (later Mrs. Betterton), Jane Long, Anne Gibbs (later Mrs. Shadwell), Mrs. Jennings, and Mrs. Norris. Of all these women, Katherine Corey, Mary Betterton, and Anne Shadwell had the most distinguished careers. None was ever a truly great actress, but Mrs. Corey was long popular in "old women" roles; Mrs. Shadwell was always competent in supporting parts; and Mrs. Betterton, eminent in Shakespearean roles, was a successful leading lady for nearly twenty-five years.

How did the managers find these pioneer actresses, and where did they come from? Again no precise answers are possible. Perhaps they came from such schools as that at Chelsea where Mrs. Pepys's maid, Mary Ashwell, once acted in a masque.[11] Perhaps they came from dancing schools and singing schools, or were recommended by musicians, choir masters, dancing masters, and actors. In the beginning the candidates can hardly have been numerous, although the requirements were modest: some measure of good looks, the ability to read and memorize lines, some small skill at singing and

[11] Pepys, February 26, April 26, 1663.

dancing, and the simple willingness to venture forth in an untried profession.

Most of the early actresses hid their family origins behind the stage curtain. We cannot even be sure that they all used their real names. Commonly—married or single—they were listed in dramatis personae only as "Mrs." (pronounced "Mistress") Marshall, or Barry, or Corbett, without a Christian name. Many Christian names can be recovered from contemporary records, diaries, and fugitive lampoons, but some may be lost forever. Mrs. Clough, Mrs. Knapper, Mrs. Norton, and Mrs. Price, to name only a few, stand in the dramatis personae of printed plays only as names, empty of personality. We do not know who they were, where they came from, or, after they had strutted their hour upon the stage, whither they went.

No "lady," of course, could consider a career on the stage; her kinfolk would rather see her starve than degrade a genteel or noble name.[12] On the other hand, the barmaid-and-brothel class lacked all education and refinement; such a natural actress as illiterate Nell Gwyn was truly a sport. There was left only a narrow middle stratum from which actresses could be drawn: the daughters of an out-of-place preacher, like the Marshall sisters, or of a notary, like Anne Gibbs (Mrs. Shadwell), or of a "decayed knight," like Charlotte Butler, or of a widowed shopkeeper, like Sarah Cooke; or an orphan like Elizabeth Barry, said to have been brought up by Lady Davenant in the odor of grease paint; or a gentleman's bastard like Moll Davis, said to have been the daughter of Colonel Thomas Howard; or the wife of such an off-color character as Mary Knep's husband, an "ill, melancholy, jealous-looking fellow . . . a kind of jockey";[13] or the wives and daughters of actors, who were themselves halfway between yeomen and gentlemen and

---

[12] Cibber (I, 75) complained that "A Lady, with a real Title, whose female Indiscretions had occasion'd her Family to abandon her," desired to be admitted as an actress, but had to be refused because of strong objections by her family. Her endeavor to "get Bread from the Stage was look'd upon as an Addition of new Scandal to her former Dishonour!"

[13] Pepys, December 8, 1665, December 11, 1668.

certainly impecunious enough. The Restoration world had little but domestic service to offer the dowerless daughters of the genteel poor. At least an actress was better paid than a waiting woman.

For example, there was Winifred Gosnell—Pepys's pretty little "Marmotte"—the younger of two sisters whose mother seems to have been a widow left badly off but with genteel family connections. Although not of gentle birth, the sisters were "gentlewomen" by courtesy. Both had been well educated; that is, they could read, write, sing, dance, and perhaps speak a little French. In December, 1662, Winifred Gosnell, hoping for advancement, became Mrs. Pepys's personal maid. Almost immediately she learned that Mrs. Pepys was not one of those ladies who haunted the Court and the playhouse daily and that she herself could not have full "liberty of going abroad" as often as she pleased. Four days later she resigned with a flimsy excuse—she had to see her uncle, the improbable Justice Jiggins, on business for her mother thrice a week. Winifred was an ambitious girl with a very small talent and some flighty ideas. There was no future in domestic service; she would look further.

Five months later Pepys was surprised to see her as a "super" in *Hamlet* at the Duke's Theatre. Probably she got started on the stage in the obvious way, by applying to Sir William Davenant, who, at that time, must have been willing to try out any likely looking wench who came along. But Mrs. Gosnell was never a good actress. According to Pepys she played a few roles of little consequence. Her name appears in the pages of a play only once, as the singer of a song in Davenant's *The Playhouse To Be Let* (1663). Better players and singers appeared, and she was relegated to the role of understudy and occasional singer. Yet she clung stubbornly to the company for twenty-seven years or more before she was finally discharged. Then she disappeared into the obscurity of failure.[14]

Mrs. Gosnell was a fairly typical candidate for the stage

[14] Pepys, December 5, 8, 9, 1662, May 28, 1663, September 10, 1664, July 28, 1668, June 21, 1669. See Sybil Rosenfeld, "Unpublished Stage Documents," *Theatre Notebook*, II, No. 3 (April–June, 1957).

in the early days of the Restoration. Probably there were many ambitious young women who, like her, chose the stage in preference to domestic service. The need for actresses was great, and the standards were low. Names which never appear in the dramatis personae of printed plays pop up in theatrical records: Jane Russell, Mary Man, Mrs. Dalton, Anne Child, and Jane Davenport, for example, all at the King's Theatre. Many women lasted only a few months and then sank into the obscurity of permanent supernumeraries or quietly drifted away.

But, after the first few years, places on the stage came to be more highly prized than in the early dawn of the Restoration theatre and were sought by women of somewhat different talents. We cannot say that stage-struck girls flocked to the companies hoping for wealth, stardom, and popular acclaim. Even for a successful actress the pay was miserable; there was no star system; and social recognition was far in the future. But young women without dowries had discovered the possibility of a theatrical career as a springboard to matrimony or "keeping." Husbands were scarce, but "keepers" swarmed. There were hundreds of lecherous gentlemen eager to seduce an actress as cheaply as possible. The foolish virgins succumbed to their blandishments and paid the usual penalty of folly. The wise ones teased their admirers into some kind of a settlement, hoping to live in clover for the rest of their lives. By her less fortunate fellows the successful Cyprian was admired rather than blamed. Chastity, after all, was a luxury that only the well-to-do could afford.

Not the most famous but probably the first successful actress-mistress was Hester Davenport of the Duke's company, an example of wisdom to all the frail ladies of the stage. Hester was the kind of woman whose beauty (said dour Anthony Wood) made men "take ill courses." She was twenty years old and already famous as Roxalana in Davenant's *The Siege of Rhodes*, Part Two (1661), when Aubrey de Vere, twentieth Earl of Oxford, saw her on the stage and fell headlong in love. Oxford was forty-four, handsome in a long-chinned way, a childless widower, wealthy,

stubborn, and exceedingly proud. He made ardent love
to the young actress, beseeching her to become his mistress—
not, of course, his wife. For an earl to marry an actress was
as unthinkable as for a king to marry a commoner. It
was not that the word "actress" had as yet acquired the
unsavory connotation it was soon to take on; the trouble
with Mrs. Davenport was that she *worked* for a living. Therefore the Earl pleaded for her love, without benefit of clergy.
But Mrs. Davenport, with remarkable resolution, held out
for a wedding ring. She was either very clever or rigidly
virtuous.

We have two accounts of Lord Oxford's courtship and its
outcome, one written by Baroness d'Aulnoy in 1694–95,
the other told by the Count de Grammont in 1713. Although
it is quite clear that the two stories were set down inde-
pendently, they agree in essentials: that after months of
frustration the lovesick Earl gave the actress a signed
promise of marriage; that a ceremony was performed with
either Oxford's trumpeter or his groom of the chamber
posing as a parson; that when the deception was discovered,
the actress, insisting that "the marriage was valid," appealed
to the King for justice; and that Oxford was ordered to
pay her a sizable pension.

Baroness d'Aulnoy, a professional writer of fairy tales,
embroidered this story with some pleasant fantasies. She
declared that the courtship covered a period of eight months
or so, during which Oxford nearly went mad. He even
contemplated abducting Mrs. Davenport and ravishing her,
declaring brutally, "All I care for is to satisfy myself,
and when I have done that I shall not trouble myself any
further about this ——— actress." Finally he pretended
to agree to marriage. A contract was drawn up, the marriage
performed and consummated. The next morning the wicked
Earl kicked the actress out of bed, snarling, "Wake up,
Roxalana, it is time for you to go." Then the story of
the tricked marriage came out. Hester screamed, raged,
tried to kill her seducer, and managed to wound herself
with his sword. Thereafter she persisted in maintaining
that the marriage was valid and appealed to the King and

Parliament. Said Mme d'Aulnoy, "Parliament contented itself with condemning him not to marry, unless he had her consent, and also to endow her with a considerable pension. Further he was also compelled to recognize as his a son that was born"—presumably of one night of love.

Behind these *chroniques scandaleuses* may lie some measure of truth. Certainly the contemporary tradition of a marriage was strong. Anthony Wood, for example, referred to Hester as "Roxalana, married to the earl of Oxon," and the author of a lampoon, "Men of Honour, 1687," scolded Oxford for "spending his estate, marrying his whore." Hester herself maintained the fiction; to the end of her days she called herself proudly "Countess of Oxford." The chances are that Oxford and his coy mistress joined hands in some kind of an irregular marriage which, in the confused state of seventeenth-century canon law, might have been proved valid had Hester cared to press her claim. For some reason she never did so, perhaps because she was aware of the odds against success, perhaps because she was satisfied with what she had achieved.

But it is highly unlikely that there were trickery, screams, and murderous assaults with consequent open scandal. According to Pepys, on May 20, 1662, Roxalana was "owned by my Lord of Oxford," that is, openly acknowledged as his mistress, a formality which gave her some social and economic standing. On January 1, 1663, Pepys saw the ex-actress at the Duke's Theatre, "in the chief box, in a velvet gown, as the fashion is, and very handsome"—seemingly content with her new role as permanent mistress and brevet wife. As far as we know she remained content and faithful to her keeper. Her son by Oxford was born April 17, 1664 (more than two years after the so-called seduction), lived a totally undistinguished life, died at the age of forty-four, and was buried as "Aubrey de Vere, Earl of Oxford." He had, of course, no right to the title.

For twelve years after his success with Roxalana, the true Earl of Oxford, apparently satisfied with his morganatic arrangement, showed no interest in marrying a more eligible bride, even though he had no legitimate heir for his title and estates. Finally, on April 12, 1673, in obedience to the King's command, he married a shopworn court lady, Diana Kirke. Oxford died in 1703, still without a son to carry on the proudest title in the peerage. Four months after his death, Hester—then sixty-two!—married one Peter Hoett, describing herself for the marriage register as "Dame Hester, Countess Dowager of Oxford." She survived Hoett, dying in 1717. In her will she called herself "Dame Hester, Countess of Oxford, late widow of Peter Hoett, Esq." and signed herself firmly "Hester Oxford," like one to the manner born. By the time of her death, of course, she had long been forgotten by the theatrical world.[15]

Hester Davenport was only the first of a long line of young women whose beauty, wit, and merit brought them preferment and hard cash. Ten years or so after the Restoration the young actress who yearned to become a rich man's darling had, besides Mrs. Davenport, a whole galaxy of stars to admire and emulate: Jane Long, mistress of a courtier, George Porter; Susannah Uphill, mistress of wealthy Sir Robert Howard; Betty Hall, mistress of Sir Philip Howard; Mrs. Johnson, mistress of Henry, Earl of Peterborough; Elizabeth Barry, mistress of John, Earl of Rochester; Peg Hughes, mistress of Prince Rupert; and those two famous luminaries, Moll Davis and Nell Gwyn, kept by His Majesty, the King.

By the 1670's, then, largely because of the exciting extra-professional opportunities open to a pretty actress, a young woman seeking a place on the stage had to use the aid of patrons and recommenders, and sometimes had to bribe an actor or manager with her virtue. In the tight circles of the Town the eager aspirant was such a well-known figure that she became a subject for dramatic commentary. For example, in Payne's *The Morning Ramble* (1672), a young woman taken by the watch excuses her late rambling thus: "Sir, I have a great mind to be a player, and have offered myself to both Houses, and truly most of the sharers have

[15] See Appendix A: Davenport, Hester; D'Aulnoy, *Memoirs of the Court of England in 1675*, trans. Mrs. W. H. Arthur (1913), pp. 269–78; Wood, I, 406; British Museum, Harleian MS. 7317, p. 150; *HMC, Portland MS*, V, 153.

had me severally at their chambers to try me, and they all say I do very well; but 'tis the envy of the women already there, that fearing I should out-do 'em, keeps me out, as I was told by two or three of the hired men of the Duke's House, with whom I have been tonight and spent all my money. But I do not doubt to find friends to bring it about, for there are two or three persons of quality have undertaken it. . . . Alas, I desire little or nothing for my pains; I would only show myself on the stage, and then, perhaps, I may get a good husband, or at least some fool that will keep me."

As usual in such cases, the would-be actress had grandiose notions about the wages of sin. Lucy, in Wycherley's *Love in a Wood* (1671), was fond of her lover, Dapperwit, because, she said (Act III, scene 1), he "taught me to rehearse, too,— would have brought me into the playhouse, where I might have had as good luck as others: I might have had good clothes, plate, jewels, and things so well about me, that my neighbours, the little gentlemen's wives of fifteen hundred or two thousand pounds a year, should have retired into the country, sick with envy of my prosperity and greatness." Of course, Lucy was naïve—very few actresses had such good luck—but probably she reflected accurately the hopes of many an aspirant for the stage. At any rate, the keeping of stage doxies became so common as to justify the envious complaint of Wycherley's Mrs. Squeamish (*The Country Wife* [1675], Act II, scene 1): "That men of parts, great acquaintance, and quality, should take up with and spend themselves and fortunes in keeping little playhouse creatures—foh!"

The little playhouse creature who was not kept was something of a rarity and an object of pity to her more fortunate sisters. In the prologue to Porter's *The French Conjurer* (1677), the woman speaker addressed the libertines in the audience thus:

> And, Gallants, though you are but seldom good,
> Yet to us women most of all you shou'd.
> No sooner comes a Beauty here in play,
> But strait your Coach and six takes her away,
> And you who cull the Flock should be so kinde
> To comfort the forlorn you leave behind.

To the companies the practice of culling the choicest lambs from the flock became a serious matter. In the epilogue to Lee's *The Rival Queens* (1677), the actors protested to the sons of Belial in the audience:

> . . . our Women who adorn each Play,
> Bred at our cost, become at length your prey:
> While green and sour, like Trees we bear 'em all,
> But when they're mellow straight to you they fall:
> You watch 'em bare and squab, and let 'em rest;
> But with the first young down, you snatch the Nest.
> Pray leave these poaching tricks, if you are wise,
> E're we take out our letters of Reprise.
> For we have vow'd to find a sort of Toys
> Known to black Fryars, a Tribe of chooping Boys . . .
> The panting Breasts, white Hands and little Feet
> No more shall your pall'd thoughts with pleasure meet.
> The Woman in Boys Cloaths all Boy shall be,
> And never raise your thoughts above the Knee.

In spite of this plaintive appeal and vain threat, the poaching continued, and the desirability of the stage as a showcase for feminine wares increased steadily. In 1685 Robert Gould wrote:

> An actress now so fine a thing is thought,
> A place at Court less eagerly is sought.
> When once in this society inrolled,
> Straight by some reverend bawd you'l hear 'em told
> "Now is the time you may your fortune raise,
> And sparke it like a lady all your days."
> But the true meaning this—now is the time
> Now in your heat of youth & beauties prime,
> With open blandishment & secret art,
> To glide into some keeping cullies hart,
> Who neither sence nor manhood understands
> And jilt him of his patrimonial lands:
> Others this way have grown both great & rich,
> Preferment you can't miss & be a bitch.

The poaching tricks continued unabated to the end of the century and beyond, in spite of the boasted *fin de siècle* reformation of morals and manners. In 1696 young Maria Allison, speaking the epilogue to Gildon's *The Roman Bride's*

Revenge, set forth without shame the ambition of the young actress:

> I, who must make my Fortune o' the Stage,
> Will ne'er expose the Vices of the Age:
> Which I expect to find my chief Support;
> And thrive by them, as Flatterers do at Court.
> 'Tis not for me to ridicule a Beau;
> I may get Good of him, for aught I know.
> Why should I call that Damme Spark a Bully,
> Or the good natur'd keeping Fool a Cully?
> When I as well as others, soon may hope
> To be maintain'd by some conceited Fop.

There were some honorable and virtuous women on the stage, but by the 1680's the tradition that every actress was at least a part time "lady of pleasure," leading a rich and glamorous life, had become firmly established. Of course the budding actress eager to sell her virginity to the highest bidder failed to realize that the kept woman's tenure depended upon the whim of the keeper: she drew no lesson from the common enough case of the damsel who, taken from the stage in the early summer, returned, usually in sad condition, before the snow flew and had to endure the jeers of her sisters. And if the young actress remembered, she took no warning from the complete failures, the actresses who, deserted by their keepers and burdened by debt or riddled with disease, turned "punks," "nightwalkers," or "fire ships," and ended their lives in the bawdyhouses of Lewkenor's Lane, Whetstone's Park, or Moorfields. The story of Elizabeth Farley, one of the earliest actresses of the King's Company, might have served as such a warning.

Elizabeth was evidently young, fresh, and beautiful when she first appeared on the stage in the winter of 1660–61. Initially her luck was amazing: the eyes of insatiable King Charles fell upon her, and she traveled the dark road that led up the Thames to Whitehall Privy Stairs, thence up the back stairs, and so into the royal bedchamber. But her dreams of glory were brief; King Charles demanded more than beauty of his permanent mistresses, and Elizabeth failed to hold his interest. Although the King "first spoiled" her (as Pepys put it), to him she was only one of the many casual doxies who went through the hands of the Chiffinches, Pages of the Back Stairs, and Pimps in Ordinary.

Once started, Elizabeth found engagements as a lady of pleasure fairly profitable, especially when they did not interfere with her acting. In 1661 she was living blissfully in sin with one James Weaver of Gray's Inn, gent. In January, 1662, her amiable keeper not only cast her off but demanded the return of £30 that he had given her and for which he had cannily taken her bond. To add to her troubles, she had been passing herself off as Weaver's wife and had run up bills on the strength of his credit. When the truth came out, various indignant tradesmen clamored for their money and sought the Lord Chamberlain's permission to sue her. Moreover, she was pregnant, and although the loose-bodied gowns and full petticoats then in vogue allowed her to continue acting much longer than was safe or proper, eventually, in the autumn of 1662, she had to turn in her parts and leave the King's Company.

Now she found herself in even worse trouble: as one of His Majesty's servants she was reasonably immune to arrest for debt, but she was no longer in the royal service. Tradesmen prepared their writs, and the debtors' prison yawned for her. Desperately continuing to represent herself as a "Comoedian," she appealed to the King for reinstatement in the company, completely misrepresenting the circumstances of her departure. As a result (or because King Charles dimly remembered her and felt he owed her a kindness), Sir Henry Bennet, Secretary of State, wrote to Killigrew ordering her reinstatement.

In Killigrew's absence Sir Robert Howard (a leading shareholder) replied, protesting that the information given His Majesty was "exactly false," that Mrs. Weaver (as Elizabeth called herself) had brought in all her parts three weeks earlier and "warn'd the Company that after such a day which is expir'd shee woud act noe more." Since that time, he said, Mrs. Weaver had appeared "big with Child," and now, since the discovery that she was not married to Weaver, "shamefully soe." There had been an open scandal. "Many women of quality," wrote Howard, "have protested they will never come to thee house to see a woman actynge all parts of vertue in such a shameful condition." Pity the poor shareholders, who saw their best customers affronted! It was not morality that made Howard protest, "Truly, S^r! wee are willinge to bringe the stage to be a place of some Creditt, and not an infamous place for all persons of honour to avoid."

By one trick or another Elizabeth managed to fend off her creditors. In October (at a guess) she gave birth to her illegitimate child, and not long afterward she was back on the stage. But the damage was done. Her reputation might have recovered, but not her purse; she could never hope to pay off her debts out of her small salary, and her market value otherwise was sadly reduced. Getting deeper and deeper in debt, she continued playing until June, 1665, when the theatres were closed by the Great Plague. Thereafter, no doubt to avoid her creditors, she disappeared into the vast underworld of London, a *memento mori* for all young actresses.[16]

We have no way of knowing how many of Mrs. Weaver's successors (if they ever heard of her) took warning from her fate. Unfortunately our information about the private lives of the Restoration actresses is painfully scanty. In the hierarchy of society they were commoners of low degree, too insignificant for contemporary historians to notice except when one of them—a Nell Gwyn or a Moll Davis—was thrust into the limelight as a royal mistress. Their public lives are recorded in the dramatis personae of some, but not all, printed plays and in the cold records of the Lord Chamberlain's office. For their private lives we have to depend on rare items in contemporary diaries, letters, and memoirs, or on the scandal-mongering of coffeehouse poets, the gossip columnists of the Court and Town. Happy was the actress who had no history.

On the basis of evidence drawn from a variety of sources we can reasonably conclude that of the eighty or so young women whose names are recorded in the annals of the

[16] See Appendix A: Farley, Elizabeth.

theatre between 1660 and 1689, at least twelve, as Downes put it, "by force of Love were Erept the Stage," i.e., left the theatre to become kept mistresses or prostitutes. Of the rest, another dozen or so—among them such famous actresses as Elizabeth Barry, Elizabeth Boutell, Charlotte Butler, Elizabeth Cox, Elizabeth James, and Rebecca Marshall—while maintaining their theatrical connections, enjoyed (and probably deserved) considerable reputations as occasional doxies. At least thirty young women were on the stage only briefly, played in one or two minor parts, and then disappeared. Perhaps they married, or died, or were dismissed for incompetence. However, to judge by the frequency of such complaints as Cibber's about the "many frail fair ones . . . who, before they could arrive to their Theatrical Maturity, were feloniously stolen from the tree,"[17] it seems much more likely that most of this group, too, joined the oldest profession. And we can be sure that there were many others, eager young girls who appeared only briefly as supernumeraries and were snatched from the stage before their names could be recorded.

We are left with not more than two dozen actresses who, as far as we know, lived respectable lives. Most of these were married, and nearly half of them—among them such important actresses as Mary Betterton, Mary Lee, Elinor Leigh, and Susanna Mountfort (afterward Verbruggen)—were married to players. Perhaps there was something to be said for Abbé Hedelin's proposal that, to insure modesty on the stage, "no single Woman shall act, if they have not their Father or Mother in the Company, and that all Widdows shall be oblig'd to marry within six months after their year is out for mourning, and in that year shall not act except they be married again."[18]

Even matrimony, however, could not save an actress from detraction. To judge from all the information about her, Anne Shadwell, wife of the poet Thomas Shadwell, lived an exemplary life. Yet the anonymous author of a verse lampoon, "A Satyr on the Players" (ca. 1684),

[17] Downes, p. 35; Cibber, II, 222.

[18] *The Whole Art of the Stage* (1657; trans. 1684), p. 173.

insisted that her chastity was enforced by old age and ugliness and that "in her Youth, none was a greater Whore." Similarly, twice-married Mary Lee (Lady Slingsby) seems to have lived quietly and decently. Yet the same anonymous poetaster accused her of an affair with "a dull Whiggish poet" —perhaps Elkanah Settle. As for unmarried Anne Bracegirdle, the "Romantick Virgin" who all her life made a fetish of chastity, there was no lack of libelers to assert that she had "yielded her Charms" to the dramatist William Congreve and after him to Robert Leake, Earl of Scarsdale.[19]

Perhaps all these accusations were true; at this distance it is impossible to prove or disprove them. But the Restoration playgoer and reader of verse lampoons needed no proof. Since so many of the early actresses lived abandoned lives, it was the general conviction that all actresses were "made of Play house flesh and bloud," unable to withstand the charms of a "powerfull Guinnee"—in short, "actress" and "whore" were effectively synonymous. From this conviction the reputation of the actress was to suffer for the following two hundred years.

[19] For details on the actresses mentioned see Appendix A.

II. *Behind the Scenes*

Like a new Eve, the first English actress came into a world made for men. Since its earliest times the stage had presented plays written and played by men and designed primarily for masculine entertainment. But, although the Restoration theatre had its serpents, it was no Eden. Merely to survive in it, a woman needed a rugged constitution and a fighting heart. To preserve her virtue intact she needed a squad of guardian angels.

Consider Killigrew's second Theatre Royal, which opened its doors for the first time on May 7, 1663. It was located in Bridges Street, just off Drury Lane in the Covent Garden neighborhood—a district of slums, alehouses, bawdyhouses, shops, and noblemen's mansions, lying cheek by jowl together. Around the corner in Russell Street was the famous Rose Tavern, a haunt for players and poets. Once, when Mr. Pepys dropped in for a drink, he found "Dryden the poet (I knew at Cambridge), and all the wits of the town, and Harris, the player, and Mr. Hoole of our college." There was much "witty and pleasant discourse."[1]

Visiting the new Theatre Royal the day after it opened, Pepys decided that it was "made with extraordinary good contrivance," and so it was for the playgoer. In modern times it would seem very small, being not more than 112 feet long by about 58 feet wide. The pit was reasonably spacious,

---

[1] Pepys, February 3, 1664.

and the backless benches were covered with matting. The boxes and the middle and upper galleries were comfortable enough, as comfort was thought of then, and the lighting was good. The stage was the latest word: a wide apron in front of a gaudy proscenium arch, behind which painted flats slid in grooves to form the scenes. There were a few faults: the rear boxes were too far from the stage; the passageways to the pit were too narrow; the "musique," being "below"—almost under the stage—was muted; and in stormy weather rain or hail beat in through the cupola over the pit. Nevertheless it was a fine theatre, much better than the first Theatre Royal.[2]

But Killigrew had given little thought to the comfort or convenience of the players. In the area behind the stage (which anyone could enter at will) was the cluttered scene room, where flats and properties were stored and where the actors rested or waited for their cues. Above was the space for the tiring rooms, divided into the "women's shift" and the men's, with small private rooms for the leading actors and actresses. The furnishings were simple necessities: chairs, tables, small mirrors, candlesticks, and chamber pots and close stools (commodes). Possibly coal fires took some of the chill from the bare, untidy tiring rooms, and at least a few of the private rooms had fireplaces. On May 4, 1667, the Lord Chamberlain ordered that Anne Quin, a leading lady, be given "a dressing roome with a chymney in it to be only for her use and whom she should admitt."[3] It was very pleasant for a leading lady to return from the draughty stage to the warmth of her private sea-coal fire. The lesser actresses, shivering bare-shouldered in their flimsy finery, shared the common misery of the tiring room. On the other hand, they had company, gallants by the score.

On March 19, 1666, while the Theatre Royal was undergoing alterations, Pepys dropped in "to see the inside of the stage and all the tiring rooms and machines." He was moved to laughter at the "mixture of things" in the tiring rooms: "here a wooden-leg, there a ruff, here a hobbyhorse, there a crown." He inspected the dressing rooms of two of the lead-

---

[2] Pepys, May 8, 1663; Nicoll, p. 296.

[3] LC 5, 138, p. 376.

ing actors, Lacy and Shatterel, and found their wardrobes contemptible. But he was struck by a sobering reflection: "to think how fine they show on the stage by candle-light, and how poor things they are to look now too near at hand, is not pleasant at all."

Had Pepys been an imaginative man he might have seen the empty tiring rooms peopled with actors preparing for the play:

> Above the rest the Prince with mighty Stalks,
> Magnificent in Purple Buskins walks:
> The Royal Robe his Haughty Shoulders grace,
> Profuse of Spangles and of Copper-Lace:
> Officious Rascals to his mighty Thigh,
> Guiltless of Blood, th'unpointed Weapon tye;
> Then the Gay Glittering Diadem put on,
> Ponderous with Brass, and starr'd with Bristol-Stone.

Impatiently he waits for his cue, while in her dressing room the leading lady makes up her face:

> His Royal Consort next consults her Glass,
> And out of Twenty Boxes culls a Face.
> The Whit'ning first her Ghastly Looks besmears,
> All Pale and Wan th'unfinish'd Form appears;
> Till on her Cheeks the blushing Purple glows,
> And a false Virgin Modesty bestows;
> Her ruddy Lips the Deep Vermilion dyes;
> Length to her Brows the Pencil's Touch supplies,
> And with black bending Arches shades her Eyes.
> Well pleas'd, at length the Picture she beholds,
> And spots it o'er with Artificial Molds.[4]

It was just as well for Mr. Pepys that he was not imaginative. He preferred to see his "Copper-Lace" under the stage candles, where it looked like gold.

But he continued to go behind the scenes. One day, a year and a half later, Mary Knep took Pepys and his wife and maid "up into the tireing-rooms; and to the women's shift, where Nell [Gwyn] was dressing herself, and was all unready,

[4] "The Play-House: A Satyr" (ca. 1698), *Poems on Affairs of State* (1705), p. 486.

and is very pretty, prettier than I thought." It was not in the least unusual for men to come into the women's shift while the actresses were undressed to their smocks. "And so walked all up and down the house above, and then below into the scene-room, and there sat down, and she [Mrs. Knep] gave us fruit; and here I read the questions to Knepp, which she answered me, through all her part of 'Flora's Figarys' which was acted today. But, Lord! to see how they were both painted would make a man mad, and did make me loath them; and what base company of men comes among them, and how lewdly they talk! and how poor the men [the actors] are in clothes, and yet what a shew they make on the stage by candlelight, is very observable." From the tiring room one could see into the auditorium; Pepys was surprised "to see how Nell cursed, for having so few people in the pit." Of course, a small audience meant a new play for the next day, and a morning spent in rehearsal.

At a still later date Pepys went backstage to fetch Mrs. Knep just as Beck Marshall, looking "mighty fine, and pretty, and noble," came off the stage at the end of *The Virgin Martyr*, in which Beck, dressed in white robes and a crown, had played the martyred Dorothea and Nell had played a guardian angel. Pepys was shocked by the contrast between the roles played by the two women and their off-stage behavior. "But, Lord!" he wrote, "their confidence! And how many men do hover about them as soon as they come off the stage, and how confident [impudent] they are in their talk!"[5]

Impudence was worth more than virtue as a defense against the blowflies of the tiring rooms, the libertines with their lewd talk, their ogling and leering and chinking the gold in their pockets. If we may judge by the epilogue to D'Urfey's *Massaniello*, Part II (1699), their approach was brutally direct. The speaker, a girl, tells us in detail how, when she came off the stage, "A Gay Town-Spark" hovered

[5] Pepys, October 5, 1667, May 7, 1668; J. H. Wilson, "Nell Gwyn as an Angel," *Notes and Queries*, CXCIII (February 21, 1948).

about her with compliments on her acting. When he begged
to kiss her hand, she was properly coy:

> Nay, Pish, Cry'd I, and put him by just so:
> Yet thank'd him, that he lik'd my Part to day.
> Burn me, says he, I like you; Damn the Play.
> Then mutter'd something softly in my Ear,
> Something of Hundreds setling by the Year.
> I colour'd like a Rose, and trembled too;
> For Heaven knows for 'em what I was to do!

The theatre was a dangerous place for any pretty girl,
whatever her function. Mrs. Knep (said Pepys) had a
"wonderful pretty maid of her own, that come to undress
her, and one so pretty that she says she intends not to keep
her, for fear of her being undone in her service, by coming to
the playhouse." Truly, as Tom Brown wrote, it was "as
hard a matter for a pretty Woman to keep her self honest
in a Theatre, as 'tis for an Apothecary to keep his Treacle
from the Flies in hot Weather; for every Libertine in the
Audience will be buzzing about her Honey-pot, and her
Virtue must defend itself by abundance of fly-flaps, or those
Flesh-loving Insects will soon blow upon her Honour, and
when once she has a Maggot in her Tail, all the Pepper and
Salt in the Kingdom will scarce keep her Reputation from
Stinking."[6]

Since their victims were of low degree, the libertines who
infested the tiring rooms considered them fair game. Woe
to the actress who resented a gentleman's lewd talk or indecent behavior. She could, of course, complain to the Lord
Chamberlain or the King, but Whitehall was some distance
from Drury Lane, and easy King Charles had a short memory
and no police. In 1665, Beck Marshall, of the Theatre Royal,
appealed to His Majesty for protection against one Mark
Trevor, a gentleman who "assaulted her violently in a Coach
and after many horrid Oathes and Threats that he would be
revenged of her for complaining to my Lord Chamberlain
formerly of him, pursu'd her with his Sword in his hand. And

[6] Pepys, April 7, 1668; Brown, II, 303.

when by flight she had secured herself in a house he continued his abusive language and he broke the windows of the adjoining house." There is no indication that Mr. Trevor was punished for his eccentric rowdyism.[7]

On a later occasion a courtier, Sir Hugh Middleton, publicly made some scurrilous remarks about the women of the King's Company. On Saturday, February 5, 1667, Sir Hugh ambled into the women's shift at the Theatre Royal. Plucky Beck Marshall "taxed him" with the "ill language" he had used and "added that she wondered he would come amongst them." At first Sir Hugh defended himself, but as Beck continued to scold he lost his temper "and told her she lyed, and concluded the injury by calling her jade, and threatning he would kick her and that his footman should kick her."

On the following Monday, understandably frightened, Mrs. Marshall went to Whitehall and complained to the King, begging his protection. It was immediately pledged; King Charles was always quick with the ready currency of promises. The grateful actress returned to the playhouse and made the mistake of bragging in the tiring rooms about the "gracious promise from his Ma^{ty} that shee should not be injured." She boasted too soon.

Late on Tuesday afternoon, as Beck was leaving the theatre after the play, she saw Sir Hugh standing "in the great Entrie going out of the Playhouse into Drurie Lane." She told "Mr. Quin who led her home"—probably her brother-in-law—"of her Apprehension that he lay in wait to doe her some mischief or affront." But Middleton was there only to point her out to the scoundrel hired for the actual assault. Rebecca went on her homeward way. "Some few doores from the Playhouse a Ruffian pressed hard upon her, insomuch that she complained first of his rudeness, and after turned about and said I thinke the fellow would rob mee, or pick my pocket. Upon wch he turned his face and seemed to slink away." Rebecca was almost home when the ruffian, who had been sliding along in the shadows, suddenly ran up behind her, picked up some excrement from the street,

[7] "The Humble Petition of Rebecca Marshall," SP 29, 142, p. 160.

smeared it over her face and hair, "and fled away in a Trice."[8]

No doubt Mr. Quin, an actor, wore a sword, but he was either too slow or too timid to draw it. Few actors were fighters. They claimed gentility and the right to bear weapons, but most of them confined their swordplay to the stage. As corporate bodies the actors did what little they could to protect the women of the theatre, just as they tried to protcet their properties from lawless men. But they were powerless against the Middletons and Trevors, the typical wild gallants of a brutal and unruly age. Even the King's proclamations against backstage abuses and "disorders in the attiring rooms" were persistently ignored by the gentlemen rakes. One proclamation, for example (February 25, 1664), ordered that "no person of what quality soever do presume to enter at the door of the attiring house, but such as do belong to the company and are employed by them." Another (January 18, 1677) ordered that "noe person whosoever presume to come between the scenes at the Royall Theatre during the tyme of Acting but only the Comoedians and such of them only as Act that day," while no one was to "sitt upon the Stage or stand there dureing the tyme of acting but the Comoedians only." In spite of repeated proclamations the abuses continued, and no actor dared to raise his voice in protest.[9]

The fact is that the actors were *déclassé* too, and just as fair game as the actresses for any titled rascal or his hired bullies. Usually they had to swallow insults and blows with a grin; resentment or retaliation could bring physical punishment or the loss of their acting rights. Only once did an actor get the better of a titled bully. As the story is told, hotheaded Jack Verbruggen struck "an illegitimate son of Charles II, behind the scenes of Drury-Lane" and called him what he was. Verbruggen was warned that unless he publicly apologized to the nobleman he could never again act in London. The next day the actor came on stage, dressed for the part of Oroonoko in the play by that name, and, "having

---

[8] "The Deposition of Mrs. Rebecca Marshall against Sᵣ Hugh Middleton. 8 Feb. 1666[7]," SP 29, 191, p. 31.

[9] Fitzgerald, I, 96; LC 5, 141, p. 521; LC 7, 1, p. 6.

first acknowledged that he had called the Duke of St.
A[lbans] a son of a w——e," he concluded, "it is true, and
I am sorry for it."[10]

Properly, no gentleman would ever soil his hands on an
actor. On April 19, 1667, when John Lacy told the Honorable
Edward Howard, a playwright, that he was "more a fool
than a poet," Howard slapped the actor in the face with his
glove, Lacy retaliated with his stick, and Howard ran to the
King to complain. Of course Howard struck the first blow,
but no matter; Lacy was arrested and confined to the Porter's
Lodge at Whitehall for a few days. Even more important was
the fact that the King's Company, of which Lacy was a leading member, was temporarily "silenced." Thus an entire
company was punished for the misdeed of one player. When
the gentry of the Town heard of Lacy's impertinence, they
were surprised "that Howard did not run him through, he
being too mean a fellow to fight with."[11]

Witty Sir Charles Sedley refused to touch an actor even
with a glove. When Edward Kynaston, who closely resembled
Sir Charles ("a handsome plump middle sized man") had the
effrontery not only to get "some laced cloathes made exactly
after a suit Sir Charles wore" but to appear so dressed on the
stage, Sedley was annoyed and promptly hired "two or three"
bullies to chastise the player. The bravos accosted Kynaston
in St. James's Park, "pretending to take him for Sir Charles,"
picked a quarrel with him, and beat him so savagely that he
was forced to take to his bed. When some moderate gentlemen, feeling sorry for Kynaston, reproached Sir Charles, "he
told them they misplaced their pity, and that 'twas he they
should bestow it on, that Kynaston's bones could not suffer
so much as his reputation, for all the town believed it was he
that was thresh'd and suffered such a public disgrace."[12]

Certainly a good many of the theatres' customers, the
libertines and rogues who swaggered backstage and talked
lewdly in the tiring rooms, were a bad lot. But it must be
admitted that most of the actors, who were, perforce, the

[10] Ryan, II, 122.

[11] Pepys, April 20, 1667; LC 5, 186, pp. 144, 146.

[12] Oldys, p. 485; Pepys, February 1, 1669.

women's close associates, were no better. Of course there were
some honorable and decent actors—Thomas Betterton, Will
Mountfort, Michael Mohun, Charles Hart, and a few more—
but most of the players did their best to deserve Robert
Gould's description of them as

> A pack of idle, pimping, spunging slaves,
> A miscellaney of Rogues, fools & knaves,
> A nest of leachers worse then Sodom bore,
> And justly merit to be punisht more.
> Diseas'd, in debt, & every moment dun'd,
> By all good Xtians loath'd & their own kin-
> dred shun'd.

This was not mere abuse. From Pepys we learn, for example, that Walter Clun, of the King's Company, murdered
by footpads on his way home one night, had spent the evening "drinking with his whore"; that William Smith, of the
Duke's Company, "killed a man upon a quarrel in play";
that when John Lacy, of the King's Company, lay supposed-
ly "a-dying of the pox," he kept "his whore by him, whom
he will have to look upon, he says, though he can do no
more: nor would receive any ghostly advice from a Bishop,
an old acquaintance of his that went to see him"; and that
Thomas Killigrew, Master of the King's Company, by his
own admission was "fain to keep a woman on purpose at 20s
a week to satisfy 8 or 10 of the young men of his house,
whom till he did so he could never keep to their business."[13]

The great Thomas Betterton complained that the actors
were often given up to "undisguised Debauchery and Drunk-
enness, coming on the very Stage, in Contempt of the
Audience, when they were scarce able to speak a word."
In his Preface to *The Relapse* (1696), Vanbrugh remarked
that George Powell, who played Worthy (the gentleman
who tries to seduce the heroine, Amanda), had spent the day
drinking Nantes brandy, and by the time "he waddled on
upon the stage in the evening had toasted himself up to such
a pitch of vigour, I confess I once gave Amanda for gone."
One is reminded of the famous story of Henry Higden's *The*

[13] Pepys, August 4, 1664, December 7, 1666, July 13, 1667, January
24, 1669.

Wary Widdow (1693), in which there were so many drinking scenes that "the actors were completely drunk before the end of the third act, and being therefore unable to proceed with this 'Pleasant Comedy,' they very properly dismissed the audience." Obviously the players were not restricted to cold tea.[14]

As one might expect, the players, both men and women, were often disorderly and given to scurrilous speech and violent behavior. Since they were all the King's servants, they were usually disciplined by the Lord Chamberlain or the Knight Marshal for their "several misdemeanors"—not always specified. For example, on April 23, 1668, Mrs. Mary Knep, "one of ye Comoedians at ye Royall Theatre," was arrested "for misdemeanors there." On November 5, 1669, Mary Meggs, fruit woman at the Theatre Royal, was arrested "for abuseing Mrs. Rebecca Marshall one of his Ma[ties] Comoedians to ye disturbance of his Ma[ties] Actors and comitting other misdemeanours." On December 9, 1669, Samuel Sandford and Matthew Medbourne of the Duke's Company were arrested for being "refractory and disorderly" —no doubt while in their cups. John Perine of the Duke's Company was arrested on September 19, 1671, "for several misdemeanors and abusing my Lady Davenant"; and on November 4, 1675, Joseph Haines was suspended from acting with the King's Company because he had abused the Knight Marshal "with ill & scandalous language & insolent carriage." The list of arrests is endless. Usually the culprits were suspended from acting for a week or two, or forced to cool their heels for a few days in the Marshalsea or the Porter's Lodge at Whitehall.[15]

The actors were not criminals; Restoration records list only two who were detected in crime. In 1681 Cardell ("Scum") Goodman, tired of living on a player's pittance, took to the King's highway and was caught red-handed in a robbery. The favor of someone in high place—probably his mistress, the Duchess of Cleveland—saved his neck. On April 18, 1681, a pardon was granted to Goodman for "all

[14] Gildon, p. 20; Ryan, I, 114.
[15] LC 5, 187, pp. 218, 175, 187; LC 5, 14, p. 77; LC 5, 141, p. 287.

Felonies, Robberies upon the Highway or elsewhere, Burglaries, Assaults, Batteries and Woundings whatsoever by him committed before the 16th day of this instant April." The second offender was less fortunate. In September, 1693, Thomas Percival was charged with clipping coins, convicted, and sentenced to death. By the intercession of his daughter, Susanna Mountfort, the penalty was changed to transportation, but he died in prison before the sentence could be carried out. Another actor who died in prison was in no sense a criminal. On March 19, 1679, Matthew Medbourne, a Roman Catholic, succumbed to the cold and filth of Newgate, a victim of the Popish Plot terror.[16]

In jail or out, most of the players—even some of the more respectable—were constantly in debt. The members of the two companies, both men and women, were sworn in either as the King's or as the Duke of York's servants; thus in effect they were all the King's servants in ordinary, without fee. As such they came under the protection of the Lord Chamberlain of the Household and could not be arrested or sued for debt without his permission. Consequently the Lord Chamberlain's books are filled with petitions from creditors seeking permission to sue for sums ranging from £2 15s. to £250, owed for "goods," clothing, rent, wine, "meate & drink," medical fees, and money lent. To judge by the number of entries, the members of the King's Company were much more improvident (or less often paid) than those of the Duke's. Of the King's Company, from 1660 to 1682, the actors John Lacy, Robert Shatterel, Walter Clun, Richard Wiltshire, Thomas Loveday, Joseph Haines, William Hughes, William Beeston, Nicholas Burt, Edward Eastland, John Coysh, Martin Powell, Cardell Goodman, Henry Hailes, Philip Griffin, and Thomas Clark, and the actresses Elizabeth Weaver, Rebecca Marshall, Elizabeth James, Margaret Rutter, Anne Reeves, and Elizabeth Youckney were all petitioned against for personal debts, some of them many times. The most consistent offender was Joseph Haines. In March, 1669, he was ordered to pay William Matthews 5s.

[16] British Museum, Add. MS. 27,277, p. 126; Borgman, p. 172; Downes, p. 170.

weekly until an unspecified debt was paid. In August of the same year he was ordered to pay Edward Sanger 10*s.* weekly until Michaelmas next, and then 15*s.* weekly until a debt of £18 was paid; plus 5*s.* weekly to John May until Michaelmas next, and then 10*s.* weekly until a debt of £9 was paid. Finally, in October he was required to pay John Curll 5*s.* weekly, beginning October 17, until a debt of £5 was paid! One wonders what he had left to live on.[17]

Of the Duke's Company during the years from 1660 to 1682, Henry Harris, John Young, Robert Turner, Samuel Sandford, James Nokes, Cave Underhill, Theophilus Westwood, Henry Norris, and Henry Wright were petitioned against for debt. All the actresses seem to have been solvent. None of the Duke's players could match the splendid record of Joseph Haines. The worst offender was Henry Harris, whose obstinate refusal to pay for the maintenance of his estranged wife, Anne, caused him a good deal of trouble.[18]

With some exceptions, then, the actors were indeed a drinking, quarreling, swaggering, wenching crew, living hand-to-mouth and avoiding the debtors' prison only by virtue of their royal master's protection. The young actress was thrown into daily contact with this raffish lot. The solid, substantial men of both companies had homes of their own—sometimes as far off as Chelsea or Hampstead—and families to whose pleasant circles they retired after the day's work was done. The lesser fry lived in lodgings near the theatres and spent their nights—sometimes with the women of the stage—drinking and gaming in the taverns and dives of Covent Garden or in little blind alehouses or bawdyhouses in Moorfields, Whetstone's Park, or the dark alleys opening off the Strand, houses kept by such notorious ladies as Mother Temple, Mesdames Cresswell, Gifford, Moseley, and Stratford, and that famous bawd, Betty Buley. Like the libertines and rakes who swarmed in the tiring rooms, the players knew intimately the dank sewers of the London

[17] For Haines see LC 5, 187, pp. 74, 157, 158, 174.

[18] For Harris see LC 5, 189, p. 92; LC 5, 190, pp. 134, 174, 182; LC 5, 191, p. 51.

underworld, into which, from time to time, some careless or foolish young actress disappeared.

The married actresses, too, had homes and families to preserve them from temptation. The unmarried women lived in lodgings as close as possible to the theatre. By day or by night the streets of London were unsafe for a young woman without escort. Chiefly for their protection, Davenant boarded four of his principal ladies, Mrs. Davenport, Mrs. Saunderson, Mrs. Long, and Mrs. Davis, in his apartments adjoining the first Duke's Theatre in Lincoln's Inn Fields. The other women of his company lived in that neighborhood, or, after the second Duke's Theatre was built in Dorset Gardens, they had lodgings off Fleet Street, in the City. The women of the King's Company found rooms in the Covent Garden–Drury Lane area. One May Day Pepys saw Nell Gwyn standing in the doorway of her lodgings in Drury Lane (just a step from the Theatre Royal), "in her smock sleeves and bodice, looking upon one." Fondly Pepys added, "she seemed a mighty pretty creature." It was still early morning, and Nell was enjoying a holiday.[19]

When the players worked, they labored hard for small wages. Unfortunately for their thin purses there were too many times when, for one reason or another, the theatres were closed and all incomes stopped. Probably no actor had work for more than thirty to thirty-five weeks out of a year. We know from Pepys that the theatres were closed for the week before Easter and that there were no plays on Fridays in Lent except when the "young men and women" (the hirelings) were given permission to act for their own benefit. In the summer the King and his Court went to Windsor or Newmarket; the gentry fled to the bucolic delights of their country estates, and attendance at the theatres fell off to the point where it was hardly worthwhile opening the doors. In addition, the theatres were closed when a member of the royal family died; when the King or a nobleman was offended by a prologue, a play, or a player; when the actors quarreled with each other (a frequent occurrence at the Theatre Royal); when there was a disturbance in a play-

[19] Downes, p. 20; Pepys, May 1, 1667.

house—no matter who was to blame; or when such calamities as fire or epidemic struck London. The longest period of closure was caused by the Great Plague and the following Great Fire—from June 5, 1665, to November 29, 1666. For nearly eighteen months the players were thrown entirely on their own meager resources.[20]

Sunday was always a day of rest. For six days the players labored mightily, rehearsing nearly every morning, playing every afternoon, and sometimes performing in the Court Theatre at Whitehall at night. In their spare time they studied their parts. Since revived plays were seldom kept on the boards for more than two or three days, and even a successful new play was lucky to have a run of three to six days, the rehearsals and constant study were highly important. (The twelve successive days' run of Shadwell's *The Sullen Lovers* [1668] was truly "a wonderful Success.") Once a part was given to a player he was expected to be ready with it at every subsequent revival, no matter how long the interval between performances. It became, in effect, his property. But memories grew rusty in time; moreover there were always some changes to be made or some new players to be led through their parts. At the Theatre Royal, a "hired man or woeman" who neglected a rehearsal could be fined a week's wages.[21]

In a normal year most of the plays presented were drawn from the companies' stocks of tried and trusted old plays— the best of Shakespeare, Jonson, Beaumont and Fletcher, Brome, Massinger, Shirley, and the few moderns whose work continued to please. New plays were infrequent, averaging (for each house) not more than four or five a year. It seems to have been the custom for an entire company to assemble

[20] Malone, I, 198; Nicoll, p. 383; Hotson (p. 232) estimates an average of two hundred acting days per year; Pepys, March 24, 1662, March 21, 1667; for an order closing the theatres because of the Duchess of York's death see LC 5, 12, p. 302; for an order suspending the players because of an affront to a peer see LC 5, 150, p. 340 (December 16, 1691); for a disturbance in the playhouse see *True News: or Mercurius Anglicus,* February 4–7, 1680; for the order closing the playhouses because of the Plague see LC 5, 138, p. 417.

[21] Downes, p. 29; Nicoll, p. 324.

while someone—usually the author himself—read a new play aloud. Once Colley Cibber heard Dryden read his *Amphitryon* to the actors. "He delivered the plain Sense of every Period," said Cibber, "yet the whole was in so cold, so flat and unaffecting a manner, that I am afraid of not being believ'd when I affirm it." On the other hand, Nathaniel Lee was "so pathetic a Reader of his own Scenes" that once, when Lee was reading to the actor Mohun at an early rehearsal, "Mohun, in the Warmth of his Admiration, threw down his Part and said, Unless I were able to play it as well as you read it, to what purpose should I undertake it.?"[22]

After the play had been read, the actor-managers, in consultation with the author, cast it and started rehearsals. Sensibly, they type-cast as much as possible. Leading roles went to leading players; lesser roles to those with less experience; and bit parts—servants, guards, soldiers, attendants, and the like—either to hirelings of some experience but small ability or to apprentices. Occasionally there was no role at all for a player, and he took an enforced holiday. Only the leading players had the privilege of refusing a role, a privilege that had to be exercised with care. In 1668, when the Theatre Royal was preparing a splendid production of Jonson's *Catiline*, Charles Hart ordered the comedian Joe Haines to play the inappropriate role of a senator. Haines was vexed. The next day, wearing a ridiculous outfit, "a Scaramouche dress, a large full Ruff . . . Whiskers from Ear to Ear . . . a long Merry Andrews Cap, and a short Pipe in his mouth," he followed Hart on stage. As Hart declaimed the prologue, Joe sat down behind him on a three-legged stool, smoked, made faces, and pointed derisively at Hart, while the audience laughed. At last Hart turned, saw Haines, and went off the stage, swearing. Haines was fired, of course —no new experience for the irrepressible comedian.[23]

A new play could not be rehearsed to the exclusion of all other work. There was always the play to be given that afternoon, and, if that failed to "take," another had to be hastily

[22] I, 113–14.

[23] *The Life of the Late Famous Comedian, Jo. Haynes* (1701), pp. 23–24.

revived and refurbished for the next day. No wonder the
authors often complained that the players were "out" in
their parts. (One poet, James Drake, expressed his indignation by printing on the title page of his play, *The Sham-
Lawyer* [1697], "As it was Damnably Acted at the Theatre-
Royal in Drury-Lane.") The actors tried hard, but sometimes
the task was too much for their overstrained memories, and
they had to fall back upon ad libbing or, worse, "loud prompt-
ing, to the eternal Disgust of the audience." Like all profes-
sions, acting is largely drudgery.[24]

By comparison with modern standards, the Restoration
players were very poorly paid. The leading actors, who were
also shareholders, did so well at first that there were some
complaints about their growing "very proud and rich." But
as the years passed, theatrical costs increased, audiences
diminished, and waste and bad management took their toll.
It has been estimated that "the celebrated tragedian"
Charles Hart gained from salary and profits about £146 a
year—or, in terms of modern purchasing power, roughly
$3,000. In 1691, when Thomas Betterton gave up his shares
to the patentees, he agreed to act for £5 a week and an
annual present of 50 guineas to help him through the summer. His wife was getting 50s. a week, and he was paid other
sums for various duties, besides living rent free over the
theatre. In 1692 the Bettertons' total income for each acting
week was estimated at £16, or (assuming thirty acting weeks
to the year) £480 a year—roughly equal to $10,000 today.
Certainly the great Bettertons were not overpaid.[25]

The hirelings, paid much less, were practically in a state of
peonage. Since they were forbidden to move from one
theatre to another without the Lord Chamberlain's permission, they could not sell their services to a higher bidder; any-
way, for a good many years there was only one theatre in
London. Occasionally, disgusted with his low pay, an actor
fled to the Dublin Theatre. There was, for example, an unknown hireling who, "being denied the Augmentation of his

[24] Gildon, p. 38.

[25] Pepys, February 23, 1661; Malone, I, 198; Nicoll, pp. 369–79.

Wages, grew angry, and said, 'If you wont, you shall see me in Ireland within two days.' "[26]

Sometimes a hireling spent months as an apprentice without any pay at all. Cibber is said to have wasted three quarters of a year before getting a part. One day

he obtained the honour of carrying a message on the stage, in some play, to Betterton. Whatever was the cause, Master Colley was so terrified that the scene was disconcerted by him. Betterton asked, in some anger, who the young fellow was that had committed the blunder. Downes replied, "Master Colley."—"Master Colley! then forfeit him."—"Why, sir," said the prompter, "he has no salary."—"No!" said the old man, "why then put him down ten shillings a week, and forfeit him 5s."[27]

A good, experienced actor was usually paid about 50s. a week. Generally women were paid less than men. If a young actress made good, she was put on the payroll at 10s. to 15s. a week—very little more than ten to fifteen dollars today. An experienced actress could command 30s. a week or more if she could bring sufficient pressure to bear on the patentees. As late as 1694 the popular Katherine Corey, after many years in the theatre, was getting only 30s. a week. At about the same time Elinor Leigh, after the death of her husband, the comedian Anthony Leigh, was raised from 20s. a week to 30s.; Mrs. Verbruggen (formerly Mountfort) was considered overpaid at 50s. a week; and even the great Elizabeth Barry had only 50s. a week plus a guaranteed £70 a year from a benefit performance. There is no reason to believe that salaries were higher in the early days of the Restoration.[28]

The underpaid players did not, however, have to provide all the clothing they wore on the stage. The theatres owned large stocks of clothes, ranging from "French gowns à-la-mode" to "garments like Romans very well." Some of these were purchased for one play and used over and over again for later plays, with no concern for historical accuracy, until they wore out. Some costumes were the castoff suits or dresses of ladies and gentlemen too proud to wear the same outfit more

[26] Richard Head, *Nugae Venales* (1686), p. 207.

[27] Davies, III, 417.   [28] Nicoll, pp. 369–79.

than once. Most other properties were furnished by the play-houses, and the player had to provide only personal items: hats, periwigs, cravats, shoes, stockings, and the like. At the King's Theatre, Hart, Mohun, and Kynaston made a special arrangement on March 6, 1672, by which they were furnished free of cost:

> Two perrywiggs to begin with, for the first year
> One perrywigg yearly afterwards, to begin a year hence
> Two Cravatts yearly
> One Lace or point Band in two years the first band to be now provided
> three paire of silk stockings yearely
> three hatts yearely
> Two plumes of ffeathers yearely
> Three shirts with Cuffs to them yearely

There is nothing to show that any of the actresses ever had such a pleasant arrangement. Presumably they were supplied only with gowns, mantles, and special articles of costume required for a play. They seem to have provided their own petticoats (often very expensive), shoes, stockings, gloves, and scarves. Probably some of these garments were the gifts of admirers.[29]

A durable young actress could find many compensations for the rigors of backstage life, the hard work, poor pay, and shabby associations. There was always the bustle and stir of the theatre, the excitement of acting, the joy in applause. A truly stage-struck girl, then as now, would work for nothing, if she could afford to, and take out her pay in handclaps and praise. Then there was the prestige of being one of "His Majesty's Servants," and the advantage to be gained by running up bills with tradesmen, happily trusting to find someone to pay them before the day of reckoning with the Lord Chamberlain. There was always the chance of slipping out after the play wearing one of the company's "French gowns à-la-mode" or some other finery. The companies frowned on this practice, complaining that their clothes were "Tarnished and Imperelled by frequent weareing them out of the Playhouse," and fined the culprit a week's pay if they

[29] *Ibid.*, pp. 50, 300, 365; LC 5, 140, p. 5.

caught her in the act. There was even some advantage (for the ladies of the King's Company, at least) in the regular gifts of materials for liveries: "foure yards of bastard scarlet cloath" for a cloak, plus "one quarter of a yard of [crimson] velvett" for the cape. Perhaps the liveries could be worn only on state occasions, but they were nice to have, and in a pinch they could always be sold.[30]

Once a month or so there was the fun of a command performance at night in the intimate little theatre at Whitehall. What a change that was from Drury Lane, Dorset Gardens, or Lincoln's Inn Fields—the great, rambling old palace twinkling with lights, the halls ornate with brocades and paintings, the brilliant audience of courtiers and ladies in blue and green and silver, with the dark, cynical King seated on a dais in their midst under a crimson velvet canopy—all mellowed by the light of the wax candles! Sometimes a young actress caught the fancy of a ruttish lord; sometimes a young actor appealed to a lecherous lady. And then there was always the King, an insatiable keeper.

If nothing else, there was luxury and plenty to eat and drink at Court. The Lord Chamberlain's records are full of warrants calling for equipment and supplies for the tiring room of the Court Theatre, listing such items as one hundred and ten yards of green baize for wall hangings; "two peices of hangings and great Curtayne rodes to make partitions between the Men and Woemen;" two pairs of andirons, two pairs of tongs, and two fire shovels (evidently for fireplaces at each end of the tiring room); twenty chairs and stools, three tables, two stands, ten candlesticks, "one Looking glasse of twenty-seven Inches for the Woemen Comoedians," and, inevitably, "two close stools and six chamber pots for the use of ye players." Warrants for food and drink were sumptuous; for example: "Twelve Quarts of Sack, twelve Quarts of Clarett, twenty foure Torches, sizes [half-ounce candles] three Bunches, Eight Gallons of Beere, four Basketts of Coales, six dishes of Meate, twelve loaves of white Bread, ——— Loaves of Brown Bread, Tallow candles foure pounds, twelve white dishes to drink in, and two Bumbards [leather

[30] Nicoll, pp. 297, 324; LC 3, 38, p. 7.

jugs] to fetch Beere"—all this for some twenty-four people.
There was good cheer at the Court of merry King Charles.[31]

Sometimes in midwinter the players were called upon to
perform at the Inner Temple before a riotous and apprecia-
tive audience of law students. Sometimes in midsummer one
of the companies went down to Oxford (a full day's journey)
for the academic "Act," set up their stage in a tavern or
tennis court, and played a week or two before townspeople
and scholars. The Oxford historian, Anthony Wood, complained that the beauty of the actresses "made the scholars
mad, run after them," and "take ill c[o]urses." Once, in July,
1674, the actors of the King's Company ran mad at Oxford,
"going about the town in the night breakeing of windows,
and committing many other unpardonable rudenesses."[32]

In London there were innocent off-stage recreations for
the young actress, alone or with a companion of either sex.
When her services were not needed in the play for the day,
she could go to the competing theatre on a busman's holiday.
So one day at the Duke's Theatre Pepys was mightily pleased
that "pretty witty Nell, at the King's House, and the younger
Marshall [Rebecca] sat next us." On Sunday mornings, aton-
ing for their sins of the week, nearly everyone went to church
to hear noble music and purple oratory. On Sunday after-
noons, in fine weather, there were Hyde Park, the Spring
Garden, Vauxhall, or boating on the Thames. Of an evening
after a play there were suppers and little parties with friends.
Only a few of the players were received "among People of
condition with Favour," but there were many small bourgeois
like Pepys who sought them out.[33]

With her excellent singing and her madcap ways, Mary
Knep of the King's Company brought a great deal of happi-
ness into Pepys' life—until Mrs. Pepys grew jealous. On a
typical evening Pepys walked to the house of Dr. James
Pierce in Covent Garden, where he found "much good com-

[31] LC 5, 137, p. 177; LC 5, 138, pp. 45, 353; Eleanore Boswell, *The
Restoration Court Stage* (1932), p. 89.

[32] Nicoll, pp. 305–7; Wood, I, 322; *Letters of Humphrey Prideaux*, ed.
E. M. Thompson (1825), p. 5.

[33] Pepys, April 3, 1665; Cibber, I, 83.

pany, that is to say, Mrs. Pierce, my wife, Mrs. Worshipp
and her daughter, and Harris the player [from the Duke's
Company], and Knipp, and Mercer, and Mrs. Barbary Shel-
don . . . and here with musique we danced, and sung and
supped, and then to sing and dance till past one in the morning." Pepys was always very free with Mrs. Knep, even in
the early days of their friendship: "I got into the coach
where Mrs. Knipp was, and got her upon my knee (the coach
being full) and played with her breasts and sung, and at last
set her at her house and so good night." On another occasion,
after a late party, Mrs. Knep stayed all night in the Pepyses'
home. Pepys saw most of his guests to the door and went up-
stairs very late with Mrs. Pierce to find Mrs. Knep in bed
asleep: "and we waked her, and there I handled her breasts
and did baiser la, and sing a song, lying by her on the bed."
Such intimacies were allowed by the easygoing morals of the
day, and were harmless enough when set to music.[34]

On the whole, in spite of many difficulties, the life of an
actress was by no means unbearable. At least it was exciting,
full of change and movement, and surely better than the drab
existence of a shopkeeper, a barmaid, or a domestic servant,
the only other occupations open to a girl of low degree and
no dowry. Although many young women displayed themselves on the boards only long enough to catch a husband or a
keeper, there were others who made acting a lifetime career.
For example, twice-married Susanna Percival had been an
actress for twenty-two years when death cut short her career.
Elizabeth Boutell had played for some twenty-six years
when, "Besides what she saved by playing, the Generosity of
some happy Lovers enabled her to quit the Stage before she
grew old." Katherine Corey played steadily for thirty-two
years, untouched by the breath of scandal. Elizabeth Barry
spent thirty-five years on the stage and then retired, en-
riched more by her extraprofessional activities than by her
playing. Frances Maria Knight was the most durable of all,
with forty-three years of acting to her credit. She must have
had a rugged constitution and a fighting heart.[35]

[34] Pepys, March 14, 1666, January 2, 1666, January 24, 1667.
[35] Curll, p. 21; Brown, II, 243–45.

III. *On Stage*

If at times the backstage seemed more like a bawdyhouse than a workshop, the forestage and the auditorium were no better. The ladies and gentlemen of the Court and Town— the small coterie which alone made theatrical entertainment possible—considered the playhouses their private property, in which they could behave as they pleased. Rugged individualists, proud, quick to take offense, often vulgar and boorish, they had not the faintest notion of audience decorum, sometimes misbehaving even in the presence of the King.

No doubt there were refined and sensible people in a typical audience, but they were outnumbered by the coarse, gross, and ill-mannered. In *The Young Gallant's Academy* (1674), Samuel Vincent gave some ironical advice to a would-be beau or wit on how to behave in a playhouse:

Let our Gallant (having paid his half Crown, and given the Doorkeeper his Ticket) presently advance himself into the middle of the Pit, where, having made his Honor to the rest of the Company, but especially to the Vizard-Masks, let him pull out his Comb, and manage his flaxen Wig with all the Grace he can. Having so done, the next step is to give a hum to the China-Orange-wench, and give her her own rate for her Oranges (for 'tis below a Gentleman to stand haggling like a Citizen's wife) and then to present the fairest to the next Vizard-Mask.

... [After the play has begun] It shall Crown you with rich Commendations, to laugh aloud in the midst of the most serious and sudden Scene of the terriblest Tragedy, and to let the Clapper (your Tongue) be tossed so high that all the House may ring of it: for by talking and laughing you heap Pelion upon Ossa, Glory upon Glory: as first, all the eyes in the Galleries will leave walking after the Players, and only follow you: the most Pedantick Person in the House snatches up your name; and when he meets you in the Street, he'l say, He is such a Gallant; and the people admire you.

Collectively the young Restoration gallants behaved like untamed savages. In the prologue to Behn's *The Debauchée* (1677) the rufflers of the pit are scolded thus:

> But you come bawling in with broken French,
> Roaring out Oaths aloud, from Bench to Bench,
> And bellowing Bawdy to the Orange-wench,
> Quarrel with Masques, and to be brisk and free,
> You sell 'em Bargains for a Repartee,
> And then cry Damn 'em Whores, who ere they be.

Even mature playgoers talked at will, indifferent to the rights of others. Pepys was once vexed by "two talking ladies and Sir Charles Sedley," who chattered so that he "lost the pleasure of the play wholly." Sometimes talk grew into a duel or a riot. We learn from a newsletter of August 30, 1675:

On Saturday last, at the Duke's playhouse, Sir Tho. Armstrong killed Mr. Scrope. . . . Their quarrel is said to be about Mrs. Uphill, the player [of the King's Company], who came into the house maskt, and Scrope would have entertained discourse with her, which Sir. T. Armstrong would not suffer, so a ring was made wherein they fought.[1]

Or we have a newspaper account of an affair on February 4, 1686:

On Munday night last happened a great disorder in the Duke's Play-house, some Gentlemen in their Cupps entring into the Pitt, flinging Links [torches] at the Actors, and using several reproachful speeches against the Dutchess of P[ortsmouth] and other persons of Honour, which has occasioned a Prohibition from farther Acting, till his Majesties farther pleasure.

[1] Pepys, February 18, 1667; *HMC, Seventh Report*, p. 465.

Apparently the only way to discipline the audience was to close the playhouse.[2]

Commonly playgoers showed their disapproval of a play, a player, or an author, not by sitting on their hands, but by interruptions, hisses, catcalls, and tumult. When Lucidor, in Boyle's *Altamira* (1664) whined,

> This scratch, which you call wound, you much miscall,
> 'Tis my great trouble that it is soe small,

it is said that the Duke of Buckingham stood up in the pit and bellowed back,

> Then greater 'twere if it were none at all.[3]

Because of a backstage quarrel with a gentleman (who was "grosly in the wrong"), the actor William Smith incurred the displeasure of the prejudiced playgoers. When Smith next appeared on the stage "he was receiv'd with a Chorus of Cat-calls, that soon convinc'd him he should not be suffer'd to proceed in his Part; upon which, without the least Discomposure, he order'd the Curtain to be dropp'd"—and retired permanently from the theatre.[4] Whenever a faction of half-wits agreed to cry down a play they followed a well-tried procedure:

> They spread themselves in parties all over the House; some in the Pit, some in the Boxes, others in the Galleries, but principally on the Stage; they cough, Sneeze, talk loud, and break silly Jests; sometimes Laughing, sometimes Singing, sometimes Whistling, till the House is in an uproar; some Laugh and clap; some Hiss and are Angry; Swords are drawn, the Actors interrupted, the Scene broken off, and so the Play's sent to the Devil.[5]

Although the typical audience was mostly male, especially in the early years of the period, many ladies went to the theatre, hiding their blushes behind their fans. Both men and women often visited the theatres only to be in fashion—to

[2] *True News; or Mercurius Anglicus*, February 4–7, 1680.

[3] See *The Theatrical Jester*, 1795, p. 15. As reported the line was "My wound is great, because it is so small" and attributed to Dryden. No such passage appears in any of Dryden's plays, but the passage I have quoted fits the context.

[4] Cibber, I, 79.

[5] Granville, *The She-Gallants* (1695), Act III, scene 1.

be seen, not to see and hear. Wits combed their blonde periwigs and chattered in Fop Corner near the stage, ignoring
the play; courtiers standing in the pit leaned their elbows on
the side-box railings and entertained the ladies seated in the
boxes; footmen guffawed in the upper gallery; and the orange
girls cried their wares. At its best the theatre was noisy; at its
worst it was a bear garden.

Since "the drama's laws the drama's patrons give," the
plays most popular on the stage reflected admirably the taste
of a typical audience. Today the plays usually chosen as
representative of Restoration drama give a false picture of a
stage dominated by soaring rhetoric and crackling wit. The
common, day-to-day fare of the theatregoer—new plays or
revivals—was bloody, erotic, low tragedy, and rough, bawdy
farce. What Steele said of the theatre in 1710 applied as well
to that of 1670: "We act murders, to show our intrepidity;
and adulteries, to show our gallantry: both of them are frequent in our most taking plays, with this difference only,
that the former are done in the sight of the audience, and the
latter wrought up to such an height upon the stage, that they
are almost put in execution before the actors can get behind
the scenes."[6]

Tragedy dealt largely in rape, incest, torture, and murder.
It created a remote world in which the wicked were incredibly
evil and the impossibly good existed only to suffer. Comedy
was outspokenly lubricous: a favorite theme was the attempt
of a young gallant to cuckold an old citizen, an undertaking
which usually succeeded, much to the gratitude of the citizen's young wife. In bedroom scenes an actress could appear
in every variety of dress and undress, while an actor often
came on stage "unbraced" or "unbuttoned" after a bedding,
or (like Blunt in Behn's *The Rover* [1677]) stimulated the
audience's libido by undressing in his mistress's bedroom
and stealing, "in his Shirt and Drawers," toward the bed
where she lay asleep. Speeches and gestures were designedly
inflammatory. In Ravenscroft's *Scaramouche* (1677), old
Spitzaferro slavers over young Aurelia, anticipating their
marriage:

[6] *The Tatler*, No. 134, February 16, 1710.

I shall then be your right owner, and master of you all over, of your pretty waggish Eyes, of that pretty little Roguish nose, of those Cherry-Cherry lips, of those little, little fritter Ears, of those pretty blub-cheeks,—of that dimpl'd, dimpl'd Chin, of those round, hard, panting Bubbies, of your soft, white Skin, of your —Euh—Oh!

Vulgarity is always relative to the taste of an age, and many of the comic situations which today seem vulgar and dull provoked hearty laughter in the Restoration theatre. Pepys, who was "not troubled at it at all" when a pretty lady in the pit of the theatre "spit backward" upon him by mistake, could only have been amused at the sight of Olivia, in Wycherley's *The Plain Dealer* (1676), spitting on the stage at every mention of "filthy china." It is unlikely that an urban audience would behave like the country bumpkin, Clay, in Belon's *The Mock-Duellist* (1675), who visits a city lady, "comes up to the Lady, makes a leg, then falls back again, spits and coughs, blows his Nose on the ground, then wipes it on his sleeve." Nevertheless they evidently found Clay's behavior not too much of a contrast to their own, and therefore amusing rather than revolting. The audiences seem, indeed, to have been amused by anything vulgar, scatological, or abnormal: physical deformities, beatings, "eating of sack possets and slabbering themselves,"[7] picturesque profanity, bawdy talk, close stools, brothel scenes, topical references to famous bawds, homosexuality, flagellation, impotence, and venereal disease.

Only the rarest of playgoers was ever upset by stage vulgarity. In 1665 a courtier, Henry Savile, wrote after seeing an alleged comedy, "I will only say that one part of it is the humour of a man that has great need to go to the close stool, where there are such indecent postures as would never be suffered upon any stage but ours, which has quite turn'd the stomach of so squeamish a man as I am."[8] Savile was squeam-

---

[7] Pepys, January 28, 1667, March 26, 1668.

[8] *Savile Correspondence* (Camden Society, 1858), p. 4. Savile wrote that he had witnessed a play by Lord Orrery, *The Widow;* evidently he was mistaken. See W. S. Clark, *The Dramatic Works of Roger Boyle, Earl of Orrery* (1937), I, 40.

ish indeed. Two years later the Theatre Royal was playing James Howard's popular *All Mistaken*, in which the indecent postures and speeches of Pinguister, a fat man who is purging to reduce, had the strong-stomached Restoration audience rolling in the aisles.

The players' task was to entertain the many-headed monster of the pit with plays which ran the gamut from absolute balderdash to Shakespeare—usually cut, altered, or "improved" with music and spectacle. It speaks well for their acting skills that they succeeded at all. Of course, under the circumstances, so-called natural acting would have been hopeless. Only by overplaying their parts could the actors hope to catch and hold the audience's attention. Essentially, then, the art that the young player had to learn was that of accentuation by tone and gesture. This was not a matter of aesthetics; acting was not considered one of the fine arts. In part it was the effect of tradition, in part of simple necessity.

At the beginning of the Restoration, the older actors (the shareholders) trained the hirelings, instructing them in the stage practices that they had learned before the Civil War. A few of the older men combined coaching with acting throughout their stage careers. In the 1690's, for example, Thomas Betterton was earning 50 guineas a year "for ye Care he took as Principall Actor in ye Nature of a Monitor in a Schole to looke after rehearsals." In addition, from 1667 to at least 1682 there were "nurseries" for young actors, maintained by one or both companies at various ancient theatres in London. In 1682 Dryden described the Nursery in the Barbican as a place,

> Where Queens are formed, and future Heroes bred;
> Where unfledged Actors learn to laugh and cry,
> Where infant Punks their tender voices try,
> And little Maximins the Gods defy.[9]

We do not know how many future queens and infant punks (prostitutes) were promoted from the nurseries to the professional theatres. On March 7, 1668, Pepys praised the

[9] Nicoll, p. 377; Dryden, *MacFlecknoe* (1682).

dancing of the new comedian, Joe Haines, at the King's Theatre, "only lately come thither from the Nursery" in Hatton Garden, but this is his only reference to the nurseries. Of course a young woman with powerful sponsors could readily bypass the training school and leap directly to the stage, and apparently most of the better-known actresses did so. But they still had to put in a period of apprenticeship, working (if the letter of the law was adhered to) "three Moneths without Sallary by Way of Approbation" before becoming regular members of the company.[10]

The amount the young actress had to learn depended, of course, on the skills with which she was equipped before she entered the company. To read well was the prime necessity, and to write after a fashion was sometimes useful (although the orthography even of ladies of high rank was often marvelous to behold). Thanks to dame schools, boarding schools, patient parents, or the local vicar, most novitiates could read well enough, but it is likely that such a child of the slums as Nell Gwyn had to learn her letters after she entered the theatre. To the end of her life her signature was a painfully traced "E. G."

Both companies kept in regular employment "Musick Masters" and "Dancing Masters" (as well as "Scene men, Barbers, Wardrobe keepers, Dore keepers and Soldiers") as much to train young players as to prepare musical numbers and dances for plays. Most of the senior actors were capable singers and dancers, and John Lacy, of the King's Company, had been a dancing master in his youth. In the early days of the Restoration theatre nearly every actress was expected to sing a ditty or dance a jig on demand, and all the players had to be able to maneuver gracefully through the country dances "by the whole company" with which many a comedy closed. Outstanding among early singers and dancers were Nell Gwyn and Mary Knep, of the King's Company, and Moll Davis and Charlotte Butler, of the Duke's. In 1667 Tom Killigrew got the notion of hiring Italian singers and English specialists like Mrs. Yates, "who," he said, "is come to sing the Italian manner as well as ever he heard any." Toward

[10] Nicoll, p. 324.

the end of the century, with the steadily increasing emphasis on sound and spectacle, most of the singing and dancing was done by expensive imported specialists.[11]

The fundamentals of acting were speaking, singing, dancing, and walking. In the highly stratified society of the seventeenth century, "behave like a lady" was much more than a warning against naughtiness. In dress, bearing, manner, and speech, a lady differed markedly from a country woman or a citizen's wife. Satiric comedy is full of bumpkins, hoydens, silly wenches, and gossipy housewives designed to be laughed at for their inability to conform to the patterns of mannered society. A stage lady was distinguished by the exaggeration of her ladylike qualities. Now most of the actresses came from the non-mannered classes and therefore had to be taught to behave like stage ladies: to stand erect with chest forward and hips back, to walk with narrow, mincing steps (the "theatrical strut," as it was later called), to curtsy gracefully, salute, take leave, and come and go like one to the manner born. A few actresses came by their manners naturally. Charlotte Butler, for instance, said to be the daughter of a "decayed knight," evidently grew up before the family decay progressed too far; at least she was said to have a "naturally genteel Air and sensible pronunciation." Elizabeth Barry, allegedly the daughter of a barrister, was said to have been reared by Lady Davenant, who introduced her to polite society, so that "by frequent conversing with Ladies of the first Rank and best Sense" she soon became "Mistress of that Behaviour which sets off the well-bred Gentlewoman." The famous stroller Tony Aston insisted ill-naturedly that Mrs. Barry was "Woman to Lady Shelton of Norfolk . . . when Lord Rochester took her on the Stage." No matter; she could have observed "Ladies of the first Rank" just as well from the back stairs.[12]

Whatever the truth about her antecedents, it seems likely that Mrs. Barry had one great advantage over her fellows:

[11] Hotson, p. 369; Pepys, September 9, 1667; Downes, p. 46.

[12] John Hill, *The Actor* (1750), p. 314; Curll, p. 14; Cibber, I, 121, 163; II, 303.

the benefit of instruction by the famous poet, profligate, and universal genius, John Wilmot, Earl of Rochester. As the story has come down to us, Elizabeth was about sixteen when she was introduced to the theatre by her patroness, Lady Davenant. At first she was a complete failure; she had "a very bad Ear" and tended to "run into a Tone [i.e., a monotone], the fault of most young players." The actors of the Duke's Company found her so difficult to teach that they gave up in despair.

Three times she was rejected; and three times, by the Interest of her Lady, they were prevailed on to try her, but with so little Success, that several Persons of Wit and Quality being at the Play, and observing how ill she performed, positively gave their Opinion she never would be capable of any Part of Acting. But the Earl of Rochester, to shew them he had a Judgment superior, entered into a Wager, that by proper Instruction, in less than six months he would engage she should be the finest Player on the Stage.

Probably the Restoration Pygmalion had already fallen in love with his Galatea, who very soon became his mistress; "and it was thought that he never loved any Person so sincerely as he did Mrs. Barry."[13]

The whole story may be apocryphal, but at least it gives us some notion of the kind of practice needed for the making of a player about the year 1675. Rochester is supposed to have trained Mrs. Barry for the role of Isabella, the Hungarian Queen, in Boyle's often revived tragedy, *Mustapha*. He made her "enter into the nature of each sentiment; perfectly changing herself, as it were, into the Person, not merely by the proper Stress or Sounding of the Voice, but feeling really, and being in the Humour, the Person she represented, was supposed to be in." Then he made her

Rehearse near 30 times on the Stage, and about 12 in the Dress she was to Act it in. He took such extraordinary Pains with her, as not to omit the least Look or Motion, Nay, I have been assured from those who were present, that her Page was taught to manage her Train, in such a Manner, so as to give each Movement a peculiar Grace.[14]

[13] Curll, pp. 14–16.   [14] *Ibid.*

As one might expect, the result was a complete triumph on the stage, and Mrs. Barry went on to become the greatest actress of her generation.

This kind of training was all very well for Elizabeth Barry, who, despite her early failures, must have had a true genius for acting. But Rochester's coaching would have been—and was—wasted on a less gifted pupil. On an earlier occasion Rochester carried down to the country with him another of his mistresses, a girl known to us only as Sarah, and "exerted all his endeavours to cultivate" in her "some disposition which she had for the stage." Eventually he recommended her to the King's Company, "and the public was obliged to him for the prettiest, but at the same time, the worst actress in the kingdom."[15] The teacher could not supply the student with talent or intelligence; he could only equip her with the stylized acting devices then in vogue.

From contemporary essays and prefaces, from the stage directions in plays, and from a collection of rules attributed to Thomas Betterton, we can learn what some of those devices were. Most of them apply only to tragic acting. Among players it was "a standing and incontrovertible Principle, that a Tragedian always takes Place of a Comedian; and 'tis very well known the Merry Drolls who make us laugh are always placed at the lower end of the Table, and in every Entertainment give way to the Dignity of the Buskin."[16] Wearers of the sock were considered lesser craftsmen; they had only to aim for briskness and verisimilitude or to exhibit their personal eccentricities. The tragedian's was an acquired skill, depending on a completely artificial set of tones and gestures.

"The warm and passionate Parts of a Tragedy," said Addison, "are always the most taking with the audience; for which Reason we often see the Players pronouncing, in all the Violence of Action, several Parts of the Tragedy which the Author writ with great Temper, and designed that they should have been so acted." Such speeches were "commonly

[15] Grammont, II, 73.

[16] Addison, *The Spectator*, No. 529, November 9, 1712.

known by the Name of *Rants*." They demanded the full power of the speaker's voice and his most musical delivery. The result, often called "heroic tone," was a kind of cadenced recitative.[17]

The musical effect of the tragedian's delivery was frequently stressed. In 1680 the playwright Elkanah Settle, deploring the downfall of the King's Company, wrote, "'Tis true the Theatre Royal was once all Harmony, the Heroic Muses sung so sweetly, and with Voices so perfectly musical, as few or no Ears could escape Enchantment." And again, "he must be a very ignorant Player, who knows not there is a Musical Cadence in speaking; and that a Man may as well speak out of Tune, as sing out of Tune." Betterton, whose own voice was "low and grumbling," pointed out that the normal variation of the human voice extended to five or six "Tones," and that the actor could form "out of these five or six Notes a just and delightful Harmony." Such musical declamations must have had strong emotional effects. Mrs. Barry said that she could never speak the line, "Ah, poor Castalio!" (from Otway's *The Orphan*) without weeping. By themselves the words would not make a turtle weep; musically intoned they might do wonders.[18]

The tones appropriate to specific emotions were fixed by traditions that had the effect of rules. Artificial though they are, it appears that the young player had to learn these precepts by heart and that his excellence on the stage was judged, not by his individual interpretation of a character, but by his ability to remember and apply the rules. The actor, said Betterton, will

express Love by a gay, soft and charming Voice, his Hate, by a sharp, sullen and severe one; his Joy, by a full flowing and brisk Voice; his Grief, by a sad, dull and languishing Tone; not without sometimes interrupting the Continuity of the Sound with a Sigh or Groan, drawn from the very inmost of the Bosom. A tremulous and stammering Voice will best express his Fear, inclining to Un-

[17] *Ibid.*, No. 40, April 16, 1711; J. H. Wilson, "Rant, Cant, and Tone on the Restoration Stage," *Studies in Philology*, LII (October, 1955), 592–98.

[18] Settle, prefaces to *Fatal Love* (1680) and *The Fairy-Queen* (1692); Gildon, pp. 40, 109.

certainty and Apprehension. A loud and strong voice, on the contrary, will most naturally show his Confidence, always supported with a decent boldness, and daring Constancy. Nor can his Auditors be more justly struck with a sense of his Anger, than by a Voice or Tone, that is sharp, violent and impetuous, interrupted with a frequent taking of the Breath, and short Speaking.

To these rules Betterton added certain other precepts, among them: "To move Compassion, the Speaker must express himself with a soft, submissive and pitiful Voice." "When you address your Speech to any Man or thing by way of Apostrophe you must raise your Voice above the ordinary and Common Tone, as to one deaf, or who want their perfect Hearing; as, 'Oh! sacred Thirst of Gold!' or 'To thee, O Jove! I make my last appeal!' " "In the Opposition or Antithesis, the Contraries must be distinguish'd by giving one a louder Tone, then the other; as, 'Truth breeds us Enemies, Flattery Friends.' "[19]

These were the instructions of a veteran actor deeply concerned about decorum and decency. But every audience loved rants. As John Crowne said in the dedication to his *Henry the Sixth* (1681), "when an Actor talks Sense, the Audience begins to sleep, but when an unnatural passion sets him a-grimacing and howling as if he were in a fit of the Stone, they immediately waken, listen, and stare." In his Preface to *Troilus and Cressida* (1679), Dryden denounced the bad taste of the audience with equal vigor: "The roar of passion, indeed, may please an audience, three parts of which are ignorant enough to think all is moving which is noise, and it may stretch the lungs of an ambitious actor, who will die upon the spot for a thundering clap; but it will move no other passion than indignation and contempt from judicious men." Unfortunately there were all too few judicious men either in the audience or on the stage. In his old age Betterton remembered with approval the acting of Cardell Goodman in a famous rant, Alexander's mad scene in Lee's *The Rival Queens:* "Mr. Goodman always went through it with all the Force the Part requir'd, and yet made not half the Noise, as some who succeeded him; who were sure to bellow it out in

[19] Gildon, pp. 43, 113–14, 118, 129, 132.

54

such a manner, that their Voice would fail them before the End."[20]

The tragic actress, too, had to learn how to express emotion in the prescribed tones and how to deliver a rant without losing her voice. Toward the end of the century female characters in tragedy became of constantly greater importance. The strain on the leading lady's lungs increased correspondingly. The following passage from Gildon's *Phaeton; or, The Fatal Divorce* (1698) is a good example of a female rant. The speaker is Queen Althea (played by Frances Maria Knight), wife to Phaeton, who is a son of Phoebus Apollo. Althea's two small sons have just been torn to bits off stage, and she has stabbed herself with a poisoned dagger. In her dying delirium she imagines that she can pick up the pieces of her son's bodies and

> carry 'em to the Gods
> To solder them together—the Gods can do it!—
> Ha! th' unequal Gods deny the Boon!
> Again disperse and scatter the dear Reliques,
> I with such Pain and Hazard have collected.
> 'Tis Guile, not Innocence is now their Care,
> And grows familiar with the partial Gods.
> (Pauses and looks upward.)

[She fancies she sees her husband, Phaeton, in the skies, taking over Apollo's chariot.]

> Ha! now he's leapt into his Father's Seat!
> He h's seiz'd the fiery Chariot of the Sun.
> But see the Steeds despise his feeble Rein,
> And swiftly whirl him o're the Azure Plain.
> (Pauses, looking fix'dly upward.)
> The Chariot burns! th' Heav'ns blaze, th' Earth's on Fire!
> See Athos, Ida, Taurus, Octa Flame!
> Hills and Valleys burn! Fountains and Streams dry up!
> Stars, Earth, and Air are swallow'd up in Fire—
> Ambition falls, see how he tumbles down!
> The Precipice of Heav'n!—Oh! shield us Jove!
> For now he comes directly on our Heads.
> (Breaks from them that endeavour to hold her, tears off her Head-Cloaths, &c, and her hair tumbles about her Shoulders.)

[20] *Ibid.*, p. 84.

Tear, tear, tear off these Flaming Tresses,
These burning Garments, this catching Fuel!
Haste, haste into the Flood, or we consume!

(Throws herself down.)

So so, hark! hark! that Thunderclap has sav'd us!
See he's faln, he's motionless, he's dead!
Ha! how freezing cold he's grown already!
I've caught the shudd'ring Fit, it chills my Heart!
Oh!

(Dyes.)

This is intolerable fustian, and it seems impossible that the arts of a player could save it from the damnation it deserved. Yet Gildon wrote in his Preface, "I'm sensible, and must own it to the World, that Mrs. Knight's admirable Action was no small advantage to me; who in playing Althea, has evidently shew'd her self one of the foremost Actresses of the Age." It was probably of such wild tragedies as this that Betterton was thinking when he said that Elizabeth Barry, a greater actress than Mrs. Knight, "has so often exerted her self in an indifferent part, that her Acting has given Succes to such Plays, as to read would turn a Man's Stomach."[21]

If the tones of a tragedian were flamboyantly artificial, his motions were even more so. He walked, posed, and gestured according to rigid conventions, acceptable on the stage but ridiculous in the context of ordinary life. We are told that in 1663, when Lord Digby spoke in Parliament against Chancellor Clarendon, everyone laughed because he pointed "like a stage-player" to various parts of his own anatomy.[22] Yet on the stage such dramatic gesturing was commonplace; the hands, arms, and body were almost constantly in motion.

For example, the actor pointed to his head .to certify thought; to his heart to emphasize emotion; toward the skies, "looking fix'dly upward," to address heaven or the gods; and toward the earth to couple hell. "Live," said Mariamme to her lover in Settle's *The Empress of Morocco* (1673), "Live, and inhabit any Seat—but This. (*Points to her Breast*)." Later she insists that she will never forget him:

[21] *Ibid.*, p. 16.   [22] Pepys, July 2, 1663.

56

"Ile to your Image dedicate this shrine. (*Points to her Breast*)." In Mrs. Boothby's *Marcelia* (1669) the heroine, torn between love and honor, cries:

> Add, add no more least reason quit this place,
> (*Points to her head.*)
> And after that, then this be left by Grace.
> (*Her heart.*)

When a player took an oath or invoked a deity, he usually raised both hands to heaven, like Arius in Lee's *Constantine* (1683) who vows:

> If ere I set my hand to such a Treason,
> May these rot off, which thus I hold to Heaven.

Surprise called for even more elaborate gesturing. Betterton described his reaction as Hamlet to the appearance of the ghost in Hamlet's scene with his mother. Of the lines,

> Save me, and hover o'er me with your wings,
> You heavenly guards!

"This," Betterton said, "is spoke with arms and Hands extended, and expressing his Concern, as well as his Eyes, and whole Face."[23] Stage directions in other plays confirm this practice: the Pedagogue in Boyle's *Mr. Anthony* (1672) cries, "You amaze me, I profess. (*Lifting up his hands*)," and Bull, in Dennis' *A Plot and No Plot* (1697), marches about the stage in amazement, "holding up his hands and his Eyes."

We see the typical actor posing gracefully, pointing here, there, and everywhere, thumping his breast, raising his arms in amazement, spreading them wide in welcome, stretching them forward in supplication, and dropping them to his sides in resignation—all while intoning his lines. Could there be too much gesturing, too much motion of arms and body? No, said Betterton, "For indeed Action is the Business of the Stage, and an Error is more pardonable on the right, than the wrong side." Better to overplay than to underplay. The inattentive audience wanted no subleties from its tragedians. It recognized heroes because they were dressed in rich clothes, with high-heeled shoes and plumed caps to make them look taller.

---

[23] Gildon, p. 74.

"The ordinary Method of making a Hero," said Addison, "is to clap a huge Plume of Feathers upon his Head, which rises so very high, that there is often a greater Length from his Chin to the Top of his Head, than to the Sole of his Foot."[24]

Similarly, the audience recognized villains because they wore black periwigs and had their faces darkened with burnt cork. "Pray," said King Charles, "what is the Meaning that we never see a Rogue in a Play, but, Godsfish! they always clap him on a black Perriwig, when it is well known one of the greatest Rogues in England [Shaftesbury] always wears a fair one?" Heroes stalked the stage, "Magnificent in Purple Buskins." Villains sneaked across the stage, like Mandricard in Saunders' *Tamerlane* (1681), whose appearance provoked the heroine to say,

> Did you not mark his black disorder'd Look?
> Between his gnashing Teeth what silent Curses
> He muttered forth, and threatned us with Frowns.

Heroines, too, wore plumes, and villainesses wore, if not black periwigs, certainly "black disorder'd Looks." These, said Betterton, were the "Contraction of the Lips and the scant Look of the Eyes" which indicated "a deriding and malicious Person," while "Shewing the Teeth and streightening the Lips on them," showed "Indignation and Anger."[25]

All this was conventional acting, designed to create a plausible illusion of reality. Incredible as it seems, it must have been successful in its time simply because playgoers were accustomed to it. To non-playgoers it would have seemed madness. Once, we are told, three highwaymen coming across the fields near London early on a summer morning saw a man "walking all alone, making all the Gestures imaginable of Passion, Discontent, and Fury, a-casting up his Eyes to the Sky, displaying his arms abroad, and wringing them together again." It was the famous player Jack Ver-

[24] *Ibid.*, pp. 74, 78; *The Spectator*, No. 42, April 18, 1711.

[25] Cibber, I, 133; Gildon, p. 45; for the appearance of villains see Addison, *The Tatler*, No. 42, July 16, 1709: "Inventory: 'The Complexion of a murderer in a band box; consisting of a large piece of burnt cork, and a coal-black peruke.'"

bruggen, rehearsing his role as the despairing Varanes in Lee's *Theodosius*. The simple highwaymen, unacquainted with stage customs and thinking they had a madman to deal with, seized him and begged him not to kill himself. Said Verbruggen, "What a Plague is all this for? I arn't going to Hang, Stab, nor Drown my self for Love; I arn't *in* Love; I'm a Player only getting my part." Properly incensed at the cheat, the gentlemen of the pad fell upon the actor, tied his hands and feet, and relieved him of ten shillings and a silver-hilted sword.[26]

Not only were there patterns for the demonstration of violent emotion; the softer passions, too, were conventionally expressed. Love, "the noblest frailty of the mind," as Dryden called it, dominated serious drama, and acting was stereotyped to show its effects. Smitten by the sight of beauty, the hero stood fixed, his world centered in his eyes. So, in Dryden's *Conquest of Granada* (1670), when Almanzor first sees the beautiful Almahide he is paralyzed, able only to stammer,

> I'm numbed and fixed, and scarce my eyeballs move;
> I fear it is the lethargy of love.

When Cupid pierced two hearts at once—male and female— both victims stared in a lethargy of love. In Otway's *Don Carlos* (1676) the Queen of Spain and Carlos twist eye-beams in the very presence of the lady's husband, King Philip, who suspects that something is wrong because Don Carlos stands in so "fixed" a posture.

As love grew stronger it demanded even more obvious demonstration with downcast looks, sighs, groans, and folded arms. So, in Boyle's *Tryphon* (1668), Demetrius "fixes his Eyes on Stratonice, folds his arms the one within the other, sighs, and goes out, still gazing on her." In Behn's *The False Count* (1681), Carlos coaches Guiliom in the bilious behavior of a romantic lover: "That's she [Isabella] in the middle; stand looking on her languishingly,—your head a little on one side,—so,—fold your arms,—good,—now and then Heave your breast with a sigh, most excellent.—(*He groans.*)" The lover who suffered from unrequited passion was a miser-

---

[26] Capt. Alexander Smith, *Lives of the Highwaymen* (1714), I, 89.

able looking object. According to Sir Positive At-all, in Shad-well's *The Sullen Lovers* (1668), "The posture of hanging" was exactly that of "a Pensive dejected Lover with his hands before him, and his head aside thus"—as if pulled to the right by the hangman's knot. Otherwise the dejected lover might, like Aurelian in Dryden's *The Assignation* (1672), wander about looking "melancholy, with Hat pull'd down, and the Hand on the Region of the Heart." This posture, or the simple "Demission or hanging down of the Head," served also to express any kind of grief or disappointment.[27] Two un-happy lovers, separated by force (or honor) always insisted on a "parting look," described facetiously to Celadon by Florimel in Cibber's *The Comical Lovers* (1707):

> So have I seen in Tragick Scenes a Lover,
> With dying Eyes his parting Pains discover,
> While the soft Nymph looks back to view him far,
> And speaks her Anguish with her Handkercher:
> Again they turn, still ogling as before,
> Till each gets backward to the distant Door,
> Then, when the last, last Look their Grief betrays,
> The Act is ended, and the Musick plays.
>
> *(Exeunt, mimicking this.)*

If a lady wished to captivate a gentleman, she made "the doux yeux" at him. This glance is defined in John Dryden, Jr.'s *The Husband His Own Cuckold* (1696) as "the hanging of the lip, and the languishing cast of an Eye half asleep"—much like the expression one sees on the faces of Lely's court beauties, described by Pope as "The sleepy look that speaks the melting soul."[28] Smitten in her turn, the lady showed her emotion by modest sighs. In Settle's *Cambyses* (1671), Prexaspes, observing Mandana, says aside,

> Her alter'd Visage wears a Mystery.
> A broken sigh, joyn'd with a fainting look!
> Just so my love its sudden birth first took.

[27] Gildon, p. 43; see also Thomas Wilkes, *A General View of the Stage* (1759), p. 132: "Disappointment is expressed by desponding down-cast looks, a gloomy eye, and the hand striking the breast."

[28] Pope, "Imitations of Horace: To Augustus" (1735).

But there were occasions when the noblest frailty of the mind had to be sternly repressed. In Ravenscroft's *King Edgar and Alfreda* (1677), Princess Matilda, whose lover has just left the stage, struggles with her love in a brief soliloquy:

> Heart, hold thy seat in spite of all his charms,
> The liberty thou strugl'st for is Bondage,
> His conquest will enslave thee—but my eyes
> Are too much thy friends, with the enemy
> They hold Intelligence, but I'le break it off. So
> (*Turns away her head laying her right hand on her Eyes.*
> (*Then starts and claps the other on her breast, then both.*)
> My heart is once more seated on its throne,
> But had he stai'd the field he must have won.

Along with bombastic speech and formalized looks and gestures went a deal of conventional stage business. In large part this was inherited and traditional; it is quite likely that most of the business of the Restoration stage came directly from the Renaissance theatre.

Since the Restoration audience, like its predecessors, loved battles, murder, and horrors, no tragedy was complete without its quota of violence. Blood was spilled by the bucketful. The aim of the tragic poet was to kill as many people as possible by swords, daggers, axes, hooks, racks, and impaling on stakes. Hanging, strangling, and "bowls" (goblets) of poison were also popular devices for poetic murder. Victims of the blade were shown with faces, breasts, arms, and clothing "bloody," and the losing fighter in a duel suddenly became spotted with blood in full view of the audience.

Of course the swords and daggers used were blunted, but even so they could be dangerous. In 1673 the actor Philip Cademan, dueling on the stage with Henry Harris, "received a Wound . . . with a foyle under the right Eye, wch touch'd his Brain by means whereof he lost his memory his speech and the use of his right side." Once when Mrs. Barry was playing Roxana to Mrs. Boutel's Statira in a revival of Lee's *The Rival Queens*, the two ladies quarreled over the ownership of a scarf just before the play began. On stage, when it came time for Roxana to stab Statira, the angry Mrs. Barry struck with such force that "tho' the Point of the Dagger was blunted, it made way through Mrs. Boutel's stays, and entered about a Quarter of an Inch in the Flesh." When Dryden and Lee's *Oedipus* was revived in October, 1692, the property man gave Sandford (the villain) a real dagger "instead of a weapon, the blade of which run up, when the point was pressed, into the handle." Powell (the victim) survived a stab some three inches deep.[29]

Ordinarily only animal blood was used for stage effects. How the blood was applied is shown by two sample stage directions. In Killigrew's *Thomaso* (1665), Don Mathias and Edwardo "cuff and struggle upon the floore, and are both bloody, occasion'd by little spunges ty'd of purpose to their middle fingers on the palmes of their hands." In Dryden's *King Arthur* (1691) the King and Oswald fight a duel: "They fight with Spunges in their Hands dipt in Blood; after some equal Passes and closeing, they appear both Wounded." Apparently women too could carry bloody sponges in their hands and appear covered with self-applied gore, to the detriment, one might think, of their finery.[30] Sometimes the injury was inflicted off stage, and the actress appeared with "her Bosom all bloody" or with "her arm wrapped in a bloody Handkercher." If she had suffered rape (a popular subject for tragedy), she appeared in a horrid condition, with "her Hair dishevel'd, and mouth Bloody, as Ravish'd."[31] The loss of her virginity led inevitably to her death by steel or poison.

Tragic distress was shown by loud lamentations, breast-beatings, and tears—the last suggested by the ostentatious use of a handkerchief. "For the moving of Pity," said Addi-

---

[29] Nicoll, p. 367; Curll, p. 21; John Doran, *Their Majesties Servants* (1888), I, 349.

[30] Perhaps the following song from Duffett's *The Mock-Tempest* (1674) explains how the actresses cleaned their garments:

> Her I'le obey whose breath's so strong, one blast
> Sent from her Lungs would lay my Castle wast;
> Come down my furies, lash no more,
> But gently poure in
> Salt and Urine
> To cleanse their Crimson Lace from Gore.

[31] Gildon, *The Roman Bride's Revenge* (1696), Act V, scene 2; Porter, *The French Conjurer* (1677), Act IV, scene 1; D'Urfey, *Massaniello* (1699), Act V, scene 2.

son, "our principal Machine is the Handkerchief; and indeed in our common Tragedies, we should not know very often that the Persons are in Distress by any thing they say, if they did not from time to time apply their Handkerchiefs to their Eyes. Far be it from me to think of banishing this Instrument of Sorrow from the Stage; I know a Tragedy could not subsist without it."[32]

The pangs of imminent death were shown by frightful grimaces and halting speech, the latter often indicated in the text of a play by dashes. In Stapylton's *The Step-Mother* (1663), Gracchus, pretending to die, "falls, and mak'st a strange Grimas like a dead man." In Boyle's *Herod* (1694), the last words of Antipater are given thus:

> These double Blessings in my Fate I meet,
> To kill her Murtherer—then—die—at—her—feet.
>
> (*Antipater dies.*)

No doubt there was an art to dying gracefully, without ludicrous sprawling on the stage or "in a chair," and without damage to expensive garments. No doubt, too, a player remembered to die, whenever possible, behind the proscenium arch, so that when the scenes closed he could get up and walk off under his own steam. If he died on the forestage, bearers had to lug him off under the eyes of the audience. Sometimes when a dead man was to lie in state a servant substituted for the actor. Once George Powell's dresser, Warren, took the actor's place on a stage bier in the last act of Rowe's *The Fair Penitent*. From his dressing room the forgetful Powell called for Warren, who replied from the bier, "Here, sir!" "Come here this moment, you Son of a Whore," roared Powell, "or I'll break all the Bones in your Skin!" Warren jumped off the bier, tripped over the draperies tied to its handles, knocked down Calista (Mrs. Barry), and "overwhelmed her with the Table, Lamp, Book, Bones, together with all the Lumber of the Charnel-house.[33]

Although there were innumerable rules for the guidance of the tragedian, there seem to have been almost none for the

[32] *The Spectator*, No. 44, April 20, 1711.

[33] Chetwood, p. 253.

comedian. "The Comedians, I fear," said Betterton, "may take it amiss that I have had little or no Regard to them in these Rules. But . . . as some have observ'd that Comedy is less difficult in the Writing; so I am apt to believe, it is much easier in the Acting."[34]

Dryden remarked that repartee was one of the "chiefest graces" of comedy: "the greatest pleasure of the audience is a chace of wit, kept up on both sides, and swiftly managed."[35] Obviously the comedian had to be skilled in rapid speech and careful timing; otherwise he was free to speak and gesture as he chose. An actor or actress with a gay, airy, ingratiating manner and a graceful person, clever at repartee and at putting the proper stress on a *double-entendre*, could often make a poor comedy sound extremely witty.

To present the low comedy characters with which plays were liberally sprinkled, a player had to be—in Downes's quaint phrase—"Aspectabund," adept at making faces. Low comedians were individualists and often famous as much for their oddities of face, figure, and gait as for their creative skill. Cave Underhill, for example, a mediocre actor, was successful as a comedian because he was tall, corpulent, and broad-faced; "his nose was flattish and short, and his Upper Lip very long and thick, with a wide Mouth and short Chin, a churlish Voice, and awkward Action, leaping often up with both Legs at a Time, when he conceived any Thing Waggish. and afterwards hugging himself at the Thought." On the other hand, James Nokes, famous for low comedy creations, was a very ordinary-looking fellow in private life, but on the stage he "had a shuffling Shamble in his Gait, with so contented an Ignorance in his Aspect and an awkward Absurdity in his Gesture, that had you not known him, you could not have believ'd that naturally he could have a Grain of common Sense."[36]

Some comediennes, too, were individualists and were famous for their specialties: Katherine Corey for such can-

---

[34] Curll, pp. 105–6.

[35] Dryden, "Essay of Dramatic Poesie" (1668).

[36] Aston, II, 307–8; Cibber, I, 145.

tankerous old women as the Widow Blackacre in Wycherley's *The Plain Dealer* (1676); Elinor Leigh, who "had a very droll way of dressing the pretty Foibles of superannuated Beauties"; and Susanna Mountfort, who "was so fond of Humour, in what low part soever to be found, that she made no scruple of defacing her fair Form to come Heartily into it." As Mary the Buxom in D'Urfey's *Don Quixote* (1694), Mrs. Mountfort made herself up as "a young Todpole Dowdy, as freckled as a Ravens Egg, with matted Hair, snotty Nose, and a pair of Hands as black as the Skin of a Tortois, with Nails as long as Kites Tallons upon every Finger."[37]

Yet this dowdy could also be a fine lady with all kinds of airs and affectations. Cibber describes her behavior as Melantha in revivals of Dryden's *Marriage A-la-Mode* as she receives Palamede, who bears a letter of recommendation from her father:

She reads the Letter . . . with a careless, dropping Lip and an erected Brow, humming it hastily over as if she were impatient to outgo her Father's Commands by making a compleat Conquest of him [Palamede] at once; and that the Letter might not embarrass her Attack, crack! she crumbles it at once into her Palm and pours upon him her whole Artillery of Airs, Eyes, and Motion; down goes her dainty, diving Body to the Ground, as if she were sinking under the conscious Load of her own Attractions; then launches into a Flood of fine Language and Compliment, still playing her Chest forward in fifty Falls and Risings, like a Swan upon waving Water; and, to complete her Impertinence, she is so rapidly fond of her own Wit that she will not give her Lover Leave to praise it: Silent assenting Bows and vain Endeavours to speak are all the share of the Conversation he is admitted to, which at last he is relieved from by her Engagement to half a Score Visits, which she *swims* from him to make, with a Promise to return in a Twinkling.[38]

Of course, no collection of rules, anecdotes, and descriptions can ever re-create the ways of long dead actors. Their art is ephemeral, vanishing at the very moment of creation. As the conventions of the theatre and the styles of acting change, that which could exalt or move an audience of a

[37] Cibber, I, 162, 166; dramatis personae of D'Urfey's *Don Quixote*.
[38] Cibber, I, 168–69.

past age merely stirs the later playgoer to laughter. We can only sympathize with the nostalgic old gentleman who in 1745 urged a contemporary actress to play Melantha as Dryden created her:

> Take, take from Dryden's hand Melantha's part,
> The gaudy effort of luxuriant art,
> In all imagination's glitter drest:
> What Bowtell, under the author's eye, exprest,
> What from her lips fantastic Montfort caught,
> And almost mov'd the thing, ye Poet thought.
> . . . Cibber will smile applause: and think again
> Of Hart, of Mohun, and all the female train,
> Coxe, Marshall, Dryden's Reeve,
> Bet. Slade, and Charles's reign.[39]

[39] *The Gentleman's Magazine*, XV (February, 1745), 98.

IV. *In Petticoats and Breeches*

When women replaced female impersonators on the stage, they brought to the theatre a new dimension in sex. Bawdry, obscenity, and vulgarity there had always been, but even the most imaginative pre-Restoration playgoer must have been constantly aware that the woman he saw in an erotic stage situation was really a boy in petticoats. To the lusty male who wanted more than gowns, wigs, make-up, and mockery, the substitution of women for boys brought a new satisfaction. Pepys had often seen Beaumont and Fletcher's spicy comedy *The Scornful Lady* with a boy playing the Lady. On February 12, 1661, he saw it again, but "now done by a woman," he said, "which makes the play appear better than ever it did to me."

After 1660 the playgoer could leave his imagination at home. Something had been added to dramatic entertainment, and the poets, quick to sense an audience reaction, took advantage of it. Restoration drama, and comedy in particular, gave the actress every opportunity to display her physical charms. The aim, however, was suggestiveness, not stark nudity. In 1711 Steele summarized the practices of the stage thus:

I, who know nothing of Women but from seeing Plays, can give great guesses at the whole Structure of the fair Sex, by being innocently placed in the Pit, and insulted by the Petticoats of their Dancers; the Advantages of whose pretty Persons are a great help to a dull Play. When a Poet flags in writing Lusciously, a pretty Girl can move Lasciviously, and have the same good Consequences for the Author.[1]

Feminine fashions in the late seventeenth century were designed to reveal, if not "the whole Structure of the fair Sex," at least provocative sections thereof. On stage in her proper costume the actress displayed her shoulders and much of her bosom (I take a frequent stage direction, "loosely dressed," to refer to such decolletage). Masquerading in male attire, she submitted her legs for public inspection. When she danced in petticoats, she tantalized the male spectators with glimpses of legs and thighs. As the prologue to Wright's *Thyestes* (1674) complains:

> She that Dances jilts the very eyes,
> Allowing only these Discoveries,
> A neat silk Leg, and pair of Holland Thighs.

To the modern playgoer all this is commonplace; to the Restoration gentleman it was fresh and exciting.

When an actress arose in the morning, the chances are that she was already wearing her chief foundation garment for the day: a loose smock (or shift or chemise) of Holland linen reaching well below her knees, with short balloon sleeves and a low-cut, lace-edged neck, adjustable with a drawstring for any desired degree of decolletage. Only the well-to-do could afford nightwear; the poor slept in their undergarments and rarely washed them. Linen was usually heavily perfumed.

After washing her face in cold water (no bath, of course), an actress put on a bodice, or corset, stiffened with wood or whalebone stays and laced either front or back. If she was a dancer, she probably donned a pair of Holland linen drawers, undergarments not commonly worn at this time, even by ladies of fashion.[2] Next came knit thread or silk

[1] *The Spectator*, No. 51, April 28, 1711.

[2] See C. W. Cunnington and P. Cunnington, *The History of Underclothes* (1951), pp. 62–66.

stockings, gartered both above and below the knee; high-heeled shoes with bright buckles; two or three full-flowing petticoats decorated with Colbertine or Flanders lace and reaching almost to the ground; and finally a short-sleeved gown made of silk or farandine (silk mixed with cheaper fibers), closed-fitted in the bodice and separated below the waist to display the petticoats.

She would spend some time on her hair, which, if done in the style favored about 1670, would be curled in long ringlets descending to her shoulders. (Twenty years later she would spend hours laboriously building up a towering "commode.") Then, after a liberal application of Spanish red to lips and cheeks and a splash of orange-flower water for her handkerchief, she would draw on perfumed gloves, pick up her purse, and be ready to sally forth.

According to the custom of the day, she would leave uncovered a considerable territory between waist and chin. A standard jest runs thus: "A Gallant once meeting in Covent-Garden with a handsome, and as it seems, smart Lass, with her Naked Breasts appearing very largely; says he, I pray, Mistress, is that Flesh to be sold? No, says she, no Money shall buy it. Well, says he, then let me advise you, if you will not sell, you should shut up your shop."[3]

Such obvious nudity was no uncommon sight, even on the streets. There were always Puritans who declaimed against the sin "of Naked Necks and Shoulders," but they prejudiced their case by overstatement. There was, for example, the writer who held up for emulation modest Lady Margaret, daughter of the Duke of Burgundy, "who by a fall from her horse having broken her Thigh, chose rather to dye than to expose herself to the inspection of the Chirurgeons."[4] But, as cynical Bernard Mandeville pointed out, morality was largely a matter of custom:

To be modest, we ought in the first place to avoid all unfashionable Denudations. A Woman is not to be found fault with for going with her Neck bare, if the Custom of the Country allows it; and

[3] *Coffee-House Jests* (1677), p. 31.

[4] *England's Vanity*, "By a Compassionate Conformist" (1683), p. 102.

when the Mode orders the Stays to be cut very low, a blooming
Virgin may, without Fear of rational Censure, shew all the World;

> How firm her pouting Breasts, that white as Snow,
> On th'ample Chest at mighty distance grow.

But to suffer her ancle to be seen, where it is the Fashion for
Women to hide their very Feet, is a Breach of Modesty.[5]

Out-of-doors women often wore "berthas," "whisks," or
large handerchiefs pinned over their shoulders and conceal-
ing their breasts. On stage an actress commonly bared her
bosom and sometimes had to endure the lecherous laying-on
of hands. If she wore a bertha or whisk, the chances were
that it would be rumpled or torn in the course of the "tumbling," "towsing," "mousing," or "ruffling" to which she was
often subjected. All these terms meant essentially the same
thing: the vigorous use of exploratory hands, chiefly above
the waist.

Stage business of this kind should not be taken as evidence
of moral decadence. Perhaps Restoration tragedy, dominated
as it was by violent and unnatural loves often culminating
in incest or rape, may be called decadent. Its appeal was to
the fervid imagination of the spectator, and its effect was
erotic overstimulation. But comedy, based on the concept
that the sole function of the female was to satisfy the male
animal, was frankly naturalistic. The physical manifestations
of lechery on the stage were little removed from the actuali-
ties of life. The actor who tumbled or towsed an actress was
merely imitating on the stage an erotic game which anyone
could see played daily in taverns and alehouses.

Mr. Pepys, for example, regularly towsed and tumbled his
numerous easy loves, sometimes recording his exploits in a
curious mixture of tongues. Of one lady he wrote, after an
episode in a tavern, that he did, "touse her and feel her all
over, making her believe how fair and good a skin she has."
Weary at last, he gave over, and "somebody, having seen
some of our dalliance, called aloud in the street, 'Sir! why
do you kiss the gentlewoman so?' and flung a stone at the
window." Of another woman Pepys wrote that he had had her

[5] *The Fable of the Bees* (1714), ed. F. B. Kaye (2 vols.; 1924), Remark
C.

"all sola a my closet, and there did baiser and toucher ses mamelles. . . ." And again, "I did in the morning go to the Swan, and there tumbling la little fille, son uncle did trouver her cum su neck cloth off, which I was ashamed of, but made no great matter of it."[6]

No great matter was made of it on the stage, either. In Behn's *The Town-Fopp* (1676), Bellmour, alone with a prostitute, Flaunt, declares, "Oh I can towse and ruffle, like any Leviathan, when I begin—come, prove my Vigor. (*Towses her*)." "Oh, Lord, Sir!" cries Flaunt, "you tumble all my Garniture." In Behn's *The Round Heads* (1681), Lady Desbro's denudation is too much for Ananias Gogle. "Who in the sight of so much Beauty," he cries, "can think of any Bus'ness but *the* Bus'ness—ah! hide those tempting Breasts, —alack, how smooth and warm they are—(*Feeling 'em, and sneering*)." A moment later, overcome by lechery, he "Takes and ruffles her." In Lacy's *The Dumb Lady* (1669), a farrier posing as a doctor meets a nurse and her husband, Jarvis. The mock doctor heads for the pretty nurse:

DOCT.: By'r lady, a pretty piece of household stuff, and a fine ornament for a couch. I do salute you, nurse, and I would I were that happy suckling that shall draw down the milk of your favour and affection, nurse.

JAR.: Her pulse beats not thereabouts, sir! Hands off, for she's my wife, sir!

DOCT.: I cry you mercy, sir. I congratulate you for having so handsome a wife, and your wife for having so worthy a husband. Your breasts, sweet nurse—

JAR.: Pray you, hold, sir! Half this courtesy would serve.

DOCT.: Worthy sir, I cannot declare enough how much I'm your servant! Delicate breasts, nurse. (*His hands upon her breasts still.*)

NUR.: At your service!

Sometimes provocative description added spice to reality. In Ravenscroft's *The Canterbury Guests* (1694), Mr. Lovell is showing off his sister Arabella (Mrs. Knight) to Captain Durzo as the pattern of a handsome woman. Facing the audience, Arabella poses quietly (perhaps simpering?) between the two men as Lovell describes her: "A Forehead high and

[6] Pepys, June 29, 1663, February 18, May 20, 1667.

fair—Eyes black and sparkling—cheeks plump, not by Art, but Nature painted—a Mouth little, red Lips and white Teeth; a Pearly Portcullis to a Ruby Gate . . . a chin dimpled . . . a Neck smooth, fat, white, and soft as the down on Swans . . . Breasts hard and round, their motions pant beholders Hearts into an exstasy; they rise and fall like Waves blown up by gentle Winds—Do but lay your hand here, Captain. (*Durzo touches Arabella's Breasts.*)"

These are typical samples of everyday business on the Restoration stage. Obviously the audience, like old Sir Jolly Jumble in Otway's *The Souldiers Fortune* (1680), loved "to see a pretty Wench and a young Fellow Towze and Rowze and Frouze and Mowze." If the actresses objected to such public manhandling, their protests have not been recorded.

To the godly (who rarely attended the theatre) all this was wickedness rampant. But to the godly, play acting itself was evil, and the mere appearance of women upon the stage, however dressed, was an abomination. Denied the right to employ women, the pre-Restoration players had dressed boys in women's garments, thereby placing themselves in a sinful dilemma. In 1633 puritanical William Prynne had argued, "If any now object, that it is farre better, farre more comendable for Boyes to act in womans attire, then to bring women-Actors on the Stage to personate female parts . . . I answer first, that the very ground of this objection is false, unlesse the objectors can manifest it to bee a greater abomination, a more detestable damning sinne, for a woman to act a females part upon the Stage, then for a Boy to put on womans apparell, person, and behaviour, to act a feminine part: which the Scripture expressly prohibits, as an abomination to the Lord our God."[7]

Damned if they employed women and damned if they used boys "to personate female parts," the frustrated players had continued to use the second alternative until King Charles came into his own again and all restraints were removed. Then the pendulum swung to the other extreme. The Restoration players not only employed women; from time to time they dressed men in women's garments (for

[7] *Histrio-Mastix* (1633), p. 214.

comic purposes only) and women in men's garments, a practice wicked enough to make Mr. Prynne's cropped ears vibrate with horror. "Dare then any Christian women be so more than whorishly impudent," he had written (at the cost of his ears), "as to act, to speak publikely on a Stage, (perchance in mans apparell, and cut haire, here proved sinfull and abominable) in the presence of sundry men and women? O let such presidents of impudency, of impiety be never heard of or suffred among Christians!"[8]

Yet, in spite of Prynne and all his tribe, of the some three hundred and seventy-five plays first produced in the London public theatres between 1660 and 1700—new plays and alterations of pre-Restoration plays—eighty-nine contained one or more roles for actresses "in Boy's Clothes," or "in Man's Clothes." (The two terms seem to have meant almost the same thing.) In at least fourteen more plays we know that women were assigned to don breeches and play parts originally written for men, not for female impersonators. At least three plays were "acted all by women," who took both the male and female roles. In addition there were many revivals of older plays with breeches parts originally played by boys. Almost every actress appeared at one time or another "dressed like a man"—as a youth, a page, a gentleman, a soldier, a shepherd, or what you will—and some became famous for their elegant appearance in breeches or pantaloons. Among those more honored in breeches than in petticoats were Nell Gwyn, Moll Davis, Pepys's friend Mary Knep, Prince Rupert's mistress Peg Hughes, Elizabeth Barry, Anne Bracegirdle, Beck Marshall, beautiful Mary Lee, Sue Percival (Mountfort), Charlotte Butler, blonde Betty Boutel, and many more. Even Katherine Corey, specialist in "old women" roles, appeared in Joyner's *The Roman Empress* (1670) "disguis'd like a Eunuch," in doublet, breeches, and periwig. The wheel had come full circle: the boys who impersonated women in Shakespeare's time were replaced in the Restoration wonderland by raffish hoydens, breeched and periwigged, with swords at their sides and masculine oaths on their lips.

[8] *Ibid.*, Table, "Women-actors."

Immodest display was only one of several reasons for the common practice of dressing actresses in men's clothing. No doubt it was made easy at first by the oddities of fashion. In 1665 Anthony Wood commented that it was indeed

A strange effeminate age when men strive to imitate women in their apparell, viz. long periwigs, patches in their faces, painting, short wide breeches like petticotes, muffs, and their clothes highly scented, bedecked with ribbons of all colours. . . . On the other side, women would strive to be like men, viz., when they rode on horseback or in coaches weare plush caps like monteros, either full of ribbons or feathers, long periwigs which men use to weare, and riding coats of a red colour all bedaubed with lace which they call vests.

At about this time also a courtier wrote to a friend in the country:

For news from Court I shall tell you that one cannot possibly know a woman from a man, unlesse one hath the eyes of a linx who can see through a wall, for by the face and garbe they are like men. They do not weare any hood but only men's perwich [periwigs] hatts and coats.[9]

These Mad Hatter fashions were not limited to Court circles. Short petticoat breeches (also called Rhinegraves or pantaloons) were quite generally worn between 1660 and 1670. These were so wide that one of Pepys's friends carelessly "put both his legs through one of his knees of his breeches, and went so all day." Male attire was effeminate, colorful, and lavishly decorated with laces and ribbons—envied, no doubt, by the women, especially by those of the middle classes, whose normal garb was sober and durable. At a hilarious party in 1666, when all Pepys's guests were "mighty merry," the host and two other men dressed like women, and Mrs. Pepys's maid, Mary Mercer, "put on a suit of Tom's like a boy, and mighty mirth we had, and Mercer danced a jigg; and Nan Wright and my wife and Pegg Pen put on perriwigs."[10]

9 Wood, I, 509; *HMC, Portland MS*, III, 293.
10 April 6, 1661, August 14, 1666.

Again we see morality determined by custom. Said Mandeville:

> If a Woman at a merry-making dresses in Man's Clothes, it is reckon'd a Frolick amongst Friends, and he that finds too much Fault with it is counted censorious: Upon the Stage it is done without Reproach, and the most Virtuous Ladies will dispense with it in an Actress, tho' every Body has a full View of her Legs and Thighs; but if the same Woman, as soon as she has Petticoats on again, should show her Leg to a Man as high as her Knee, it would be a very immodest Action, and every Body will call her impudent for it.[11]

The immediate reason for epicene dress on the stage was the fact that at the Restoration the two patent companies inherited a number of older plays with romantic or comic plots involving a girl disguised as a boy. The role of the girl was originally designed, of course, to be played by a boy; now, with the substitution of women for boys in breeches parts, the hackneyed old plots took on new life. Actresses discovered a new freedom of movement, an additional opportunity for coquetry; dramatists found that the disguise formula, upon which they thought all the changes had been rung, now had a new appeal; and the male playgoer discovered that women had legs. Whether an actress wore the short jackanapes doublet and Rhinegraves of the early Restoration, or the vest, long coat, and knee breeches of a later period, or a fantastic Roman toga, "wide-sleev'd, and loosely flowing to the knees,"[12] or the Elizabethan doublet and trunk hose which remained the stock costume of a page—she showed her legs. To the Restoration gentleman, accustomed to seeing ladies in petticoats and skirts which brushed the floor, and only occasionally tantalized by the sight of an "ancle," or a dancer's "neat silk Leg, and pair of Holland Thighs," this was a treat indeed.

Obviously a successful actress had to have shapely legs. As William Mountfort said in the prologue to D'Urfey's *The Marriage-Hater Match'd* (1692) when his companion, Anne

[11] Kaye (ed.), *op. cit.*, Remark P.

[12] See the Preface to Flecknoe's *Erminia* (1661).

Bracegirdle, pretended to be ashamed of her appearance in boy's clothes,

> That's very strange, faith, since thy Legs are straight;
> For if thou hadst a thousand Lovers here,
> That very Garb, as thou dost now appear,
> Takes more than any Manto we can buy,
> Or wir'd Comode, tho' Cocked Three Stories high.

Mountfort's judgment is confirmed by Anthony Aston, who asserted that modest Anne was "finely shap'd, and had very handsome Legs and Feet; and her Gait, or Walk, was free, man-like, and modest, when in Breeches."[13] To play breeches parts, then, an actress had to have youth (or the appearance thereof), a good shape, "handsome Legs and Feet," and the ability to walk with a "free, manlike, and modest" gait. A good stock of impudence was a help, too.

From the point of view of the playgoer, we have two comments on legs by Pepys. On October 28, 1661, he saw a revival of Glapthorne's *Argalus and Parthenia* at the Theatre Royal, "where a woman acted Parthenia and came afterward on the stage in mens clothes, and had the best legs that ever I saw, and I was very well pleased with it." Again, at the Duke's Theatre on February 23, 1663, he was much taken with Moll Davis' appearance "in boy's apparel, she having very fine legs, only bends in the hams [knock-kneed?], as I perceive all women do"—a grudging compliment.

The players themselves were properly complacent about the limbs of their actresses. In the epilogue to Corye's *The Generous Enemies* (1671), Elizabeth Boutel, showing off her handsome legs in a page's costume, is made to say,

> As Woman let me with the men prevail,
> And with the Ladies as I look like Male.
> 'Tis worth your Money that such legs appear;
> These are not to be seen so cheap elsewhere:
> In short, commend this play, or by this light,
> We will not sup with one of you tonight.

Since Mrs. Boutel created at least twelve breeches parts and no doubt inherited a goodly number as well, we may

[13] II, 305.

take it that the legs were very fine indeed and continued to be worth the money during her entire stage career, roughly 1668 to 1695. Another notable male impersonator was Sue Mountfort, who, said Cibber,

> While her Shape permitted . . . was a more adroit pretty Fellow than is usually seen upon the Stage. . . . People were so fond of seeing her a Man, that when the Part of Bays in *The Rehearsal* had for some time lain dormant, she was desired to take it up, which I have seen her act with all the true coxcombly Spirit and Humour that the Sufficiency of the Character required.

Alas, as Mrs. Mountfort grew older she had to give up breeches parts because she developed "thick Legs and Thighs, corpulent and large Posteriours."[14] It may well be that Mary Betterton and Anne Shadwell, both popular in breeches parts in their younger days, had to give them up because of middle-aged spread.

No great histrionic ability was needed to play the simplest breeches role, that of a love-lorn maiden in disguise. This stock character had a lengthy dramatic pedigree, but the immediate model seems to have been Bellario in Beaumont and Fletcher's ever popular romance, *Philaster*. Usually the romantic girl put on the costume of a page to pursue or serve the man with whom she was in love, or to whom she was contracted, or by whom she had been seduced—or hoped to be seduced. Her male disguise could get her into some very embarrassing situations: she could be accused of the unlikely feats of seduction or rape, for instance; or, as a "pretty boy," she could find herself pursued by a lecherous lady or by an even more lecherous gentleman of unnatural tastes. Nevertheless, her responses were always so feminine that sometimes her girlish face or behavior revealed her sex to others in the play (of course the audience knew who she was all along). She always got her hero, or, failing him, a handsome and handy second lead.

Any wide-eyed young actress with good legs could play this simple role, but it was the forte of "chestnut-man'd" Betty Boutel, who was "low of Stature, had very agreeable

14 Cibber, I, 167; Aston, II, 313.

Features, a good Complexion, but a Childish Look."[15] It is very likely that Wycherley tailored his Fidelia in *The Plain Dealer* (1676) to her specifications. Timid, long-suffering Fidelia, serving as page to the blustering plain dealer, Captain Manley, is forced to act as his procuress with his ex-mistress Olivia, narrowly escapes the lecherous attentions of both Olivia and her husband Vernish (who discovers Fidelia's sex), and eventually gets Manley for a husband. The role of youth and innocence in what was, in effect, a brothel could be played only by an actress who looked the first and could pretend the second. Others who had this gift were Jane Long, Anne Marshall, Charlotte Butler, and Anne Bracegirdle.

The heroic, or tragic, version of the lovelorn damsel usually required an actress of more force. In tragedy the woman in breeches was often a sinner who came to a bad end. Her love was an all-consuming passion that, frustrated, could turn to fiendish fury. The actress had to know how to deliver a rant, to handle a sword with some skill, and generally to personate a swashbuckling male. Mary Lee (Lady Slingsby), particularly effective in such tragic roles, must have been anything but an innocent-looking beauty, if we can believe a description of her as Bellamira in Lee's *Caesar Borgia* (1679):

> Oh such a skin full of alluring flesh!
> Ah, such a ruddy, moist, and pouting lip;
> Such Dimples, and such Eyes, such melting Eyes,
> Blacker than Sloes, and yet they sparkl'd fire.

One of Mrs. Lee's best breeches parts was Tarpeia in *Romulus and Hersilia* (Anon., 1682). For the love of a Sabine general, Curtius, Tarpeia betrays a Roman fort to the Sabines. Then, when Curtius refuses to marry her, she comes to him "in Mans apparel," wounds him with his own sword, is wounded in turn by his guards, and escapes to aid the Romans in the recapture of the fort. When her treason is finally disclosed and her father dooms her to spend the rest of her life as a vestal, Tarpeia, overcome by remorse and horror, falls on her sword and dies. A character of this kind

[15] Curll, p. 21.

called for considerable acting skill, strong lungs, and an
active body, as well as good-looking legs. Mrs. Lee's only
serious rival in such tragic roles was Elizabeth Barry.

The most popular, and in some ways the most difficult,
variety of breeches part was that played by a comedienne.
In comedy the intention seems to have been, at least in part,
to poke fun at the extremes of male dress and behavior, so
that the appeal of the pretty girl in breeches was both sensu-
ous and comic. When Pepys saw Nell Gwyn in breeches as
Florimel in Dryden's *Secret Love* (1667), he wrote ecstatically
that she had "the motions and carriage of a spark the most
that ever I saw any man have." Her part, he decided, was
"the most comicall that ever was made for woman."[16] Dryden's intention is suggested by Florimel's soliloquy as she
admires herself in a pocket mirror: "Save you, Monsieur
Florimel! Faith, methinks you are a very jaunty fellow,
poudré et adjusté as well as the best of 'em. I can manage the
little comb, set my hat, shake my garniture, toss about my
empty noddle, walk with a courant slur, and at every step
peck down my head. If I should be mistaken for some courtier now, pray where's the difference?" Mistaken for a courtier she is, as she swaggers about the stage mimicking the
airs of a beau, makes impudent love to Olinda and Sabina,
and completely fools her lover, Celadon.

Florimel was the prototype of the mad girl in breeches, a
comic character which was, in the main, a Restoration inven-
tion. As succeeding dramatists developed the type, the mad
girl became increasingly a female rakehell, swaggering, bully-
ing, fighting, invading taverns and brothels, and making violent love to her sisters in petticoats. The ultimate character
of this kind is Lucia in Southerne's *Sir Anthony Love* (1690),
a part written especially for Sue Mountfort. Lucia, an adventuress, dresses "in Man's attire," sets up as a rich young
gallant, attracts all the girls within a ten-mile radius, goes
through a mock marriage with one of them, fights off a homo-
sexual abbé who thinks her a "pretty boy," changes to her
real form long enough to spend a night with a favored lover,
invades a nunnery to get a wife for said lover, engages in a

[16] March 21, May 25, 1667.

pitched battle with a band of bravos and wins, tricks a fool into marrying her, and then bullies him into giving her a separate maintenance. Lucia is the complete female libertine.

In his dedication to the play Southerne wrote:

I am pleased, by way of thanks, to do [Mrs. Mountfort] that public justice in print, which some of the best judges of these performances, have, in her praise, already done her, in public places; that they never saw any part more masterly played: and as I made every line for her, she has mended every word for me; and by a gaiety and air, particular to her action, turned everything into the genius of the character.

Of course Mrs. Mountfort was unique; in the opinion of contemporaries she was "a Miracle."[17] The other actresses notable for comic breeches parts—Betty Boutel, Charlotte Butler, Betty Currer, and Anne Bracegirdle—were all her inferiors.

Women in breeches appealed so strongly to the males in an audience that many epicene roles were forced into plays, sometimes with rhyme but rarely with reason. With an eye to profits, the managers dressed their women as men on the slightest pretext, employing them for a miscellany of purposes: to do an after-play dance, to speak a prologue or epilogue, to play a role written originally for a man, or to play the part of a boy. As Pepys wrote cynically after seeing Moll Davis dance a jig and announce the next day's play at the close of Caryl's *The English Princess* (March 7, 1667), "it come in by force only to please the company to see her dance in boy's clothes."

The reason for appointing a woman in breeches to deliver a prologue or epilogue was not merely to give everyone a "full View of her Legs and Thighs"; the costume provided the writer with a subject for risqué wit. When Charlotte Butler spoke the epilogue to Harris' *The Mistakes* (1690) "in mans cloaths," she was evidently wearing some sort of uniform. She began:

As Malefactors brought to Execution,
Have leave t'Harrangue before their Dissolution:

[17] Wells, p. 106.

Such favour your poor Criminall beseeches,
Something to say to justify her Breeches.
To strut with Feather, Tilter, Lace and Blue,
I have as good pretence as most of you.
'Twas time to take this War like Dress in Vogue;
To guard my Dang'rous Post of Epilogue;
Where lurching Wits like Rapperees appear:
And Coward Critique still attacks our Rear.
I stand your Shot—To storm this little Fort,
Let's see who dares—I've that shall find you sport.
Damn your French way of shooting on the Stretch,
Give me the Man bears up and mounts the Breach.
Entrench'd i' th' Pit you sit securely Rageing,
You know who'l have the odds in close Engaging.

The chief reason for casting women in leading roles written
for men was, of course, to capitalize upon their effectiveness
in breeches parts. Thus Jane Long played Prince Osiris in
Settle's *Cambyses* (1671), Mary Knep and Elizabeth Corbet
were the mock-heroic Prince Nicholas and King Andrew in
Duffett's *Psyche Debauch'd* (1675), Mary Lee and Elizabeth
Barry acted the shepherds Astatius and Philicides in *The
Constant Nymph* (Anon., 1677), Sue Verbruggen (Mountfort)
played Achmet, a eunuch, in Pix's *Ibrahim* (1696), and Mary
Kent played Young Fashion in Vanbrugh's *The Relapse*
(1696). The practice of casting women in leading male roles
continued well into the next century. Peg Woffington, an
actress noted for her promiscuity, was very popular as Sir
Harry Wildair in Farquhar's comedy by that name: "Once,
after playing the role, she came into the Green-room and said
pleasantly, 'In my Conscience! I believe Half the Men in
the House take me for one of their own Sex.' Another Actress
reply'd, 'It may be so, but in my Conscience! the other Half
can convince them to the contrary.' "[18]

Occasionally, perhaps on the principle that one can't have
too much of a good thing, a Restoration company produced
a play with women playing every part. These productions
seem to have been provocative and therefore popular. On
October 11, 1664, Pepys heard "what a bawdy loose play"

[18] Chetwood, p. 252.

Killigrew's *The Parson's Wedding* was, as "acted by nothing but women at the King's House," and confessed his pleasure at the news. In 1672, after the Theatre Royal burned down, the King's Company turned for a time to presenting older plays "acted by nothing but women," as a sure means of attracting playgoers to their makeshift theatre in Lincoln's Inn Fields. At least three plays were so presented: Killigrew's *The Parson's Wedding*, Dryden's *Secret Love*, and Beaumont and Fletcher's *Philaster*. The prologues and epilogues to these, written for the occasion and spoken by Betty Boutel, Beck Marshall, and Anne Reeves, all "in Mans Cloathes," testify to the provocative intention. There are apologies to the ladies in the audience for presenting "Youth and Beauty" lacking in virility ("You'd find the cheat in the empty Pantaloon"); appeals to the gentlemen to note that the actresses' "Legs are no ill sight"; and promises that, unlike the boys who played women's roles in the last age, the actresses "can hold out women to our Lodgings too."[19]

Not to be completely outdone, the Duke's Company tried this device at least once, with a very poor anonymous tragedy, *Piso's Conspiracy* (1675)—perhaps reasoning that only novelty and legs could save the play from damnation. Announcing that the men of the company were tired of heroic roles, the speaker of the prologue, a woman in breeches, advised her hearers that women were to play the male roles, and warned them to

> Expect grave Strut, big Looks, and thund'ring Speeches,
> From Hero, made up by the Force of Breeches.
> Aye, and a good Shift too; For, under the Rose,
> Whilst we look big by Virtue of our Cloathes,
> And, Hero like, talk what We cannot do,
> We're much such Blusterers as some of you.

Finally, it seems to have been a fairly common practice to assign young actresses to play certain minor roles—pages, attendants, and the like—which ordinarily would have been

---

[19] Thorn-Drury, pp. 1–5, 19–20, 113, 129. Early in the following century Congreve's *Love for Love* was "acted all by women" at the Haymarket Theatre, January 9, 1706, and Settle's *Pastor Fido* was similarly produced at the Dorset Garden Theatre, October 30, 1706 (Genest, II, 347, 355).

played by youths. Usually, since these roles were played
without stage discovery, our only evidence of the casting is
the appearance of a woman's name after a male part in the
dramatis personae of a play. Thus, disguised in doublet and
trunk hose, Anne Reeves played Ascanio, a page, in Dryden's
The Assignation (1672); Anne Gibbs played Garcia, a page,
in Otway's *Don Carlos* (1676); and Betty Allison, in coat,
vest, and breeches, played "A very young Beau" in Dennis'
A Plot and No Plot (1697). Perhaps this practice resulted
more from a chronic shortage of young males than from a
desire to show off girls' legs. Even so, the actors were often
suspiciously quick to call attention to the epicene disguise
and make a virtue of necessity. For example, the role of
young Hippolito in the Davenant-Dryden version of *The
Tempest* (1667) was played by a girl (probably Moll Davis
or Jane Long). The prologue begged the audience to pity the
poor players,

> Who by our dearth of Youths are forc'd t'employ
> One of our Women to present a Boy.
> And that's a transformation you will say
> Exceeding all the Magick in the Play.
> Let none expect in the last Act to find,
> Her Sex transform'd from man to Woman-kind.
> What e're she was before the Play began,
> All you shall see of her is perfect man.
> Or if your fancy will be farther led,
> To find her Woman, it must be abed.

Almost invariably, when an actress dressed in man's
clothing performed an important plot function, some kind
of revelation was necessary toward the end of the play. The
audience, of course, had been aware of her sex all along, but
the other players, an incredibly stupid lot, had taken her to
be a page, a youth, or a young gentleman. Eventually in a
kind of obligatory scene, the actress pulled off her hat and
periwig at a climactic moment or lost both in a struggle or a
duel. As she stood there blushing, with her hair about her
ears, the astounded players raised their hands heavenward
and called her name or chorused, "A Woman!"

The origin of this device is, of course, Elizabethan; for example, in Jonson's *Epicœne; or The Silent Woman* Dauphine "takes off Epicoene's peruke and other disguises" at the climax of the comedy. But the Restoration periwig was vastly different from the woman's wig worn by a boy actress in Jonson's time. Almost universally worn by gentlemen after 1660, the periwig was a huge mass of hair, usually blonde, closely framing the face and falling in heavy curls on the shoulders. Beneath it the wearer kept his head shaved, partly for coolness and partly as a protection against lice and nits. The actress who donned a periwig for disguise could have her own long hair arranged under it for a spectacular disclosure. Thus, in Boyle's *Guzman* (1669), a marriage is performed by a woman disguised as a priest. The imposture is discovered when "Francisco pulls off her Perruque, and her Woman's Hair falls about her ears." Or we have at the conclusion of Granville's *The She-Gallants* (1695) the disguised girl, Constantia, dragged upon the stage, "her Perruque off, and her Hair about her Ears."

Although de-wigging was the commonest discovery device, the poets rang the changes on the trick and tried whenever possible to remind the audience that, even in breeches, actresses were mammals. Discovery could be achieved simply by demonstrating this fact. For example, in Behn's *The Younger Brother* (1696), Olivia (Sue Verbruggen) has been serving Mirtilla as a page. When she is accused by Prince Frederick of having designs on her mistress, Mirtilla "Opens Olivia's Bosom, shews her Breasts." "Ha!" cries the Prince, "By Heav'n, a Woman!" Again, in Shadwell's *Bury Fair* (1689), when Philadelphia (Charlotte Butler), who has been serving Lord Bellamy as a page, "Swoons and falls down upon a chair," Gertrude cries, "Your page is in a swoon, Help, help! Open his breast. Oh Heaven! this is a woman!" Idiotically, Bellamy and his friend Wildish chorus, "A woman!"

The two discovery devices could be combined into one, as in Wycherley's *The Plain Dealer* (1676), when poor Fidelia, captured by Vernish in Olivia's lodgings, confesses that she is a woman. "How!" says Vernish, "a very handsome woman, I'm sure then: here are witnesses of it too, I confess—(*Pulls off her peruke and feels her breasts*)." In the search for variants upon these two devices, some poets achieved memorable results. Noteworthy is the discovery scene in Hopkins' *Friendship Improv'd* (1699), in which Princess Locris (Anne Bracegirdle), dressed as a man in a helmet and tunic, after refusing to duel with Maherbal, the man she secretly loves, discloses her sex:

LOCRIS: Here's my bare Breast, now if thou dar'st, strike here. (*She loosens her robe a little, her Helmet drops off, and her Hair appears.*)
MAHERBAL: O all ye Gods! what Wonders do I see!

All this indelicate capitalizing on breasts and limbs seems to have disturbed no one, either the reformers who attacked the stage so bitterly toward the end of the century, or the audience, or the actresses so exploited. In fact there is a surprising dearth of comment on practices which, to a moralist, must have seemed outrageous. Probably the reformers never committed the mistake of going to the theatre and contented themselves with reading selected plays and culling out choice specimens of verbal obscenity. No doubt most of the male playgoers were earthy enough to enjoy the show, and the more delicate minded were so inured to it by custom as to see no immorality in it. The ladies, of course, rivaled the actresses in their display of bosoms and shoulders. As for their attitude toward epicene garb, we have Mandeville's word for it that "the most Virtuous Ladies will dispense with it in an Actress."

One would hardly expect the actresses themselves to complain about having to appear in breeches, or in petticoats "undrest . . . loosely to the Winds."[20] Most of them were made of playhouse flesh and blood, and they were encouraged by managers and spectators alike to display themselves provocatively. Even the great Doctor Samuel Johnson was not immune to their attractions. In 1750, while his *Irene* was in rehearsal, Johnson frequented the Green Room and en-

[20] Behn, *The Rover*, Part I (1677), Act V, scene 1.

joyed chatting with the players. But at last he "denied himself this amusement, from considerations of rigid virtue," saying to Garrick, "I'll come no more behind your scenes, David; for the silk stockings and white bosoms of your actresses excite my amorous propensities."[21]

[21] Boswell's *Life of Johnson* (Oxford, 1904), I, 135.

V. *The Actress and the Play*

In the course of a discussion of stage improvements at the time of the Restoration, William Archer remarked, almost casually, "But the great step in advance lay, of course, in the assignment of female parts to women instead of boys. I need not enlarge upon the immense significance of this reform."[1] Too many stage historians have been content to make similar airy statements, apparently assuming that the substitution of women for boys was a benefit to the theatre and a boon to Restoration drama. Only the first of these assumptions is correct

In 1739 Colley Cibber insisted that the early Restoration actors had two "critical Advantages" over all other players in theatrical history: the first that they spread a feast of drama before audiences made hungry by the "so long Interdiction of Plays during the Civil War and the Anarchy that followed it," and the second that women replaced boys in female roles.

The Characters of Women on Former Theatres were perform'd by Boys or young Men of the most effeminate Aspect. And what Grace or Master-strokes of Action can we conceive such ungain Hoydens to have been capable of? . . . The additional objects then,

[1] *The Old Drama and the New* (1923), p. 144.

of real, beautiful Women could not but draw a Proportion of new Admirers to the Theatre.[2]

The assumption that many male playgoers came to admire the women rather than the plays and continued to come to gaze hungrily on beauty is supported by Restoration evidence. In 1671, for example, Edward Howard wrote in the Preface to his *The Six Days Adventure*, "Scenes, Habits, Dancing, or perhaps an actress, Take more with Spectators, than the best Dramatick Wit." In the epilogue to Shadwell's *The Libertine* (1675), certain promises are made to the gallants of the pit, among them:

> Item, you shall appear behind our Scenes,
> And there make love with the sweet chink of Guinnies,
> The unresisted Eloquence of Ninnies.
> Some of our Women shall be kind to you,
> And promise free ingress and egress too.
> But if the Faces which we have w'on't do,
> We will find out some of Sixteen for you.
> We will be civil when nought else will win ye;
> We will new bait our Trap, and that will bring ye.

Again, the prologue to a lost play called *Fools Have Fortune* (ca. 1680) introduced a new actress, Charlotte Butler, with these lines:

> 'Tis seldom a new play with you prevails,
> But a new woman almost never fails.
> New did I say? Nay though the town before
> Had rumpled, read, & thumb'd her oer & oer,
> But on the stage no sooner she appears,
> But presently the sparks prick up their ears,
> And all in clusters round the scenes betake,
> Like boys about a bush to catch a snake.[3]

And in 1681, at a revival of Lee's *Mithridates*, Cardell Goodman spoke a new epilogue in which, after crying, "Pox on this Play-house, 'tis an old tir'd Jade," he debated how best to please the audience, decided at last that a woman was needed, and went off to

> . . . scoure the Scene-room and Engage
> Some Toy within to save the falling Stage.

[2] II, 222.   [3] Collier, p. 202.

He returned with beautiful Elizabeth Cox, who had just re-joined the King's Company after a long absence and was ready with some neatly suggestive verses to save the day, the play, and the stage all at once.

Further evidence of the drawing power of the new women is the large number of prologues and epilogues written for them to deliver. Sometimes the speaker of one of these dramatic appendages is named; sometimes we are told only that the speaker was "A Woman"; but even without tags it is easy to identify the recitations intended for women by their substance and tone.[4] Usually delivered by popular actresses (often "in mans cloaths"), they were designed to give full scope for coquetry and suggestiveness, so that a clever young woman could coax an audience into a good humor. Sometimes a poet gave a new actress a chance to call attention to her fresh attractions and to the fact that she was available for extraprofessional engagements. Sometimes a writer built a prologue or epilogue so closely about the known personality of the speaker (including the use of her name in the lines) that it could not be spoken by anyone else without drastic revision. For example, the epilogue to Dryden's *Tyrannic Love* (1669), spoken by Nell Gwyn, contains the following highly personal lines:

> I come, kind gentlemen, strange news to tell ye:
> I am the ghost of poor departed Nelly. . . .
> To tell you true, I walk because I die
> Out of my calling, in a tragedy.
> O poet, damned dull poet, who could prove
> So senseless to make Nelly die for love! . . .
> As for my epitaph when I am gone,
> I'll trust no poet, but will write my own:
> "Here Nelly lies, who, though she lived a slattern,
> Yet died a princess, acting in Saint Cattern."

Of the women who became actresses before 1689, at least twenty-six were intrusted with one or more prologues and epilogues. Of these Anne Bracegirdle was easily the champion, with at least nine prologues and twenty-two epilogues

[4] See Autrey Nell Wiley, "Female Prologues and Epilogues," *Publications of the Modern Language Association*, XLVIII (1933), 1060–79.

to her credit. (Mrs. Barry was runner-up with six prologues and twenty-one epilogues.) Of course Anne was not only beautiful; as "the Romantick Virgin" she was a perennial curiosity.

From the box-office point of view there can be no doubt that the substitution of women for boys was a master stroke. Even after the first novelty had worn off, the women continued to attract spectators by their acting skills, by their beauty, by the often daring display of their persons, and especially by their demireputations. Constantly, allusions in prologues and epilogues reminded the sparks and wits in the pit that the women of the theatre were ripe for the picking. For example, in the epilogue to *The Conquest of Jerusalem* (Part I, 1677), John Crowne felt constrained to apologize for the ostentatious virtue of his heroines, Clarona and Berenice:

> And last, to take away all sad Complaints,
> These Plays debauch our Women into Saints,
> Forgive it in the Plays, and we'll engage
> They shall be Saints no where but on the Stage.

Since the women who played the two roles were Elizabeth Boutel and Rebecca Marshall, both noted Cyprians, this was a safe enough promise.

As creators of character there can be little doubt that the new actresses were superior to their juvenile predecessors. Of course it was unfair of Cibber to damn so thoroughly the boy-actresses of the previous age; he knew nothing about the original creators of Shakespeare's great women characters. Moreover, he should have remembered young Kynaston, who was no "ungain Hoyden," and who, in women's clothes, "was clearly," said Pepys, "the prettiest woman in the whole house."[5] Nevertheless, it is inconceivable that a boy, no matter how talented, could compete with such gifted mature women as the great Mary Betterton, the famous Elizabeth Barry, or the accomplished Anne Bracegirdle. The stage life of the female impersonator was usually short, and his interpretation of a character could never be more than superficially correct. Allardyce Nicoll suggests that the actresses

[5] January 7, 1661.

made possible "a more charming presentation of Shakespearean tragedy and comedy, shedding a fresh light upon
the Desdemonas and Ophelias of the past."[6] No doubt he is
right—although there is no assurance that the light shed was
always pure and clear. Certainly the players themselves were
convinced that the women were more effective than boys.
In the prologue to Settle's *The Conquest of China* (1675),
Mary Lee ("in male attire") is made to say,

> Did not the Boys Act Women's Parts last Age?
> Till we in pitty to the Barren Stage
> Came to Reform your Eyes that went astray,
> And taught you Passion the true English Way.
> Have not the Women of the Stage done this?
> Nay, took all Shapes, and used most means to Please.

In the main, then, we must agree with Cibber that the
substitution of women for boys not only made the theatre
more attractive (at least for a certain kind of playgoer), but
also made possible "Master-strokes of Action" in the interpretation of female characters. The advent of actresses was
indeed a benefit to the theatre.

But what of dramatic literature? Did the new actresses influence the playwrights of the new era, and, if so, was the influence good or bad? Did the imagination of the Restoration
poet body forth the forms of girls unknown, or did he use as
his models the women of the Court and Town? Or did his
creative eye, in a fine frenzy rolling, steady at last upon some
stage Nell, or Anne, or Betty?

Without information from the Elysian fields it is difficult
to answer these questions precisely. The advent of women
on the stage was only one of many factors influencing the
development of Restoration drama; in addition there were
Elizabethan, French, and classical influences, the changed
climate of morality, the new stagecraft, and the tastes of the
small coterie that dominated the theatres. Nevertheless, the
introduction of women was a factor of considerable importance, and there is reason to believe that the new actresses
influenced the poets to a greater degree than has been recog-

[6] P. 71.

nized. Regrettably, we must add, their influence was not always good, morally or dramatically.

Before considering the relations of poet and player, we must remember that the Restoration poet, like his predecessors, wrote for stock companies. For twenty-two years after the return of Charles II there were two companies in London, the King's and the Duke's. Each kept in regular employment some eight actresses. For thirteen years, from 1682 to 1695, only the United Company, with eight to ten regular actresses, presented plays. From 1695 to 1708 two companies competed again for the favor of the Town.

A play submitted for production was read by the actor-managers of a company with an eye, first, for profits. Since the actresses were stellar attractions, it is obvious that the dramatist had to provide roles for as many women as feasible and opportunities for those women to exercise their provocative arts and display their persons. This constant dwelling upon the impurely physical, so apparent in most Restoration plays, did not develop immediately after the Restoration. The women's roles in plays written in the first three or four years could just as well have been played by boys. Probably Dryden's *The Rival Ladies* (1664), with its emphasis on female anatomy, led the way to the new era of open impudicity.

Although an amateur playwright could free-lance and offer his play to the theatre of his choice (when there were two companies), most of the professionals wrote specifically for one company or another, shaping their characters and plots to suit the abilities of the chosen players. Some professionals were under contract to write for one company only, and such contracts were usually enforced. In 1671 Elkanah Settle, who had engagements with the Duke's Company, thought to better himself by offering his new play, *The Empress of Morocco*, to the King's Company, at that time a very able troupe "in the height of Mr. Hart's Health and Excellence." But the Duke's players protested, authority intervened, and the play went to the contract company.[7] Did Settle have to revise it to fit it to the actors of the Duke's

---

[7] *A Narrative Written by E. Settle* (1683).

Company? Very likely. Cibber informs us that Congreve had his *Love for Love* (1695) all ready for the United Company when the Betterton-Barry-Bracegirdle group seceded and set up their own theatre in Lincoln's Inn Fields. After some hesitation the author decided to let his play "take its Fortune with those Actors [the seceders]" for whom he had first intended the parts.[8] Cibber himself had to rewrite his *Woman's Wit* (1697). In his Preface he apologized for certain inconsistencies in the comedy. The reason for these, he said, was that while he was writing the first half of the play he was engaged (as an actor) by the Lincoln's Inn Fields Company, and therefore prepared his characters "to the Taste of those Actors." Before he completed the play he returned to the Drury Lane Company, "and was then forc'd," he said, "to confine the business of my persons to the Capacity of different People."

Since the famous low comedian Thomas Dogget was then a member of the Drury Lane Company, Cibber, "not to miss the advantages of Mr. Dogget's excellent Action," wrote a part especially for him, which, said the poet, "I knew from him cou'd not fail of diverting." Evidently it was a common practice to create characters designed to make the most of some player's "excellent Action," especially when the player had become typed. The famous stage villain Samuel Sandford initially played villains because he was "Round-shoulder'd, Meagre-fac'd, Spindle-shank'd, Splay-footed, with a sour Countenance, and long lean Arms." In the course of time he became so completely typed that once when he was cast as an honest man and remained virtuous throughout the action the audience fairly damned the play, "as if the Author had impos'd upon them the most frontless or incredible Absurdity."[9] We can be sure that the playwrights took care to fit their creations to the known abilities of heroes like Hart and Betterton, heroines like Mrs. Marshall and Mrs. Barry, villains like Sandford, and comedians like Nokes, Underhill, Leigh, Dogget, Mrs. Leigh, and Mrs. Mountfort. Occasionally, if we may judge from one example, they even consulted with the player in advance. On May 9,

[8] I, 197.   [9] Aston, II, 306; Cibber, I, 133.

1693, Dryden wrote to his friend Walsh describing the play he was then preparing for the United Company, *Love Triumphant*. "This morning," he concluded, "I had their chief Comedian whom they call Solon [Dogget] with me; to consult with him concerning his own Character: and truly I think he has the best Understanding of any man in the Playhouse."[10]

All our information leads to the conclusion that playwright and player were very closely associated. The poet who had had a play produced was given thereafter the freedom of the house and entered at any time without paying. One important professional writer, Thomas Shadwell, was married to an actress and numbered the chief players of the Duke's Company among his friends. A few poets, notably the Earl of Rochester, Sir Charles Sedley, John Dryden, and William Congreve, chose mistresses from among the actresses. The masters of the two original companies, Davenant and Killigrew, were playwrights, as was Sir Robert Howard, a chief shareholder in the King's Company. In addition we have a long list of playwrights who were also successful actors: Betterton, Cibber, Dogget, Haines, Harris, Horden, Jevon, Lacy, Medbourne, Mountfort, and Powell (both Otway and Lee failed as actors). All these men, of course, knew the theatres and the players intimately.

Poets were not only consulted about the casting of their plays; they had what amounted to veto power, even for revivals. In her Preface to *The Dutch Lover* (1673), Aphra Behn complained about the ad-libbing of Angel, who played the low comedy role of Haunce. Admitting that she had known he customarily spoke "a great deal of idle stuff," she concluded, "I gave him yet the Part, because I knew him so acceptable to most o' th' lighter Periwigs about the Town." In the summer of 1684, when the United Company was planning revivals of *All for Love* and *The Conquest of Granada*, Betterton and Dryden discussed the casts for each. The final lists were sent to Dryden in the country. He gave his approval with provisos: "Only Octavia was to be Mrs. Buttler, in

[10] C. E. Ward (ed.), *The Letters of John Dryden* (1942), p. 54.

case Mrs. Cooke were not on the Stage. And I know not whether Mrs. Percivall who is a Comedian will do so well for Benzayda."[11]

Occasionally we have complaints that the cast was not that planned by the author, or that an actor for whom a part was designed failed to play it. Mrs. Behn's literary executor asserted in the Preface to her posthumous *The Widow Ranter* (1685) that the play failed because many of the parts were "false cast, and given to those whose Tallants and Genius's suited not our Author's Intention." In his Preface to *Cuckolds-Haven* (1685), Tate complained that Nokes, for whom he had designed the leading role, had been unable to play it. To make sure that the reader understood his intentions, Tate inserted this line in the dramatis personae of the printed play: "Alderman Touchstone, intended for Mr. Nokes—Mr. Percivall."

On the other hand, we often find prefatory praise for a leading actor or actress, sometimes accompanied by the smug suggestion that the poet planned the play to give the player his big chance. So (to deal only with women) William Joyner, in his Preface to *The Roman Empress* (1670), said modestly of the leading character, Fulvia, "If my art has fail'd in the writing of it, it was highly recompenc'd in the scenical presentation; for it was incomparably acted"—by Rebecca Marshall. In his dedication to *Sir Anthony Love* (1690), Thomas Southerne gave high praise to Mrs. Mountfort as "the original Sir Anthony," concluding with a double boast, "and as I made every line for her, she has mended every word for me; and by a gaiety and air, particular to her action, turned everything into the genius of the character." He was almost as kind to Mrs. Barry when she played Isabella in *The Fatal Marriage* (1694): "I made the play for her part, and her part has made the play for me."

The intimate, day-by-day association of poets and actresses resulted inevitably in some liaisons. It is not easy to determine what effect theatrical love affairs may have had on plays, but it is clear that some playwrights wrote parts for their favorites. The tradition that pretty Anne Reeves

[11] *Ibid.*, p. 24.

owed her roles in Dryden's plays to her intimacy with the poet is underscored by a passage in Buckingham's *The Rehearsal* (1672), in which Bayes (Dryden) is made to say of Amaryllis (Anne Reeves), "Ay, 'tis a pretty little rogue; I knew her face would set off armour extremely; and, to tell you true, I writ that part only for her. You must know she is my mistress."

We are on surer ground with two other poets, Thomas Otway and William Congreve. It is generally believed that Otway, hopelessly besotted with Elizabeth Barry, created for her two of the finest characters in Restoration tragedy, Monimia in *The Orphan* (1680) and Belvidera in *Venice Preserved* (1682), modeling them not so much on the real Mrs. Barry as on his passionate idealization of that mercenary lady. His loving labors went unrewarded; William Oldys commented indignantly that Mrs. Barry "could get bastards with other men, though she would hardly condescend to grant Otway a kiss, who was as amiable in person and address as the best of them."[12] If we can believe the gossips, Congreve had better fortune with his inamorata, Anne Bracegirdle, for whom he wrote the parts of Cynthia in *The Double-Dealer* (1693), Angelica in *Love for Love* (1695), Almeria in *The Mourning Bride* (1697), and Millamant in *The Way of the World* (1700), roles that made all possible capital of Mrs. Bracegirdle's presumed character and known abilities.[13]

To these examples of playwrights associated with actresses we may add Betterton, Mountfort, and Shadwell, all married to leading actresses. Conjugal fidelity if not conjugal love required these gentlemen to write good parts for their respective spouses, and some of the best roles the three ladies played were written by their husbands.

But a poet could write roles for an actress without the inspiration of either connubial pride or a tender passion. Every major actress had her forte. In the early years of the period the audiences enjoyed the impudence of Nell Gwyn, the tragic intensity of Rebecca Marshall, the sweet dignity

12 P. 397; R. G. Ham, *Otway and Lee* (1931), pp. 82–94.

13 John C. Hodges, *William Congreve, the Man* (1941), pp. 43–45, 49–50.

of Mary Betterton, the romantic charm of Elizabeth Boutel, the whimsical drolleries of Elinor Leigh, and so on. It was simply practical good sense for a playwright to exploit the known abilities of an actress. Although the stock female characters repeated again and again in Restoration drama owe their existence to a number of components, certainly not the least of those was the actress herself.

In the King's Company, for example, after the theatres reopened in November, 1666, tall, dark, queenly Rebecca Marshall became the recognized leading lady. In a sizable body of plays, Dryden, Lee, Wycherley, and others made capital of her fire and passion. Usually playing opposite her was the romantic ingénue, blonde Betty Boutel, who represented goodness and chastity in opposition to Mrs. Marshall's pictures of evil and lechery. Little Betty Boutel, "celebrated for the gentler parts in tragedy,"[14] usually played supporting roles in major productions. Notable paired roles for Marshall and Boutel were wicked Lyndaraxa versus faithful Benzayda in Dryden's *The Conquest of Granada* (1670–71), lustful Poppea versus chaste Cyara in Lee's *Nero* (1674), lecherous, hypocritical Olivia versus pure, simple Fidelia in Wycherley's *The Plain Dealer* (1676), and passionate, cruel Roxana versus soft, mild Statira in Lee's *The Rival Queens* (1677). Marshall and Boutel were typed, and their successors (especially Barry and Bracegirdle) conformed in the main to the molds created by the two originals.

Here, then, is a mass of evidence to show that most of the Restoration dramatists knew and associated (often intimately) with the players, tried in general to fit their plays to the capacities of an acting company, chose or helped choose the casts for their own plays, sometimes consulted with actors during the writing of a play, and wrote parts for actors and actresses who were popular, personally favored, or typed. Under such conditions, it was almost inevitable that the player should influence the playwright.

The actual process of creation remains, of course, a mystery, open to conjecture. No dramatist has told us precisely how he went about his job. In the writing of heroic or tragic

[14] Davies, II, 404.

plays, imagination was highly valued, especially for plays dealing with the past. In his dedication prefixed to *Lucius Junius Brutus* (1680) Lee wrote, "When Greece or old Rome come in play . . . the Poet must elevate his Fancy with the mightiest Imagination, he must run back so many hundred Years, [and] take a just Prospect of the Spirit of those Times without the least thought of ours." The tragic poet drew a character from history or fiction, distilled it in the alembic of his imagination, blended the distillate with his knowledge of comparable characters in older drama, and modified it by his awareness of the player for whom he designed the role. The result was a fantastically heightened character, remote from reality but theatrically effective.

The comic poet, on the other hand, prided himself on his reportorial accuracy. As Southerne informed his audience in the epilogue to *The Disappointment* (1684),

> In Comedy your little Selves you meet,
> 'Tis Covent-Garden drawn in Bridges-Street.

But such statements should be taken with a large grain of salt. Restoration comedy was not truly realistic, even though at times it caricatured known personalities. As Allardyce Nicoll points out, the comic dramatist created real characters and situations "freely, always subserving a theatrical purpose."[15] His characters were a blend of journalistic observation and his knowledge of comparable characters in older plays modified by his awareness of the player for whom he was writing. The result was not realism; the mirror held up to nature was always distorted by the poet's preconceptions.

In these creative processes the actress was the new modifier. The actor merely carried on a consistent tradition of conventional acting. The poets of the sixties, watching Hart or Mohun at work in the revival of an old play, saw characters reproduced much as they had been in the days of Lowin

---

[15] P. 281.

and Taylor before the Civil War.[16] But the actresses went beyond the roles written for boys and set their own tradition of acting. The new playwrights, watching Rebecca Marshall or Nell Gwyn in a revived play, saw something new and strove to embody it in their own creations.

Some support for this theory may be found in the history of two important stock characters, "the pair of lovers, witty, gay, anti-moral and sprightly,"[17] who came to dominate Restoration comedy. In his Preface to *The Sullen Lovers* (1668), Shadwell describes this pair as "a Swearing, Drinking, Whoring Ruffian for a Lover, and an impudent, ill-bred tomrig for a mistress." No doubt this couple somewhat resembled people in real life, although attempts to find their exact counterparts at the court of Charles II are usually pointless. (The argument, for example, that King Charles and his famous mistress, Lady Castlemaine, were models for the "ruffian" and the "tomrig" is patently ridiculous.)[18] More important is the fact that the ancestors of the gay couple appear in earlier plays; the lines of descent are clear, and the fumbling attempts of early Restoration poets to bring new life to them are easily discernible.[19]

In large measure the Restoration gay couple owe their existence to Charles Hart and Nell Gwyn. Hart, a handsome, debonair actor of long experience, played the wild gallant to perfection. Nell, who was in her own person "an impudent, ill-bred tomrig," was a first-rate comedienne during those formative years when the new poets were searching for the right vein in comedy. Of the two players it was Nell who brought novelty to roles in revived plays. Hart had only to play his parts much as he had seen them played when he was a boy at the Blackfriars Theatre. Nell, with no acting models

---

[16] See James Wright's "Historia Histrionica" (1699; reprinted in Cibber, I, xxiv–xxv). According to Downes (p. 21), Betterton was taught how to play Hamlet by Sir William Davenant, who remembered how Taylor had played the part at the Blackfriars.

[17] Nicoll, p. 194.   [18] *Ibid.*, p. 228.

[19] See J. H. Smith, *The Gay Couple in Restoration Comedy* (1948), pp. 3–58.

to limit her, could, and evidently did, create new stage effects.

Hating serious parts, Nell did them very badly, but as a comedienne she was supreme. Pepys was constantly astonished "to think how ill she do any serious part . . . just like a fool or changeling; and, in a mad [i.e., comic] part, do beyond all imitation almost."[20] Even as a beginner playing small roles she must have made an impression. On April 3, 1665, Pepys (who had seen her on the stage but not yet met and talked with her) called her "pretty, witty Nell." Surely by "witty" he meant her gay, inventive style of acting.

But John Dryden, the most enterprising of the new playwrights, perfected the gay couple. Well-read in drama, fiction, and history, fully aware of the life about him, intimately acquainted with the players of the King's Company, and with the team of Hart and Nelly before his eyes as sophisticated lovers in revived plays and in one or two moderately successful new plays, Dryden created the first true pair of witty, antimoral lovers in Restoration comedy: Celadon and Florimel in *Secret Love* (February, 1667). For Hart, Celadon was, in the main, merely a familiar role; for Nell, Florimel was a creation and a triumph. "So great performance of a comical part," wrote Pepys on March 2, 1667, "was never, I believe, in the world before as Nell do this." That Dryden wrote the part especially for Nell is clearly shown by Celadon's description of the masked Florimel, a description that agrees precisely with Mrs. Gwyn's authentic portraits: "an Oval Face, clear Skin, hazel Eyes, thick brown Eye-brows and Hair . . . a turn'd up Nose . . . a full neather Lip, an out-mouth . . . the bottom of your cheeks a little blub, and two dimples when you smile; for your stature 'tis well [enough], and for your wit 'twas given you by one that knew it had been thrown away upon an ill face." The one who gave the wit was not God but John Dryden.

In subsequent comedies Hart and Nelly continued to shine as the model gay couple: as Philidor and Mirida in James Howard's *All Mistaken* (ca. September, 1667); probably as Wildish and Olivia in Sedley's *The Mulberry Garden*

[20] December 27, 1667.

(May, 1668); and certainly as Wildblood and Jacintha in Dryden's *An Evening's Love* (June, 1668). By 1669, when Nell left the stage to become the King's mistress, the pattern of the gay couple was firmly established. Had it not been for Nell Gwyn, it might have been something very different.

For further evidence that the new actresses strongly affected the work of the playwrights we may glance briefly at the Restoration practice of altering and adapting Elizabethan plays. Stage historians have concluded that older plays were altered to make them conform to the classical unities or to the vogue for heroic love, to fit them to the new stagecraft and make room for scenes, machines, and songs, or, sometimes, to modernize and simplify old-fashioned speech.[21]

No one has examined in detail the possibility that at least some changes were made to fit an old play to the demands of the new actresses. For example, when Davenant altered *Macbeth* (ca. 1664), he greatly increased Lady Macduff's role. Hazelton Spencer has argued that his purpose was to set up Lady Macduff as a good woman—"a most sanctified dame" —in opposition to wicked Lady Macbeth.[22] Allardyce Nicoll suggests on the contrary that "Lady Macduff's part is enormously lengthened, purely for the sake, apparently, of giving opportunity to some rising actress [Jane Long] of the Duke's Theatre."[23] But might not both reasons be equally valid?

Whenever possible, in almost every major alteration of an old play, the adapter either added new roles for women or heightened and lengthened the existing ones. Ordinarily, male roles were enlarged significantly only when the adapter was himself an actor and sought to fatten the part he intended to play. (See, for example, John Lacy's alteration of *The Taming of the Shew* as *Sauny the Scot* [1667], in which Lacy, an excellent comedian, played Sauny, and Cibber's alteration of *Richard III* [1699], in which the actor-poet played Richard.) But usually there were only three or four roles for women in older plays, and of these one or two were often only

[21] See A. C. Sprague, *Beaumont and Fletcher on the Restoration Stage* (1926); and Hazelton Spencer, *Shakespeare Improved* (1927).

[22] Spencer, p. 195.   [23] P. 176.

bit parts. Moreover the roles written to be played by boy-actresses were frequently inadequate for popular leading ladies or unsuited to women who had become typed in stock roles. These were matters which any good theatrical crafts-man had to bear in mind when he set about adapting an old play for the Restoration stage. He was writing for a company employing eight or more rather temperamental women; theatrical economy demanded that he keep them busy; and there was always the ticket seller to remind him that many spectators paid admission as much to look on beauty bare as to see a play.

Examining a few altered plays from this theatrical point of view, we may be able to offer some additional explanations for certain changes. For instance, it is no doubt true, as Spencer argues, that Shadwell's addition of a love story to Shakespeare's *Timon* (1687) "adds greatly to our interest in the central figure" and "exercises throughout the play a unifying force,"[24] but it is also true that it adds two important female characters, Evandra (Mrs. Betterton) and Melissa (Mrs. Shadwell), plus a maid, Chloe (Mrs. Gibbs). The original play had only two bit roles for women; the alteration has five roles, two of them major. Similarly, D'Urfey's addition of three new women to the original five Amazons in his alteration of Fletcher's *The Sea Voyage* as *A Commonwealth of Women* (1685) was surely motivated by the fact that at the time the United Company was rich in talented and beautiful actresses. Eight handsome women, "all drest in Amazonian Habits" (probably helmets and knee-length tunics), grouped before "a Rosy Bower, placed in the midst of a pleasant Country," must have been a sight to behold. Again, the only reason Davenant could have for adding a new character, the "very young" Viola, to his amalgam of *Measure for Measure* and *Much Ado about Nothing* as *The Law against Lovers* (1662) was that he wanted to introduce little Miss Davis, a talented singer and dancer. Pepys saw the play on February 18, 1662, and thought it "a good play and well performed, especially the little girl's (whom I never saw act before) dancing and singing." Finally, when Crowne intro-

[24] *Op. cit.*, p. 286.

duced into *The Misery of Civil War* (1680), a blend of *II Henry VI* and *III Henry VI*, a new character, Lady Elianor Butler, he seems to have done so only to create a breeches part for Betty Currer, who had very handsome legs. Lady Elianor's sole function is to wander about in male attire bemoaning the loss of her lover, Edward.

These are only a few examples of additional roles made necessary or desirable by theatrical conditions. In addition we have some roles that were obviously altered or enlarged for the benefit of a popular actress or for one typed in comic or heroic parts. To illustrate, in 1679, when Otway altered *Romeo and Juliet* into a political play, *The History and Fall of Caius Marius*, he made very considerable changes in the plot and reduced the love story to a subplot. The character of Romeo (Marius, Jr., played by Smith) was changed very little, but Juliet (Lavinia, played by Mrs. Barry) was no longer a naïve, straightforward child who had "not seen the change of fourteen years." She was now sixteen (a mature woman by seventeenth-century standards), capable of heroic action and given to noble sentiments and ranting speeches —the kind of speeches for which Mrs. Barry was already famous. Here, for example, is Juliet's poignant reaction to the death of Romeo in the Capulet tomb:

> What's here? a cup, closed in my true love's hand?
> Poison, I see, hath been his timeless end.
> O churl! drunk all, and left no friendly drop
> To help me after?—I will kiss thy lips;
> Haply some poison yet doth hang on them,
> To make me die with a restorative. (*Kisses him.*)
> Thy lips are warm!

This was too quiet and simple for the extravagant, declamatory style of Mrs. Barry. Here is Lavinia in the same situation:

> He's gone; he's dead; breathless: alas! my Marius.
> A Vial too: here, here has bin his Bane
> Oh Churl! drink all? not leave one friendly Drop
> For poor Lavinia? Yet I'll drain thy Lips.
> Perhaps some welcom Poison may hang there,
> To help me to o'retake thee on thy Journy.

Clammy and damp as Earth. Hah! stains of Bloud?
And a man murther'd? 'Tis th'unhappy Flamen.
Who fix their Joys on any thing that's Mortall,
Let 'em behold my Portion, and despair.
What shall I doe? how will the Gods dispose me?
Oh! I could rend these Walls with Lamentation,
Tear up the Dead from their corrupted Graves,
And dawb the face of Earth with her own Bowels.

It is hard to imagine unhappy Juliet entertaining such a gruesome notion at that moment.

By a comparable process, the Duke of Buckingham, in his alteration of Fletcher's *The Chances* (1667), enlarged the role of the Second Constantia, a whore, to give scope for the audacities of impudent Nell Gwyn in a scene with Charles Hart as Don John. Nahum Tate's reason for introducing a love affair between Cordelia and Edgar into his alteration of *King Lear* (1681) may have been only (as he said in his Preface) "to rectifie what was wanting in the Regularity and Probability of the Tale," but the effect, of course, was to enlarge Cordelia's part. Tate does not explain why he heightened Regan's villainy and gave her a luscious love scene with Edmund. No doubt the facts that Mary Lee, long the leading tragedienne and villainess of the Duke's Company, played Regan, while her ambitious young rival, Elizabeth Barry, played Cordelia, had something to do with the terms of the alteration. Again, when the Earl of Rochester revised Beaumont and Fletcher's *Valentinian* in 1676 or 1677, he increased the lines of Lucina, the victim of Valentinian's lusts, by one-fourth and so heightened the emotional tone of her speeches as to give full play for the passionate style of Rebecca Marshall, for whom he designed the part. When the play was finally produced in 1685, the part of Lucina was played by Mrs. Barry, who inherited Mrs. Marshall's roles.[25] These are only samples. A complete re-examination of Restoration adaptations of plays by Shake-

[25] See the dramatis personae in the manuscript version, British Museum, Add. MS. 2869. Montague Summers (*The Playhouse of Pepys* [1935], pp. 290–91) argues that the alteration was first produced at the Theatre Royal in 1677–78. There is no proof of this. Rebecca Marshall left the King's Company in the spring of 1677.

speare, Beaumont and Fletcher, Marston, Massinger, Brome, and other older dramatists would reveal still more female roles heightened or enlarged to fit the needs and tastes of the new actresses.

One more point remains to be considered: was the influence of the actress good or bad? Regretfully we must admit that it was as good or as bad as the private character of the actress. The fact is that, in the small, intimate theatrical world, it was difficult for an audience to separate the stage character of an actress from her real character. As Elizabeth Farley discovered in 1662, there were always some Tartufes to protest against an actress playing "all parts of virtue" while in a "shameful condition." Ordinary playgoers might not protest, but they were certainly aware of the moral character of an actress, her past misdeeds and present liaisons, and they were quick to see any incongruity between the reality and the stage make-believe. As Colley Cibber declared:

The private Character of an Actor will always more or less affect his Publick Performance. I have seen the most tender Sentiment of Love in Tragedy create Laughter, instead of Compassion, when it has been applicable to the real Engagements of the Person that utter'd it. I have known good Parts thrown up, from a humble Consciousness that something in them might put an Audience in mind of—what was rather wish'd might be forgotten: Those remarkable Words of Evadne, in *The Maid's Tragedy*—A maidenhead, Amintor, at my Years?—have sometimes been a much stronger Jest for being a true one.[26]

William Chetwood, for many years a prompter, told an anecdote that illustrates Cibber's point:

I remember a virtuous Actress, or one reputed so [Mrs. Bracegirdle], repeating two Lines in King Lear, at her Exit in the Third Act,

> Arm'd in my Virgin Innocence I'll fly,
> My Royal Father to relieve, or die,

receive a Plaudit from the Audience, more as a reward for her reputable Character, than, perhaps, her Acting claim'd; where a different Actress [Mrs. Barry] in the same Part, more fam'd for her

[26] I, 250.

Stage Performance than the other, at the words *Virgin Innocence*, has created a Horse-laugh (no Reflection on the Audience, since a Theatrical Term), and the Scene of generous Pity and Compassion at the Close turn'd to Ridicule.[27]

Such audience reactions, while human, were obviously unfair. In 1698, when the stage was under fire from a battery of reformers, an anonymous writer pointed out that the argument that "the actors are generally debauch'd and of lewd Conversation" had nothing to do with the merits or demerits of the playhouse, because on the stage "they are confin'd to the Poet's language." Therefore (he continued), "If we shou'd see Mr. Powel acting a Brave, Generous and Honest Part; or Mrs. Knight, a very Modest and Chaste one, it ought not to give us Offence; because we are not to consider what they are off the Stage, but whom they represent: We are to do by them as in Religion we do by the Priest, mind what they say, and not what they do."[28] This was all very reasonable, but apparently, like most logic, completely futile.

Now if an audience could not forget that George Powell was a profane rip and Frances Maria Knight a harlot, how could the playwright? He had to depend upon the players to interpret his dramatic creations; he dared ignore their private characters no more than their dramatic skills. Perhaps in a tragedy, in which the poet's creations were so remote from reality as to be completely incredible, it made little difference whether the players were saints or sinners, so long as the writer avoided those unfortunate lines which could suddenly expose the incongruity between stage character and actor character and arouse a "Horse-laugh." In so-called realistic comedy there was usually no problem: the real character of George Powell differed very little from that of the swearing, wenching, drinking "fine gentleman" of Restoration comedy, and Mrs. Knight, the sinner, was extremely like the sinful and would-be sinful heroines. But no dramatist in his right mind would have dreamed of writing the realistic character

[27] P. 28.

[28] *A Letter to A. H. Esq: Concerning the Stage* (1698) (Augustan Reprint No. 3 [1946], p. 12).

of "a Brave, Generous and Honest" man for Powell, or that of a "Modest and Chaste" woman for Mrs. Knight. Their off-stage personalities were too well known.

It follows, then, that the lives and characters of the players affected the free choice of the playwright. Since most Restoration actresses were "generally debauch'd, and of lewd Conversation," the female roles available to the playwright were distinctly limited. When we remember also that many actresses were trivial-minded women, interested in acting not as a career but only as a means of displaying their wares to prospective buyers, we can only conclude that their chief effect on dramatic literature was to push it steadily in the direction of sex and sensuality. This is not to blame the ladies alone for the general atmosphere of immorality that pervades Restoration drama. Their shoulders are too frail for that heavy burden. The greater share of the blame must be laid upon those forces usually cited: the reaction against Puritan morality and restriction, the libertine spirit of Court and King, and the general cynicism of an aristocratic coterie audience. The actresses afforded the poet models for "impudent tomrigs," demimondaines, and harlots and by their provocative acting underscored his suggestive lines. In short, they helped the dramatist to "heap the steaming ordure of the stage."

In summary, then, all available evidence indicates that Restoration dramatists, writing for stock companies, created characters at least partly designed to capitalize on the drawing power of attractive women, wrote parts for favored or popular women or women typed as stock characters, and altered old plays to suit the needs or abilities of stage prima donnas. If these statements are true, perhaps we have a partial explanation for the fact that the Restoration playwrights produced so few female characters comparable with the great women's portraits in the Elizabethan gallery. Shakespeare's women were the creations of a teeming imagination; his poetic pen gave to airy nothing a local habitation and a name, and its only limitation was the number of competent, well-trained boys available at a given time. His interpreters of female roles were ephemeral and impersonal, and the word was more important than the speaker. But the Restoration playwright, working in an age when the speaker had become more important than the word, confined by the necessity of writing not just for actresses but for a specific Nell, Anne, or Betty, and influenced during the creative process by the acting styles of those women, had to suit his roles to their abilities, their types, and, worst of all, to their personal reputations.

Appendix A: The Actresses 1660-89

Unless otherwise noted, the information on roles played comes from the earliest quarto of each play cited. All dates are New Style and are based on Nicoll's "Hand-List of Restoration Plays" (pp. 386–447).

ARIELL, MRS. (Duke's Company, 1676?–80?). When "Little Mrs. Ariell" spoke the epilogue to Behn's *Abdelazar*, ca. September, 1677, her opening line was, "With late Success being blest, I'm come agen." Her "late Success" must have been at least a year earlier, for she concluded:

> Since then I'm grown at least an Inch in height,
> And shall e'er long be full-blown for Delight.

The epilogue of Otway's *Don Carlos*, ca. June, 1676, was "spoken by a Girl" who may have been Mrs. Ariell, since much is made of her extreme youth. No doubt she was only nine or ten years old on her first appearance. It is possible that Mrs. Ariell played "Fanny, a child of seven Years old," in Behn's *Sir Patient Fancy*, January, 1678. She may also have been "the little Girl" who played Cordelio, a page, in Otway's *The Orphan*, ca. March, 1680. Curll (p. 26) assigns this part to Anne Bracegirdle, but he is very unreliable.

BAKER, FRANCES and *KATHERINE* (King's Company, 1677–78). The identities of the two Bakers are so confused that it seems best to deal with them together. Since they twice appeared together and one was called "Mrs. Baker, Jun.," it is likely that they were mother and daughter. The Mrs. Baker who played young Parisatis in Lee's *The Rival Queens*, March, 1677, was probably Katherine, the daughter. Probably it was Katherine, too, who played Margaret, a young girl, in Leanerd's *The Country Innocence*, ca. March, 1677. Both Bakers appeared in Chamberlayne's *Wits Led by the Nose*, ca. July, 1677, "Mrs. Baker" (the mother?) playing Amazia, a role for a mature woman, and "Mrs. Baker, Jun." playing Heroina, a juvenile. "Mrs. Frances Baker," presumably the elder, played the mature Alfreda in Ravenscroft's *King Edgar and Alfreda*, ca. October, 1677. In the same play "Mrs. Katherine Baker" played young Hilaria. In all likelihood it was Katherine who played Jocalin, a juvenile lead, and delivered the epilogue in E. Howard's *The Man of Newmarket*, ca. March, 1678.

In Ravenscroft's *Dame Dobson*, June, 1683, the role of Mrs. Frances, an old servant, was played by "Mr. Baker." This could be an error for Mrs. Baker, probably Frances. The Mr. Francis Baker named in the list of actors constituted by King James in 1688 (Nicoll, p. 332) seems to have been in Ireland at this time. On the London stage he is first listed in the dramatis personae of a revival of *Rollo*, ca. 1685.

BARRY, ELIZABETH (Duke's, United, Lincoln's Inn Fields, and Second United companies, 1674–1709). Mrs. Barry, undoubtedly the greatest Restoration actress, was born in 1658. According to Curll (pp. 13–17) she was the daughter of one Robert Barry, a barrister, who ruined his estate fighting for King Charles I. Lady Davenant, a friend of the family, took her in, gave her a genteel education, and, about 1674, put her on the stage (Downes, p. 35). This, we may presume, was Mrs. Barry's own version of her parentage and background. Anthony Aston (II, 303) wrote, "She was woman to Lady Shelton of Norfolk (my Godmother)—when Lord Rochester took her on the Stage; where for some Time, they could make nothing of her.—She could neither sing nor dance, no, not in a Country-Dance." According to Cibber (I, 159) she was so unsuccessful that she was discharged at the end of the first year. Curll insists that she was rejected three times and did not succeed until her lover, the Earl of Rochester, gave her private lessons for about six months.

Her first recorded performance was in the small part of Draxilla in Otway's *Alcibiades*, September, 1675. If she ever had a period of training with Rochester, it may have been in the autumn and winter of 1675–76. Downes (p. 36) asserts that she played the major role of Mrs. Loveit in Etherege's *The Man of Mode*, March, 1676, but it is more likely that the role was created by Mary Lee and inherited by Mrs. Barry after Mrs. Lee's retirement in 1685. Mrs. Barry played Theodocia in Rawlins' *Tom Essence*, ca. August, 1676; Elvira in Ravenscroft's *The Wrangling Lovers*, ca. September, 1676; Constantia in D'Urfey's *Madam Fickle*, November, 1676; Phoenice in Otway's *Titus and Berenice* and Lucia in the accompanying farce, *The Cheats of Scapin*, ca. December, 1676; Clorinia in Porter's *The French Conjurer*, ca. March, 1677; Hellena, a breeches part, in Behn's *The Rover*, March, 1677; Emilia in D'Urfey's *A Fond Husband*, May, 1677; Philisides, a breeches part, in *The Constant Nymph* (Anon.), ca. July, 1677; and Leonora in Behn's *Abdelazar*, ca. September, 1677. In December, 1677, she took time out to give birth to a daughter, fathered by the Earl of Rochester. She seems to have been at the time a protégée of Nell Gwyn (*Rochester-Savile Letters*, ed. J. H. Wilson [1941], p. 52).

She returned in the following year to play Mrs. Goodvile and the epilogue in Otway's *Friendship in Fashion*, April, 1678; Clara, a breeches part, and the epilogue, in Leanerd's *The Counterfeits*, May, 1678; Sophia in D'Urfey's *Squire Oldsapp*, ca. June, 1678; Polyxena, the heroine, in Banks's *The Destruction of Troy*, November, 1678; Cornelia in Behn's *The Feign'd Curtezans*, ca. March, 1679; the epilogue to Behn's *The Young King*, ca. September, 1679; Olivia, a breeches part, and the prologue with Nokes and Leigh in D'Urfey's *The Virtuous Wife*, ca. September, 1679; Lavinia and the epilogue in Otway's *Caius Marius*, September, 1679; Mrs.

Gripe, a breeches part, and the epilogue in Shadwell's *The Woman Captain*, September, 1679; Monimia (one of her most famous roles) in Otway's *The Orphan*, March, 1680; Lady Dunce in Otway's *The Souldiers Fortune*, March, 1680; Leonora, Queen of Arragon, in Dryden's *The Spanish Friar*, March, 1680; Camilla, a breeches part, and the epilogue (Wiley, p. 329) in Maidwell's *The Loving Enemies*, ca. March, 1680; Corina, "the whore," in Behn's *The Revenge*, ca. June, 1680; Athenais in Lee's *Theodosius*, ca. September, 1680; Teraminta and the epilogue in Lee's *Lucius Junius Brutus*, December, 1680; Cordelia and the epilogue in Tate's *King Lear*, ca. March, 1681; La Nuche, a courtesan, and the epilogue in Behn's *The Rover*, Part II, ca. April, 1681; the epilogue with Leigh to Shadwell's *The Lancashire Witches*, ca. September, 1681; The Princess of Cleve in Lee's *The Princess of Cleve*, ca. September, 1681; the epilogue to Behn's *The False Count*, November, 1681; Arabella, the prologue, and the epilogue (with others) in Ravenscroft's *The London Cuckolds*, November, 1681; Belvidera (another famous role) in Otway's *Venice Preserved*, February, 1682; Lady Galliard and the prologue in Behn's *The City Heiress*, March, 1682; Anna Bullen in Banks's *Vertue Betray'd*, April, 1682; Marmoutier in Dryden and Lee's *The Duke of Guise*, November, 1682.

By this time, as Downes (p. 38) says, she had earned the name of "Famous Mrs. Barry, both at Court and City." The virtual retirement of Mrs. Betterton, and Mrs. Barry's superiority over Mary Lee (Lady Slingsby) made her the undisputed leading lady of the new United Company. She continued to play indefatigably, creating the roles of Porcia, a rich widow, in Otway's *The Atheist*, ca. July, 1683; Fausta in Lee's *Constantine the Great*, November, 1683; Lucina in Rochester's *Valentinian*, February, 1684 (Downes, p. 40); Mrs. Fitchow in Brome's *The Northern Lass*, ca. 1684; Leonora in Crowne's *Sir Courtly Nice*, May, 1685 (Downes, p. 40); Laura in D'Urfey's *The Banditti*, February, 1686; Lady Fulbank in Behn's *The Lucky Chance*, ca. December, 1687; Princess Oryala in Mountfort's *The Injur'd Lovers*, ca. March, 1688; Barzana and the epilogue in Crowne's *Darius*, April,

1688; Almeyda in Dryden's *Don Sebastian*, November, 1689; Princess Marguerite in Lee's *The Massacre of Paris*, November, 1689; Alcmena in Dryden's *Amphitryon*, October, 1690; Orundana in Settle's *Distress'd Innocence*, November, 1690; Eugenia in Shadwell's *The Scowrers*, ca. December, 1690; Isabella, the Queen Mother, in Mountfort's *King Edward III*, ca. December, 1690; Dorinda in Mountfort's *Greenwich Park*, April, 1691; Mrs. Friendall and the epilogue in Southerne's *The Wives Excuse*, December, 1691; Cassandra in Dryden's *Cleomenes*, April, 1692; Lady Subtle in D'Urfey's *The Marriage Hater Match'd*, June, 1692; Fulvia in Crowne's *Regulus*, June, 1692; Queen Eleanor in Bancroft's *Henry the Second*, September, 1692; Lady Malapert and the prologue in Southerne's *The Maid's Last Prayer*, January, 1693; Sophronia, a female plain dealer, in D'Urfey's *The Richmond Heiress*, ca. February, 1693; Laetitia and the epilogue in Congreve's *The Old Bachelor*, March, 1693; Lady Touchwood in Congreve's *The Double-Dealer*, October, 1693; Isabella in Southerne's *The Fatal Marriage*, February, 1694; Princess Victoria in Dryden's *Love Triumphant*, March, 1694; and Celestina, the villainess, in Settle's *The Ambitious Slave*, March, 1694.

In 1695 Mrs. Barry was one of the leaders of the group of players who revolted against the patentees and organized a new company at Lincoln's Inn Fields. She continued to play leading roles which called for a mature woman, turning over the juvenile leads to Mrs. Bracegirdle. She played Mrs. Frail in Congreve's *Love for Love*, April, 1695; Panthea in Banks's *Cyrus the Great*, ca. December, 1695; Lady Dorimen, a fading, lewd woman, in Granville's *The She-Gallants*, ca. December, 1695; Lady Testie and the prologue in Dogget's *The Country-Wake*, ca. April, 1696; Princess Homais, the villainess, in Manley's *The Royal Mischief*, ca. April, 1696; Lady Single in Motteux's *Love's a Jest*, June, 1696; Urania, a secondary role, in "Ariadne's" *She Ventures and He Wins*, ca. September, 1696; the prologue "to Her Royal Highness" for Ravenscroft's *The Anatomist*, ca. November, 1696; Lady Grumble in Dilke's *The City Lady*, January, 1697; Zara, a captive queen, in Congreve's *The Mourning Bride*, February, 1697;

Mme de Vandosme and the epilogue in D'Urfey's *The In-trigues at Versailles*, ca. February, 1697; Lady Brute and the epilogue with Mrs. Bracegirdle in Vanbrugh's *The Provoked Wife*, May, 1697; Elvira in "The Unfortunate Couple," Act IV of Motteux's *The Novelty*, June, 1697; Bellinda in Pix's *The Innocent Mistress*, ca. June, 1697; Boadicea in Hopkins' *Boadicea*, ca. November, 1697; Chruseis in Granville's *Heroic Love*, ca. December, 1697; Olivia in Pix's *The Deceiver Deceived*, ca. December, 1697; Laura in Motteux's *Beauty in Distress*, ca. April, 1698; Lamira and the epilogue in Trot-ter's *Fatal Friendship*, ca. May, 1698; Queen Catherine in Pix's *Queen Catherine*, ca. June, 1698; Armida in Dennis' *Rinaldo and Armida*, ca. November, 1698; Tamira in Cib-ber's *Xerxes*, February, 1699; Adellaida in Pix's *The False Friend*, ca. May, 1699; Semanthe, a mother role, in Hopkins' *Friendship Improv'd*, November, 1699; Queen of the Scyth-ians in Dennis' *Iphigenia*, December, 1699; Julia in Smith's *The Princess of Parma*, 1699; Mrs. Marwood in Congreve's *The Way of the World*, March, 1700; Favonia and the epi-logue in Southerne's *The Fate of Capua*, ca. March, 1700; Artemisa in Rowe's *The Ambitious Step-Mother*, ca. Decem-ber, 1700; Lady Lovetoy in Burnaby's *The Ladies Visiting-Day*, ca. January, 1701; Zarrianna in Pix's *The Czar of Muscovy*, ca. March, 1701; Queen of Bayonne in Gildon's *Love's Victim*, ca. April, 1701; Princess Leamira in Pix's *The Double Distress*, ca. May, 1701; Altemira in Charles Boyle's *Altemira*, ca. December, 1701; and Arpasia in Rowe's *Tamer-lane*, ca. December, 1701.

Now in her forties but still vigorous, Mrs. Barry refused to step aside in favor of younger women. She continued to play in numerous revivals and created many new characters: Lucasia, the heroine, in Centlivre's *The Stolen Heiress*, De-cember, 1702; Leodice in Wiseman's *Antiochus the Great*, 1702; Clorinda in *The Fickle Shepherdess* (Anon.), ca. March, 1703; Villaretta and the epilogue in Burnaby's *Love Betray'd*, March, 1703; Eugenia in Boyle's *As You Find It*, April, 1703; Calista in Rowe's *The Fair Penitent*, ca. May, 1703; Issame-nea in Oldmixon's *The Governour of Cyprus*, 1703; Sakia, a romantic Huron, in Dennis' *Liberty Asserted*, February, 1704;

Mrs. Clever in Rowe's *The Biter*, December, 1704; Lady Wealthy in Centlivre's *The Gamester*, ca. January, 1705; Clarissa and the epilogue in Vanbrugh's *The Confederacy*, October, 1705; Penelope in Rowe's *Ulysses*, November, 1705; Zelmane, the heroine, in *Zelmane* (Anon.), 1705. Constantia in Trotter's *The Revolution of Sweden*, February, 1706; Arcanon, an enchantress, in Granville's *The British Enchanters*, February, 1706; Clarinda in Pix's *The Adventures in Madrid*, ca. June, 1706; Almyna in Manley's *Almyna*, December, 1706; Phaedra in Smith's *Phaedra and Hippolitus*, April, 1707; Princess Rhodogune in Rowe's *The Royal Convert*, November, 1707; Lady Wronglove in Cibber's *The Lady's Last Stake*, December, 1707; and Sultana Valide in Goring's *Irene*, February, 1708.

The uniting of the two companies in January, 1708, seems to have contributed to Mrs. Barry's decision to retire. However, she had been off the stage less than a year when she was called back to play (and speak the epilogue) in a revival of Congreve's *Love for Love* (April 7, 1709) for Betterton's benefit. She played thereafter in various revivals in the season of 1709–10. Her final appearance was as Lady Easy in a revival of Cibber's *The Careless Husband*, June 13, 1710 (Genest, II, 454). She died at Acton on November 7, 1713, aged 55.

According to Anthony Aston (II, 302), "Mrs. Barry was middle-siz'd, and had darkish Hair, light Eyes, dark Eyebrows, and was indifferently plump." Although Aston insisted that she was not handsome, "her mouth op'ning most on the Right side, which she strove to draw t'other Way," the gossips all agreed that she was irresistibly attractive to men and that her lovers were beyond numbering. They asserted also that she was hard, miserly, mercenary, and vicious. Said Tom Brown (III, 39), "Should you lie with her all night she would not know you next morning, unless you had another five pounds at her service."

Such evidence must be taken with a grain of salt, and some of the statements made about her are demonstrably untrue. For instance, Oldys (p. 186) asserted that Mrs. Barry had a daughter by Sir George Etherege, who "settled 6 or 7000 pounds on her." Probably Etherege never had that much money in all his life, and the only child known to be born of Mrs. Barry was her daughter by the Earl of Rochester.

The mixed view of Mrs. Barry is expressed in the following passage from Wells, p. 13:

SULLEN: What think you of the renowned Cleopatra?

CRITIC: By that Nickname, so unfortunate to poor Anthony, as the other has been to many an honest Country Gentleman, I shou'd guess whom you mean.

SULLEN: You take me right.

CRITIC: In her time she has been the very Spirit of Action every way; Nature made her for the delight of Mankind; and till Nature began to decay in her, all the Town shar'd her Bounty.

RAMBLE: I do think that Person the finest Woman in the World upon the Stage, and the ugliest Woman off on't.

SULLEN: Age and Intemperance are the fatal Enemies of Beauty; she's guilty of both, she has been a Riotter in her time, but the edge of her Appetite is long ago taken off, she still charms (as you say) upon the Stage, and even off I don't think so rudely of her as you do: 'Tis true, Time has turn'd up some of her Furrows, but not to such a degree.

The lampoons of the Restoration often touched upon Mrs. Barry's private life, sometimes in the foulest possible terms. When her daughter died in 1689, the author of "To the most Virtuous and most devoted Overkind, Notorious Mad^m Barry" ("Choyce Collection," p. 303) offered ironical consolation and suggested:

> Retyre thou Miser from thy Shop the Stage
> Retyrement will befit thy Sins and Age:
> The Vitious Treasure thy base ways have gain'd,
> Which for thy Daughters sake was still obtain'd,
> Give to some Pious Use, or thou'lt be damn'd.

Whatever she may have been in private life, there can be no doubt that Mrs. Barry was the greatest actress of her age. Cibber (I, 160) admired her extravagantly:

Mrs. Barry, in Characters of Greatness, had a Presence of elevated Dignity, her Mien and Motion superb and gracefully majestick; her Voice full, clear, and strong, so that no Violence of Passion could be too much for her: And when Distress or Tenderness possess'd her, she subsided into the most affecting Melody and Softness. In the Art of exciting Pity she had a Power beyond all the Actresses I have yet seen, or what your Imagination can conceive.

BATES, MRS. (King's Company, 1678) Mrs. Bates's name appears only in the dramatis personae of Leanerd's *The Rambling Justice*, March, 1678; she had the small part of Emilia, daughter of Sir Arthur Twilight. She was probably a beginner; to judge by the rest of the cast and the date, this was a Lenten play performed by the "young" actors.

BETTERTON, MARY, nee *SAUNDERSON* (Duke's and United companies, 1660–94). Evidently one of the first women to join Davenant's company, Mary Saunderson may have been the first regular English actress. However, her first known role was as Ianthe in Davenant's *The Siege of Rhodes*, Parts I and II, June, 1661. Downes (pp. 21, 22) lists her in revivals in 1661 as Ophelia in *Hamlet* and Juliet in *Romeo and Juliet*. She played also Mrs. Aurelia in Cowley's *Cutter of Coleman Street*, December, 1661 (Downes, p. 25); The Duchess in *The Duchess of Malfi* (Downes, p. 25; Pepys, September 30, 1662); and Bellmont in Porter's *The Villain*, October, 1662 (Downes, p. 23).

On December 24, 1662, Thomas Betterton, "of Westminster, gent., bachelor, about 30," took out a license to marry Mary Sanderson, "of St. Giles, Cripplegate, spinster, about 25, with the consent of her widowed mother" (*London Marriage Licences*, ed. Joseph Foster [1887], col. 123).

Mrs. Betterton continued playing, creating the roles of Porcia in Tuke's *The Adventures of Five Hours*, January, 1663 (Downes, p. 22); Pyramena in Stapylton's *The Slighted Maid*, February, 1663; Cesarina in Stapylton's *The Step-Mother*, ca. November, 1663; Queen Catherine in *Henry the Eighth*, December, 1663 (Downes, p. 24); Graciana in Etherege's *The Comical Revenge*, March, 1664 (Downes, p. 25); Princess Katherine in Boyle's *Henry the Fifth*, August, 1664; probably Heraclia in Davenant's *The Rivals* (Pepys, December 2, 1664); and Roxalana in Boyle's *Mustapha*,

April, 1665. No doubt Downes (p. 26) was in error when he said that she succeeded Mrs. Davenport in this last role.

After the Plague and the Fire, Mrs. Betterton played Virginia in Betterton's *Appius and Virginia*, May, 1669 (Downes, p. 30); Julia in Caryll's *Sir Solomon*, ca. 1669 (Downes, p. 30); Queen Parisatis in E. Howard's *The Womens Conquest*, ca. November, 1670; Erminia in Behn's *The Forc'd Marriage*, ca. December, 1670; Lady Laycock in Betterton's *The Amorous Widow*, ca. 1670 (Downes, p. 30); Princess Mandana in Settle's *Cambyses*, ca. January, 1671; Serina in E. Howard's *The Six Days Adventure*, ca. March, 1671; Empress Laula in Settle's *The Empress of Morocco*, July, 1671; Princess Juliana, a breeches part, and the epilogue (shared) in Crowne's *Juliana*, August, 1671; Duchess Isabella in Crowne's *History of Charles the Eighth*, November, 1671; Isabella in Boyle's *Mr. Anthony*, ca. March, 1672; Lucia in Ravenscroft's *The Citizen Turn'd Gentleman*, July, 1672; Eugenia in Payne's *The Fatal Jealousy*, August, 1672; Jilt in Shadwell's *Epsom Wells*, December, 1672 (Downes, p. 33); Lady Macbeth in Davenant's *Macbeth*, February, 1673; Juliana in Arrowsmith's *The Reformation*, September, 1673; Aphelia in Settle's *Love and Revenge*, November, 1674; Orunda, Princess of China, in Settle's *The Conquest of China*, May, 1675; Timandra in Otway's *Alcibiades*, September, 1675; Lady Faddle in Crowne's *The Country Wit*, January, 1676; Isabella in Settle's *Ibrahim*, March, 1676; Bellinda in Etherege's *The Man of Mode*, March, 1676 (Downes, p. 36); Amaryllis in Settle's *Pastor Fido*, ca. December, 1676; Octavia in Sedley's *Antony and Cleopatra*, February, 1677; Florinda in Behn's *The Rover*, March, 1677; Iphigenia, Priestess of Diana, in C. Davenant's *Circe*, May, 1677; Alveria in *The Constant Nymph* (Anon.), ca. July, 1677; Statira and the epilogue in Pordage's *The Siege of Babylon*, ca. September, 1677; Florella in Behn's *Abdelazar*, ca. September, 1677; Isabella in Behn's *Sir Patient Fancy*, January, 1678; Evandra, the heroine, in Shadwell's *Timon of Athens*, ca. January, 1678; Jocasta in Dryden and Lee's *Oedipus*, ca. November, 1678; Andromache in Banks's *The Destruction of Troy*, November, 1678; Andromache in Dryden's *Troilus and*

Cressida, ca. April, 1679; Lady Grey in Crowne's *Misery of Civil War*, ca. March, 1680; Elvira in Dryden's *The Spanish Friar*, March, 1680; Pulcheria in Lee's *Theodosius*, ca. September, 1680; Lucretia in Lee's *Lucius Junius Brutus*, December, 1680; Eleanor of Glocester in Crowne's *Henry the Sixth*, September, 1681; Elianor, a cheating wife, in Lee's *The Princess of Cleve*, ca. September, 1681; and Camilla in D'Urfey's *The Royalist*, January, 1682.

After the union of the two companies, Mrs. Betterton created only a few new roles and played less frequently in her usual romantic roles. At forty-five she had lost much of her attractiveness. She played the Queen Mother in Lee's *The Massacre of Paris*, November, 1689; Amalazontha, a queen mother, in Brady's *The Rape*, February, 1692; Crate-siclea, a mother part, in Dryden's *Cleomenes*, April, 1692; Wishwell, a bawd, in Southerne's *The Maid's Last Prayer*, January, 1693; and Queen Ximena, a mother part, in Dryden's *Love Triumphant*, March, 1694.

In December, 1694, the patentees complained that although Mrs. Betterton's salary was 50s. a week, "constantly pd her in Complemᵗ to Mʳ Betterton," she was almost a dead loss to the company, not appearing "in any pts to yᵉ satisfaction of yᵉ Audience" (Nicoll, p. 378). She seems to have left the stage for good when Betterton seceded from the United Company in 1695.

Betterton died in April, 1710. Davies (III, 397) remarked that Mrs. Betterton, a woman "of a thoughtful and melancholy temper, . . . was so strongly affected with [Betterton's] death that she ran distracted, though she appeared rather a prudent and constant than a fond and passionate wife. They had no children." According to Cibber (I, 162) Queen Anne gave Mrs. Betterton a pension. She survived her husband nearly two years and on April 13, 1712, was buried beside him in Westminster Abbey.

In her heyday Mrs. Betterton must have been a very attractive woman. Dryden described her as Elvira in *The Spanish Friar* (Act I, scene 2): "She is of a middle stature, dark-coloured hair, the most bewitching leer with her eyes, the most roguish cast! her cheeks are dimpled when she smiles, and her smiles would tempt a hermit." All contemporaries agree that she was an honorable and generous woman, and even the most licentious libelers have nothing to say against her. Appropriately, she usually played the roles of good women.

Cibber (I, 162) said of Mrs. Betterton:

> She was, to the last, the Admiration of all true Judges of Nature and Lovers of Shakespeare, in whose Plays she chiefly excell'd, and without a Rival. When she quitted the Stage several good Actresses were the better for her Instruction. She was a Woman of an unblemish'd and sober life, and had the Honour to teach Queen Anne, when Princess, the Part of Semandra in [Lee's] *Mithridates*, which she acted at Court in King Charles's time.

BOUTELL, ELIZABETH (King's, United, and Lincoln's Inn Fields companies, 1670–96). Although Downes lists "Mrs. Boutel" as one of those who "came into the Company some few Years after" 1660, and casts her (in presumably early revivals) as Estifania in Beaumont and Fletcher's *Rule a Wife and Have a Wife*, Aspatia in their *The Maid's Tragedy*, and Lilia Bianca in Fletcher's *The Elder Brother*, there are no records of her membership in the company until about 1670. It is very likely that she played the roles cited by Downes in later revivals and that he (or Charles Booth) remembered her better than her predecessors.

Probably Mrs. Boutell replaced Mrs. Hughes, who left the company in 1669–70. Downes (p. 12) gives Mrs. Hughes the role of Theodosia in Dryden's *An Evening's Love*, June, 1668, but the quarto of 1671 has "Mrs. Bowtell" in the part. On the other hand Downes (p. 10) gives Mrs. Boutell the role of St. Catherine in Dryden's *Tyrannic Love*, June, 1669, but the quarto of 1670 has Mrs. Hughes. No doubt Mrs. Hughes created both roles.

According to Curll (p. 21), "Mrs. Boutel was . . . a very considerable Actress; she was low of Stature, had very agreeable Features, a good Complexion, but a Childish look. Her Voice was weak, tho' very mellow; she generally acted the young, innocent Lady whom all the Heroes are mad in Love with; she was a Favorite of the Town." She was particularly popular in breeches parts.

Mrs. Boutell played Aurelia, a breeches part, in Joyner's *The Roman Empress*, August, 1670; Benzayda, a breeches part, in Dryden's *Conquest of Granada*, December, 1670–January, 1671; Christina in Wycherley's *Love in a Wood*, ca. March, 1671; Semina, a breeches part, and the epilogue in Corye's *The Generous Enemies*, ca. July, 1671; the prologue, in breeches, to a revival of Dryden's *Secret Love*, played by women only, spring, 1672 (Thorn-Drury, p. 1); Melantha, a breeches part, in Dryden's *Marriage A-la-Mode*, April, 1672; Laura in Dryden's *The Assignation*, ca. November, 1672; Alcinda and the prologue in Duffett's *The Spanish Rogue*, ca. March, 1673; Clara, a breeches part, in Duffett's *The Amorous Old Woman*, March, 1674; Princess Cyara, a breeches part, in Lee's *Nero*, May, 1674; an epilogue at Oxford, July, 1674; Mrs. Pinchwife, a breeches part, in Wycherley's *The Country Wife*, January, 1675; Rosalinda, a breeches part, in Lee's *Sophonisba*, April, 1675; Bellinganna in Fane's *Love in the Dark*, May, 1675; Fidelia, a breeches part, in Wycherley's *The Plain Dealer*, December, 1676; Clarona in Crowne's *The Destruction of Jerusalem*, January, 1677 (Downes, p. 18); Statira in Lee's *The Rival Queens*, March, 1677; Princess Glorianda in Chamberlayne's *Wits Led by the Nose*, ca. July, 1677; Matilda in Ravenscroft's *King Edgar and Alfreda*, ca. October, 1677; Cleopatra in Dryden's *All for Love*, December, 1677; Semandra in Lee's *Mithridates*, February, 1678; and Cellida in D'Urfey's *Trick for Trick*, ca. March, 1678.

Although Downes (p. 39) says that Mrs. Boutell was one of the "Remnant" of the King's Company taken into the United Company, there is no record of her appearance between 1678 and 1688. On May 5, 1688, Lord Granville wrote to Sir William Leveson that "Mrs. Boute[ll] . . . is again come upon the stage, where she appears with great applause" (*HMC, Fifth Report*, p. 197). She played Aurelia in D'Urfey's *A Fool's Preferment*, ca. April, 1688; Mrs. Termagant, a breeches part, in Shadwell's *The Squire of Alsatia*, May, 1688; Mrs. Fantast in Shadwell's *Bury Fair*, April, 1689;

Queen Semanthe in Powell's *The Treacherous Brothers*, February, 1690; and Lady Credulous in Crowne's *The English Frier*, March, 1690.

It is possible that Mrs. Boutell retired from the stage in 1690; at least her name appears in no more dramatis personae until the winter of 1695, when she joined her friends at the new theatre in Lincoln's Inn Fields. There she played Queen Thomyris in Banks's *Cyrus the Great*, ca. December, 1695; Constantia, a breeches part, in Granville's *The She-Gallants*, ca. December, 1695; Francelia in Motteux's *Love's a Jest*, June, 1696; Clara in Harris' *The City Bride*, ca. March, 1696; Dowdy, a comic role, in *She Ventures and He Wins* (Anon.), ca. September, 1696; and Estifania in Fletcher's *Rule a Wife and Have a Wife*, ca. 1696 (Genest, II, 122). After this she retired permanently. Wrote Curll, "Besides what she saved by Playing, the Generosity of some happy Lovers enabled her to quit the stage before she grew old." Probably she was in her early forties when she retired.

Perhaps, as Summers suggests (Downes, p. 98), Mrs. Boutell was the wife of "Boutell, one of the French musicians attached to the Court between 1661–1675." She is referred to as a widow in "Lampoons":

> Betty Bowtall is true to whom she pretends
> Then happy is hee whom she Chuses for freind
> Shee faine would hang out Widdows peak for a signe
> But ther's noe need of Bush where there is so good wine.

The implications of this are reinforced in later satires. "The Session of Ladyes: 1688" (p. 148) dismissed her abruptly as "Chesnut-man'd Boutel, whom all the Town F——ks." In "Satyr on Bent——g &c. 1688/9" ("A Choyce Collection," p. 301) she is labeled a "Whore" who

> Poor Armstrong's Life betray'd,
> And past upon Maccarty for a Maid.

BRACEGIRDLE, ANNE (United and Lincoln's Inn Fields companies, 1688?–1707). If the Funeral Book of Westminster Abbey is correct, Mrs. Bracegirdle was eighty-five when she died on September 12, 1748 (J. L. Chester, *Westminster Abbey Registers* [1869]). If so, she was born in 1663. Because

her father, Richard Bracegirdle of Wolverhampton, Stafford-
shire, was blessed with a large brood of children, he was
happy to have her brought up in the family of Thomas Betterton, "whose Tenderness," says Curll (p. 26), "she always
acknowledges to have been Paternal." Curll adds that "she
performed the Page in *The Orphan* [March, 1680] . . . before
she was six Years old." The "six" could be Curll's slip for
sixteen, or he could be right about her age. If Anne was at
least sixteen in March, 1680, we may well wonder that she
did not embark fully upon her stage career at that time.
However, she is not listed among the women of any company
until January 12, 1688 (Nicoll, p. 332). When Cibber joined
the United Company in 1690, Mrs. Bracegirdle, he said
(I, 170), "was now but just blooming to her Maturity; her
Reputation as an Actress gradually rising with that of her
person." The implication is that in 1690 she was still quite
young.

Anne's first recorded performance was as young Antelina
in Mountfort's *The Injured Lovers*, ca. March, 1688. Thereafter she played a number of ingénue roles. She was Lucia,
a young girl, in Shadwell's *The Squire of Alsatia*, May, 1688;
the Indian Queen, a breeches part, in Behn's *The Widow
Ranter*, ca. November, 1689; Biancha and the prologue in
Mountfort's *The Successful Strangers*, ca. December, 1689;
Marcelia in Powell's *The Treacherous Brothers*, February,
1690; Julia in Crowne's *The English Frier*, March, 1690;
Rosania and the epilogue in Shadwell's *The Amorous Bigotte*,
spring, 1690; the prologue to Dryden's *Amphitryon*, October,
1690; Cleomira in Settle's *Distress'd Innocence*, November,
1690; Urania in Powell's *Alphonso King of Naples*, December,
1690; Charlotte and the prologue in Southerne's *Sir Anthony
Love*, December, 1690; Clara in Shadwell's *The Scowrers*, ca.
December, 1690; Maria and the epilogue in Mountfort's
King Edward III, ca. December, 1690; and Miranda in
Harris' *The Mistakes*, ca. December, 1690.

Apparently Anne inherited Mrs. Boutell's roles in 1690,
among them Statira in Lee's *The Rival Queens*, a part in
which she became famous. In D'Urfey's *The Richmond
Heiress* (Act I, scene 1), ca. February, 1693, Sir Quible says:

And Mrs. Bracegirdle, prithee where is she now? . . . Well, I'll
say she acts Statira curiously.

> From every Pore of him a Perfume falls.
> He kisses softer than a Southern Wind:
> Curls like a Vine, and touches like a God.

> *(Speaks this affectedly.)*

Mrs. Bracegirdle's further creations were Mirtilla in
D'Urfey's *Love for Money*, ca. December, 1690; Tamira in
D'Urfey's *Bussy D'Ambois*, ca. March, 1691; Emmeline and
the epilogue in Dryden's *King Arthur*, May, 1691; Mrs.
Sightly in Southerne's *The Wives Excuse*, December, 1691;
Eurione and the epilogue in Brady's *The Rape*, February,
1692; Cleora and the epilogue in Dryden's *Cleomenes*, April,
1692; Amidea in Rivers' *The Traytor*, May, 1692; Phoebe, a
breeches part, and the prologue with Mountfort in D'Urfey's
The Marriage Hater Match'd, June, 1692; Rosamond and the
epilogue in Bancroft's *Henry the Second*, September, 1692;
Clara and the prologue in Shadwell's *The Volunteers*, ca.
November, 1692; Lady Trickitt and the epilogue in Southerne's *The Maid's Last Prayer*, January, 1693; Fulvia and the
epilogue in D'Urfey's *The Richmond Heiress*, ca. February,
1693; Araminta and the prologue in Congreve's *The Old
Bachelor*, March, 1693; Mariana in Wright's *The Female
Vertuosos*, ca. April, 1693; Cynthia and the prologue in Congreve's *The Double-Dealer*, October, 1693; Victoria and the
prologue in Southerne's *The Fatal Marriage*, February, 1694;
Celidea in Dryden's *Love Triumphant*, March, 1694; Princess
Clarismunde in Settle's *The Ambitious Slave*, March, 1694;
and Marcella in D'Urfey's *Don Quixote*, ca. August, 1694.

In the following year Mrs. Bracegirdle was one of the
players who founded a theatre in Lincoln's Inn Fields. In
Congreve's *Love for Love*, with which the new company
opened on April 30, 1695, she played Angelica, the lead, and
gave the epilogue. Thereafter she played Lausaria in Banks's
Cyrus the Great, ca. December, 1695; Angelica, a breeches
part, and the epilogue in Granville's *The She-Gallants*, ca.
December, 1695; Mrs. Purslew in Dilke's *The Lover's Luck*,
December, 1695; the epilogue to J. Dryden, Jr.'s, *The Husband His Own Cuckold*, ca. February, 1696; Flora in Dogget's

The Country-Wake, ca. April, 1696; Princess Bassima in Manley's *The Royal Mischief*, ca. April, 1696; Christina in Motteux's *Love's a Jest*, June, 1696; Charlot, a breeches part, in "Ariadne's" *She Ventures and He Wins*, ca. September, 1696; Princess Almeria and the epilogue in Congreve's *The Mourning Bride*, February, 1697; Duchess de Sanserre in D'Urfey's *The Intrigues at Versailles*, ca. February, 1697; Venus in Motteux's *The Loves of Mars and Venus*, ca. March, 1697; Bellinda, the prologue, and the epilogue with Mrs. Barry in Vanbrugh's *The Provok'd Wife*, May, 1697; Mrs. Beauclair, a breeches part, in Pix's *The Innocent Mistress*, ca. June, 1697; Camilla in Hopkins' *Boadicea*, ca. November, 1697; Briseis in Granville's *Heroic Love*, ca. December, 1697; Ariana in Pix's *The Deceiver Deceived*, ca. December, 1697; Placentia and the epilogue in Motteux's *Beauty in Distress*, ca. April, 1698; Felicia in Trotter's *Fatal Friendship*, ca. May, 1698; Isabella in Pix's *Queen Catherine*, ca. June, 1698; Louisa in Pix's *The False Friend*, ca. May, 1699; Locris, a breeches part, in Hopkins' *Friendship Improv'd*, November, 1699; Iphigenia in Dennis' *Iphigenia*, December, 1699; Almira and the epilogue in Smith's *The Princess of Parma*, 1699; Isabella in Gildon's *Measure for Measure*, ca. February, 1700; Mrs. Millamant and the epilogue in Congreve's *The Way of the World*, March, 1700; Amestris and the epilogue in Rowe's *The Ambitious Step-Mother*, ca. December, 1700; Fulvia, a breeches part, in Burnaby's *The Ladies Visiting-Day*, ca. January, 1701; Guinoenda in Gildon's *Love's Victim*, ca. April, 1701; Cytheria in Pix's *The Double Distress*, ca. May, 1701; Portia in Granville's *The Jew of Venice*, ca. May, 1701; Selima and the epilogue in Rowe's *Tamerlane*, ca. December, 1701; Amintas, a breeches part, in *The Fickle Shepherdess* (Anon.), "Play'd all by Women," ca. March, 1703; Caesario, a breeches part, in Burnaby's *Love Betray'd*, March, 1703; Orinda in Boyle's *As You Find It*, April, 1703; Lavinia and the epilogue in Rowe's *The Fair Penitent*, ca. May, 1703; Abra-Mulé and the epilogue in Trapp's *Abra-Mulé*, January, 1704; Irene in Dennis' *Liberty Asserted*, February, 1704; Mariana and the epilogue in Rowe's *The Biter*, December, 1704; Julia and the epilogue in *Squire Trelooby*,

1704; Angelica, a breeches part, in Centlivre's *The Gamester*, ca. January, 1705; Flippante in Vanbrugh's *The Confederacy*, October, 1705; Semanthe and the epilogue in Rowe's *Ulysses*, November, 1705; Oriana in Granville's *The British Enchanters*, February, 1706; Phillis in Motteux's *The Temple of Love*, March, 1706; Mrs. Ford in *The Merry Wives of Windsor*, April, 1706 (Downes, p. 47); Laura, a breeches part, in Pix's *The Adventures in Madrid*, ca. June, 1706; Lucinda in Centlivre's *The Platonick Lady*, November, 1706; Zoradia in Manley's *Almyna*, December, 1706; Melantha, a breeches part, in Cibber's *The Comical Lovers;* and the Countess of Rutland in a revival of Banks's *The Unhappy Favourite*, February 20, 1707 (Genest, II, 365). According to Cibber (I, 173), "She retir'd from the Stage in the Height of her Favour from the Publick, when most of her Cotemporaries whom she had been bred up with were declining." She returned to the stage only once after *The Unhappy Favourite*, on April 7, 1709, when she appeared in *Love for Love* for Betterton's benefit. She died September 12, 1748, and was buried in Westminster Abbey.

Testimonies to Mrs. Bracegirdle's success as an actress are legion. She usually played "good" woman roles and was notably successful in Shakespearean revivals, especially as Desdemona and Ophelia (Hazelton Spencer, *Shakespeare Improved* [1927], pp. 26, 69). She was also an excellent singer. According to Downes (p. 45), Crowne's unprinted *Justice Busy*, 1699, was a failure. "However Mrs. Bracegirdle, by a Potent and Magnetick Charm in Performing a Song in't; caus'd 'The Stones of the Streets to fly in the Men's Faces.' "

Aston (II, 305) described her thus: "She was of a lovely Height, with dark-brown Hair and Eye-brows, black sparkling Eyes, and a fresh blushy Complexion; and, whenever she exerted herself, had an involuntary Flushing in her Breast, Neck and Face, having continually a chearful Aspect, and a fine set of even white Teeth; never making an *Exit*, but that she left the Audience in an Imitation of her pleasant Countenance."

She was much sought after by would-be "keepers," one of whom was the vicious Captain Hill who murdered the ac-

tor Mountfort in 1692 (Borgman). Presumably successful
lovers were William Congreve and, after him, Robert Leke,
third Earl of Scarsdale, who bequeathed her £1,000 in 1708
(*Westminster Abbey Registers*). In spite of her popular reputation for chastity, she was attacked in a number of contemporary lampoons. The attitude of the skeptics is summarized
in the following passage from Wells (p. 106):

RAMBLE: And Mrs. Bracegirdle . . .

CRITIC: Is a haughty conceited Woman, that has got more
Money by dissembling her Lewdness, than others by professing it.

SULLEN: But does that Romantick Virgin still keep up her great
Reputation?

CRITIC: D'ye mean her Reputation for Acting?

SULLEN: I mean her Reputation for not acting; you understand
me—.

CRITIC: I do; but if I were to be sav'd for believing that single
Article, I cou'd not do it; 'Tis all, all a Juggle, 'tis Legerdemain; the
best on't is, she falls into good Hands, and the secrecy of the
Intrigue secures her, but as to her Innocence, I believe no more on't
than I believe of John Mandevil.

BROWN, MRS. (Duke's Company, 1662). Mrs. Brown is
listed for the role of Dorothea in Parkhurst's translation of
Ruggles' *Ignoramus*, November, 1662 (Hotson, p. 214). Her
name does not appear elsewhere.

BURROUGHS, MRS. (Duke's Company, 1672–73). Mrs.
Burroughs played Marina, the second lead, in Ravenscroft's
The Citizen Turn'd Gentleman, July, 1672. Marina was described as short but "well shaped," with black eyes, "a wide
mouth," and dimples. Mrs. Burroughs' only other known
role was as Jacinta, a lead, in Ravenscroft's *The Careless
Lovers*, March, 1673.

BUTLER, CHARLOTTE (Duke's and United companies,
1680–92). According to Cibber (I, 163), Mrs. Butler, "who
had her Christian name of Charlotte given her by King
Charles, was the Daughter of a decay'd Knight, and had the
Honour of that Prince's Recommendation to the Theatre."
She sang and danced "to perfection," and in such dramatic

operas as Betterton's *The Prophetess*, ca. June, 1690, and Dryden's *King Arthur*, April, 1691 (in which she played Philidel), "she was a capital and admired performer." She had a "sweet-ton'd Voice," and a "naturally genteel Air and Sensible Pronunciation."

The date of her joining the Duke's Company is uncertain. Downes (p. 35) listed her with a group who joined about 1673–74. A "Mrs. Butler" who doubled the roles of Plenty and an African woman in Crowne's *Calisto*, February, 1675, is identified as Charlotte by Eleanor Boswell (*The Restoration Court Stage* [1932], p. 198). Collier (p. 202) claims that Mrs. Butler made her debut in a lost comedy called "Fools have Fortune, or Luck's All," ca. 1680, and quotes from the prologue, in which her name was marginally inserted (see also Downes, p. 221). Unlike most of Collier's quotations, this one rings true.

Mrs. Butler's first recorded appearance at the Duke's Theatre was as Serina and the epilogue in Otway's *The Orphan*, March, 1680. Thereafter she played Marinda in Behn's *The Revenge*, ca. June, 1680; Charlot and the epilogue in Behn's *The City Heiress*, March, 1682; the prologue to Behn's lost play "Like Father, like Son," 1682 (Wiley, p. 97); the prologue and possibly Feliciana in *Romulus and Hersilia* (Anon.), August, 1682; Mrs. Clerimont in Ravenscroft's *Dame Dobson*, June, 1683; Lucretia, a breeches part, in Otway's *The Atheist*, ca. July, 1683; and Constance and the epilogue in a revival of Brome's *The Northern Lass*, 1684.

At about this time she seems to have left the stage to try her fortune as a singer. The author of "A Satyr on the Players" (p. 292) wrote:

> Fam'd Butlers Wiles are now so common grown
> That by each Feather'd Cully, she is known
> So that at last to save her Tott'ring Fame
> At Music Club she strives to get a Name
> But Mony is the Syren's chiefest Aym.

She returned to the United Company, playing Sophia in Carlile's *The Fortune-Hunters*, March, 1689; Philadelphia, a breeches part, in Shadwell's *Bury Fair*, ca. April, 1689; Statilia, a breeches part, and the epilogue in Powell's *The*

Treacherous Brothers, February, 1690; Airy, a courtesan, in Crowne's *The English Frier*, March, 1690; Levia, a courtesan, a breeches part, and the prologue in Shadwell's *The Amorous Bigotte*, spring, 1690; "Night" in Dryden's *Amphitryon*, October, 1690; Floriante, a breeches part, and the epilogue in Southerne's *Sir Anthony Love*, December, 1690; Astella, a breeches part, and the epilogue in Harris' *The Mistakes*, ca. December, 1690; Betty Jiltall and the epilogue with Mountfort in D'Urfey's *Love for Money*, ca. December, 1690; the epilogue in Smith's *Win Her and Take Her*, 1691; Prince Agilmond, a breeches part, in Brady's *The Rape*, February, 1692; and La Pupsey and the epilogue in D'Urfey's *The Marriage-Hater Match'd*, June, 1692. At this time, according to Cibber (I, 165), Mrs. Butler was getting only 40s. a week. When her request for 10s. more was refused she went to the Dublin Theatre, never to return.

Mrs. Butler was a handsome, black-eyed brunette (see the frequent references to her black eyes in D'Urfey's *Love for Money*). Usually she played only secondary roles, especially those calling for singing and dancing. She was often cast as a courtesan. In "Satyr on both Whigs and Toryes: 1683" (p. 242) we are told that

> Whorwood, whom Butler clapt & made a Chiaux,
> To save his Stake, marry'd, & clapt his Spouse,

and the author of "The Wedding," ca. 1689 (Harvard MS Eng. 633), asks:

> But Butler oh thou Strumpet Termagant
> Durst thou pretend to husband or gallant
> Ev'n to thy owne Profession a disgrace
> To sett up for a Whore with such a face
> Who but an Irish Fool would make this Choice?

CHILD, *ANNE* (King's Company, 1666). Mrs. Child's name appears only in the Lord Chamberlain's livery warrant for June 30, 1666.

CLOUGH, *MRS.* (Duke's Company, 1670–73). Mrs. Clough's first known part was the small role of Isillia in Behn's *The Forc'd Marriage*, ca. December, 1670. She ap-

peared also as the Second Lady in E. Howard's *The Six Days
Adventure*, ca. March, 1671, and as Hillaria, a breeches part,
in Ravenscroft's *The Careless Lovers*, March, 1673. Probably
she was the "Mrs. Caff" who played Mariana in Arrowsmith's *The Reformation*, September, 1673.

A passage in "Lampoons" (p. 276) offers a possible clue
to her career after she left the stage:

> Clough and Jackson yee Whores debaucht by fine Cloathes
> Have a care of returning to packthred in Shoos
> Silly Jackson is poor and has gott a Clapp
> Bloody Clough makes Tarse ware a Cardinalls Capp.

COOKE, SARAH (King's and United companies, 1677–88).
Mrs. Cooke seems to have been of humble origin, if we can
believe the author of "Satyr on the Players" (p. 291):

> Impudent Sarah thinks she's prais'd by all,
> Mistaken Drab, back to thy Mothers Stall
> And sell there Savin, which thou'st prov'd so well.

Her first part was the small role of Gillian in Leanerd's
The Country Innocence, ca. March, 1677. In September of
that year she was listed among the younger actors with whom
Charles Killigrew made a new agreement (Hotson, p. 261).
Thereafter she played a variety of roles: Flora and the prologue in Leanerd's *The Rambling Justice*, March, 1678; the
epilogue to Tate's *Richard the Second*, December, 1680; Livia
in D'Urfey's *Sir Barnaby Whigg*, ca. September, 1681; the
Countess of Rutland in Banks's *The Unhappy Favorite*, ca.
September, 1681; and Semanthe, the heroine, and the epilogue in Southerne's *The Loyal Brother*, February, 1682.

For the United Company she played Estiphania in Fletcher's *Rule a Wife and Have a Wife*, 1682 (Downes, p. 39); the
epilogue to Dryden and Lee's *The Duke of Guise*, November,
1682; Serena and the epilogue in Lee's *Constantine*, November, 1683; the first and second days' prologues to Rochester's
Valentinian, February, 1684; Erminia in Southerne's *The
Disappointment*, April, 1684; Portia in *Julius Caesar*, ca.
1684; Aminta, the lead, in D'Urfey's *A Commonwealth of
Women*, ca. August, 1685; Edith in *Rollo*, ca. 1685; Donna

Elvira in D'Urfey's *The Banditti*, February, 1686; Lady
Lovemore in Jevon's *The Devil of a Wife*, March, 1686;
Elaria and the epilogue in Behn's *The Emperor of the Moon*,
ca. March, 1687; Quisaria in Tate's *The Island Princess*,
April, 1687; and Leticia in Behn's *The Lucky Chance*, ca.
December, 1687. She died in April or May, 1688 (*HMC,
Fifth Report*, p. 197).

Mrs. Cooke was highly regarded as a player, especially for
romantic or tragic roles. In August or September, 1684, Dryden, writing about the casts for two of his plays to be revived
in the winter, remarked that in *All for Love* "Octavia was to
be Mrs. Buttler, in case Mrs. Cooke were not on the stage,"
a comment that indicates that he thought Mrs. Cooke superior to Mrs. Butler for the role (*The Letters of John Dryden*,
ed. C. E. Ward [1942], p. 23). On February 27 / March 8,
1688, evidently after hearing of Mrs. Cooke's illness and
approaching death, Etherege (p. 337) paid her a backhanded
compliment when he wrote to a friend, "Sarah Cooke was
always fitter for a player than for a Mrs., and it is properer
her lungs should be wasted on the stage than that she should
die of a disease too gallant for her." Presumably she died of
a veneral disease.

CORBETT, MRS. (King's Company, 1675–81). Very little
is known about Mrs. Corbett; she was unimportant both as
a player and as a subject for gossip. Downes (p. 8) was probably confusing a late with an early cast when he listed her
as Portia in *Julius Caesar*, ca. 1669–70. More probably she
appeared in a revival of that play in December, 1676 (4to,
1684; Nicoll, p. 346). Her first assured role was Mrs. Dainty
Fidget in Wycherley's *The Country Wife*, January, 1675.
Thereafter she played King Andrew, a breeches part, in Duffett's *Psyche Debauch'd*, May, 1675; Melesinda in Dryden's
Aurenge-Zebe, November, 1675; Narcissa in Lee's *Gloriana*,
January, 1676; Monimia in Lee's *Mithridates*, February,
1678; Clevly in J. Howard's *The Man of Newmarket*, ca.
March, 1678; Sabina in D'Urfey's *Trick for Trick*, ca. March,
1678; Gratiana in D'Urfey's *Sir Barnaby Whigg*, ca. Septem-
ber, 1681; and the Countess of Nottingham in Banks's *The*

Unhappy Favourite, ca. September, 1681. These were all supporting roles.

It is barely possible that the Mrs. Corbett who was a cousin of Mrs. James Pierce and whom Pepys first met on November 9, 1666, later joined the King's Company and became Mrs. Corbett the actress. Mrs. Pierce seems to have had a wide acquaintance in theatrical circles.

COREY, KATHERINE (King's and United companies, 1660–92). In "The humble petition of Katherine Corey," March 11, 1689, Mrs. Corey said of herself that "she was the first and is the last of all the actresses that were constituted by King Charles the Second at His Restauration" (A. S. Borgman, "The Killigrews and Mrs. Corey," *Times Literary Supplement*, December 27, 1934). She claimed, further, to have served the Killigrew family faithfully for twenty-seven years. If she made due allowance for the eighteen-month theatrical interregnum, June, 1665, to November, 1666, this figure agrees well enough with a beginning date in the autumn of 1660.

Although Downes, too, lists her first among Killigrew's seven original actresses, her name does not appear either in the cast of Flecknoe's *Erminia*, 1661, or in the Lord Chamberlain's list of comedians for the autumn of 1663. Her name ("Mrs. Corey") is attached to the role of Mrs. Whitebroth in the MS of Wilson's *The Cheats*, ca. March, 1663, but it may have been added some time after the production of that play (see Nahm, p. 62). The first reliable contemporary reference to her is the appearance of her name ("Core") as Anna, a bawd, in the MS of Thomas Killigrew's *Thomaso*, ca. November, 1664 (Van Lennep, p. 805). It is possible that Katherine Corey was originally the Katherine Mitchell who was cast as Althea, a waiting woman, in Flecknoe's *Erminia* and was listed in the Lord Chamberlain's troupe of comedians for the autumn of 1663. Nothing is heard of Mrs. Mitchell after that date.

Mrs. Corey was a big woman with a gift for comedy. She was popular in a variety of roles, but especially in old women parts: scolding wives, mothers, governesses, waiting women, and bawds. Downes (pp. 4–6) listed her in early revivals of old plays as Lady Would-be in Jonson's *Volpone*, Mrs. Otter in Jonson's *Epicœne; or The Silent Woman*, Arane, the queen mother, in Beaumont and Fletcher's *A King and No King*, Abigail in Beaumont and Fletcher's *The Scornful Lady*, Duchess Sophia in Fletcher's *Rollo*, and Doll Common in Jonson's *The Alchemist*. Her great admirer, Pepys, called her only "Doll Common" (December 27, 1666).

After the reopening of the theatres in November, 1666, Mrs. Corey played a large number of roles: Melissa in Dryden's *Secret Love*, late February, 1667; Cleorin in Boyle's *The Black Prince*, October, 1667; Quisania in *The Island Princess*, November, 1668; Sempronia in *Catiline*, January, 1669 (imprisoned for imitating Mrs. Harvey; see Pepys, January 15, 1669); Sophonia in Joyner's *The Roman Empress*, August, 1670; Mrs. Joyner, a bawd, in Wycherley's *Love in a Wood*, ca. March, 1671; Julia in Corye's *The Generous Enemies*, ca. July, 1671; Teresa in Duffett's *The Spanish Rogue*, ca. March, 1673; an English Woman in Dryden's *Amboyna*, ca. May, 1673; Strega, the lead, in Duffett's *The Amorous Old Woman*, March, 1674; Agrippina in Lee's *Nero*, May, 1674; Lucy, the maid, in Wycherley's *The Country Wife*, January, 1675; Cumana, a priestess, in Lee's *Sophonisba*, April, 1675; Redstreak in Duffett's *Psyche Debauch'd*, ca. May, 1675; Widow Blackacre and the epilogue in Wycherley's *The Plain Dealer*, December, 1676; Arane, the queen mother, in Beaumont and Fletcher's *A King and No King*, ca. 1676; Sysigambis in Lee's *The Rival Queens*, March, 1677; a school-mistress in Ravenscroft's *Scaramouche*, May, 1677; Octavia in Dryden's *All for Love*, December, 1677; Quickthrift in E. Howard's *The Man of Newmarket*, ca. March, 1678; Begona in Southerne's *The Loyal Brother*, February, 1682; Dame Dobson in Ravenscroft's *Dame Dobson*, June, 1683; Mrs. Trainwell in Brome's *The Northern Lass*, ca. 1683; the Mother in Southerne's *The Disappointment*, April, 1684; Mrs. Touchstone in Tate's *Cuckolds-Haven*, ca. June, 1685; Roselia, chief of the Amazons, in D'Urfey's *A Commonwealth of Women*, ca. August, 1685; Eugenia in D'Urfey's *The Banditti*, February, 1686; Mopsophil in Behn's *The Emperor of the*

Moon, ca. March, 1687; and Ruth, a governess, in Shadwell's *The Squire of Alsatia*, May, 1688.

In the early spring of 1689, Mrs. Corey seems to have been one of a group of players who planned to form a new company under Henry Killigrew. When the project failed, Mrs. Corey was refused readmission to the United Company (under Charles Killigrew) and was forced to petition the Lord Chamberlain, who ordered her reinstated (Nicoll, pp. 333–34). Thereafter she played Lady Fantast in Shadwell's *Bury-Fair*, April, 1689; Mrs. Flirt in Behn's *The Widow Ranter*, ca. November, 1689; Farmosa in Mountfort's *The Successful Strangers*, ca. December, 1689; Belliza, the bigot, in Shadwell's *The Amorous Bigotte*, spring, 1690; Bromia in Dryden's *Amphitryon*, October, 1690; Doranthe in Settle's *Distress'd Innocence*, November, 1690; Priscilla in Shadwell's *The Scowrers*, December, 1690; Crowstich in D'Urfey's *Love for Money*, December, 1690; Teresia, a governess, in D'Urfey's *Bussy D'Ambois*, ca. March, 1691; Aunt to Dorinda in Mountfort's *Greenwich Park*, April, 1691; Mrs. Teazall in Southerne's *The Wives' Excuse*, December, 1691; Mrs. Bumfiddle in D'Urfey's *The Marriage Hater Match'd*, June, 1692; Mother Morossa in Rivers' *The Traytor*, May, 1692; and the Abbess of Charlton in *The Merry Devil of Edmonton*, 1692 (Genest, II, 15).

In spite of her popularity and long service, to the end of her career Mrs. Corey never received more than 30*s.* a week salary (Nicoll, p. 379). The gossips found nothing at all to say about her private life.

COX, ELIZABETH (King's Company, 1671–82). The first known part created by Betty Cox was Lydia in Wycherley's *Love in a Wood*, ca. March, 1671. She played thereafter romantic parts, which slowly increased in importance: Palmyra in Dryden's *Marriage A-la-Mode*, ca. April, 1672; Violetta in Dryden's *The Assignation*, ca. November, 1672; Constantia in Duffett's *The Amorous Old Woman*, March, 1674; Octavia in Lee's *Nero*, May, 1674; Desdemona in a revival of *Othello*, ca. 1674 (4to, 1687); Sophonisba in Lee's *Sophonisba*, April, 1675, and the epilogue at Oxford (Wiley, p. 333); Indamora in Dryden's *Aurenge-Zebe*, November, 1675; and Panthea in a revival of Beamont and Fletcher's *A King and No King*, 1676 (4to, 1676).

She seems to have deserted the theatre some time in 1676. Although she was cast for the role of Claudia in the MS version of Rochester's *Valentinian*, ca. 1676 (British Museum, Additional MS, 2869), there is no evidence that the play was performed before February, 1684. At a revival of Lee's *Mithridates* in the autumn of 1681 Mrs. Cox spoke a new epilogue (with Goodman), making much of the fact that she had just returned to the stage after a protracted absence (Wiley, p. 45). However, she created only one new role, Artemira in Settle's *The Heir of Morocco*, March, 1682, before the union of the two companies, and none thereafter.

There can be little doubt about her off-stage occupation. Among those seeking the favor of Apollo in "The Session of the Ladies. 1688" was "Lord Lumley's cast player the fam'd Mrs. Cox." In "Satire to Julian. 1683" ("A Choyce Collection," p. 134) she was said to be the mistress of Cardell Goodman.

CROFTS, MRS. (Duke's Company, 1679–81). Mrs. Crofts created two waiting woman roles, Teresa in Dryden's *The Spanish Friar*, March, 1680; and Aurelia in Behn's *The Rover*, Part II, ca. April, 1681.

CURRER, ELIZABETH (Duke's and United companies, 1675–89). Although Downes (p. 35) listed Mrs. Currer with those who joined the Duke's Company ca. 1673–74, her first recorded performance was as Alcinda, a small part, in Settle's *The Conquest of China*, May, 1675. Thereafter she played Betty Frisque in Crowne's *The Country Wit*, January, 1676; and Asteria in Settle's *Ibrahim*, March, 1676.

On May 25, 1676, for an unknown reason, the Lord Chamberlain issued a warrant for the arrest of "Mrs. Elisabeth Currer, Comoedian at His Royall Highnesses Theatre" (LC 5, 190, p. 150). She continued playing steadily: Mrs. Hadland, a breeches part, and the prologue in Behn's *The Counterfeit Bridegroom*, ca. September, 1677; Lady Fancy in

Behn's *Sir Patient Fancy*, January, 1678; Madam Tricklove and the epilogue in D'Urfey's *Squire Oldsapp*, ca. June, 1678; Marcella and the prologue in Behn's *The Feign'd Curtezans*, ca. March, 1679; Jenny Wheadle, a whore, in D'Urfey's *The Virtuous Wife*, ca. September, 1679; the Queen and the epilogue in Tate's *The Loyal General*, ca. December, 1679; Lady Elianor Butler, a breeches part, in Crowne's *Misery of Civil War*, ca. March, 1680; Ariadne, a breeches part, in Behn's *The False Count*, November, 1681; Eugenia and the epilogue (with others) in Ravenscroft's *The London Cuckolds*, November, 1681; Lady Medler in *Mr. Turbulent* (Anon.), January, 1682; Aquilina in Otway's *Venice Preserved*, February, 1682; Diana in Behn's *The City Heiress*, March, 1682; an unnamed role in Behn's lost play, "Like Father, like Son," ca. 1682 (Wiley, p. 98); Mrs. Testy and the prologue in Ravenscroft's *Dame Dobson*, June, 1683; Sylvia in Otway's *The Atheist*, ca. July, 1683; and Duchess Isabella in Tate's *A Duke and No Duke*, November, 1684.

It is likely that in 1684 Mrs. Currer joined the Dublin company for a time. The author of "A Satyr on the Players," wrote:

> Currer 'tis time thou wert to Ireland gone
> Thy utmost Rate is here but half a Crown
> Ask Turner if thou art not fulsom grown.

She was off the London stage for about five years. She returned to play the Widow Ranter, a breeches part, in Behn's *The Widow Ranter*, ca. November, 1689. Apparently she then had a quarrel with the management of the United Company. The Lord Chamberlain set March 8, 1690, for the hearing of a "difference betweene Mr Killigrew & Mrs Currer" (LC 5, 150, p. 366). Thereafter nothing more is heard of her.

Mrs. Currer's most famous role was Aquilina in Otway's *Venice Preserved*. According to Davies (III, 215), "When Leigh and Mrs. Currer performed the parts of doting cully and rampant courtezan, the applause was as loud as the triumphant Tories, for so they were at that time, could bestow."

DALTON, MRS. (King's Company, 1666). Mrs. Dalton's name appears only in the Lord Chamberlain's livery warrant for June 30, 1666.

DAVENPORT, ELIZABETH (King's Company, 1667–69). Mrs. Davenport's full name appears in the livery warrants for July 22, 1667, and February 8, 1668, and probably she was the "Mrs. Davenport" listed in the warrant for October 2, 1669. She created two small roles: Sabina (a "little, innocent" girl) in Dryden's *Secret Love*, February, 1667; and a lady in Boyle's *The Black Prince*, October, 1667. She may have been the sister of Frances and Jane Davenport (q.v.).

DAVENPORT, FRANCES (King's Company, 1664–68). Frances Davenport may have been the oldest of three sisters, Frances, Elizabeth, and Jane, all of the King's Company. It is unlikely that she was related to Hester Davenport, the famous "Roxalana" of the Duke's Company. Frances was first mentioned by Thomas Killigrew, in November, 1664, as "Franki" in the MS cast of his *Thomaso*, ca. 1665 (Van Lennep, p. 805). Her full name is given in three livery warrants. She played the small parts of Flavia, a maid of honor, in Dryden's *Secret Love*, February, 1667, and Valeria, a breeches part, in Boyle's *The Black Prince*, October, 1667. On April 8, 1668, Pepys wrote, "The eldest Davenport is, it seems, gone from the [King's] house to be kept by somebody; which I am glad of, she being a very bad actor."

It is possible that Mrs. Davenport was the "Fr. Damport" (a common spelling of Davenport) who, with her mother, also "Fr. Damport," was involved in some complicated intrigues with the Duke of Buckingham and others in the summer of 1667 (see J. H. Wilson, *A Rake and His Times* [1954], pp. 83–85).

DAVENPORT, HESTER (Duke's Company, 1660–62). Mrs. Davenport was listed by Downes as one of Davenant's original actresses. Her birth date is variously given as March 2, 1641 (British Museum, Sloane MS. 1684, p. 6) and March 23, 1642 (Bodleian Library, Ashmole MS. 243, p. 194). According to Downes (pp. 20–22) in 1661 she played

Roxalana in the second part of Davenant's *The Siege of Rhodes;* Lady Ample in Davenant's *The Wits;* the Queen in *Hamlet;* and Evandra in Davenant's *Love and Honour.* Pepys (April 2, 1662) implies that she also played Cleora in Massinger's *The Bondman.* From July 3 to July 13, 1661, she was with the Duke's players at Oxford, acting at The King's Arms (Wood, I, 406).

Sometime in 1661 or 1662 she went through a form of marriage with Aubrey de Vere, Earl of Oxford, a widower (Grammont, II, 54). According to Evelyn her last appearance before she left the stage was as Roxalana on January 9, 1662. On February 18 and April 12, 1662, Pepys spoke with regret of her loss, and on May 19 he wrote that she was "now owned by my Lord of Oxford." On January 1, 1663, Pepys was glad to see "the old Roxalana" in the chief box at the Duke's Theatre, "in a velvet gown, as the fashion is, and very handsome." There is no reliable evidence that she ever returned to the stage, although Downes (pp. 22, 26) states that she appeared as Camilla in Tuke's *The Adventures of Five Hours,* January, 1663, and as Roxalana in Boyle's *Mustapha,* April, 1665.

Mrs. Davenport's son by the Earl of Oxford was born April 17, 1664 (Bodleian Library, Ashmole MS 243, p. 194) and christened May 15 as Aubrey de Vere (*Complete Peerage,* ed. Doubleday *et al.* [1945], *s.v.* Oxford). Mrs. Davenport seems to have lived obscurely after leaving the stage, but perhaps, since Oxford lost most of his money gambling, not very well. Although Oxford was scolded in a satire called "Men of Honour. 1687" (British Museum, Harleian MS. 7317, page 158) for

> His spending his estate, marrying his whore,
> Suffering his son to perish at the door,

the son lived forty-four years. He was buried June 4, 1708, as "Aubrey de Vere, Earl of Oxford, from Grays Inn." The true Earl of Oxford, his father, died on March 12, 1703. Four months later, on July 25, 1703, the marriage of "Dame Hester, Countess Dowager of Oxford" to Peter Hoet, of Gray's Inn, was recorded. Hoet was buried May 8, 1717, at St.

Dionis Backchurch, and "Hester, called Countess of Oxford," was buried November 20, 1717, at St. Anne's, Soho. Cf. J. H. Wilson, "Lord Oxford's 'Roxalana,'" *Theatre Notebook*, XII (Autumn, 1957), 14–16.

DAVENPORT, JANE (King's Company, 1667–68). Jane was probably the youngest sister of Frances Davenport (q.v.). Although her name appears in the livery warrants for July 22, 1667, and February 8, 1668, there are no other records of her.

DAVIS or *DAVIES, KATHERINE* (Duke's and United companies, 1681–91). Mrs. Davis' first recorded appearance was as Julia, a leading role, in Behn's *The False Count*, November, 1681. Presumably Julia's lover, Don Carlos, was describing Mrs. Davis when he said to Julia, "What Eyes you have like Heaven blue and charming, a pretty Mouth, neck round and white as polisht Alabaster, and a Complexion beauteous as an Angel." This beauteous creature seems to have played very rarely. Presumably she was the Katherine Davies whose name is listed with the band of royal comedians constituted by James II on January 12, 1688 (Nicoll, p. 332). Her only other known role was as the hoyden Molly in D'Urfey's *Love for Money*, ca. December, 1690.

DAVIS, MARY, or *"MOLL"* (Duke's Company, 1662–68). Mrs. Davis was said to be an illegitimate daughter of Colonel Thomas Howard, who became third Earl of Berkshire (Pepys, January 14, 1668). It is supposed that she was a native of Charlton, near Malmesbury, where the Berkshire family had a country seat. Although Downes listed Moll as one of Davenant's four "Principal Actresses" in 1660, Pepys, who for some time called her simply "the little girl," wrote on February 18, 1662, after seeing her as Viola in Davenant's *The Law against Lovers*, that he had never seen her before that date. On February 23, 1663, he was pleased to see "the little girl dance in boy's apparel" in Stapylton's *The Slighted Maid*. On March 8, 1664, he saw a translation of Corneille's *Héraclius* and commented, "The little girl is come to act very prettily, and spoke the epilogue most admirably." Probably

Pepys did not learn her name until 1666. On April 17 of that year he wrote, "This day I am told that Moll Davis, the pretty girl, that sang and danced so well at the Duke's House, is dead." The report proved false.

Mrs. Davis must have been a child when she joined the company; as late as March 7, 1667, Pepys was still calling her "Miss," a term then applied properly to a child or an adolescent girl. She played Violinda in Stapylton's *The Step-Mother*, ca. November, 1663; Aurelia in Etherege's *Love in a Tub*, March, 1664 (Downes, p. 25); Princess Anne in Boyle's *Henry the Fifth*, August, 1664; and the Queen of Hungary in Boyle's *Mustapha*, April, 1665 (Downes, p. 26). She danced a jig at the close of Caryll's *The English Princess*, March, 1667 (Pepys, March 7, 1667); danced "in a shepherd's clothes" in a revival of Shirley's *Love Tricks* (Pepys, August 5, 1667); played Mrs. Millisent in Dryden's *Sir Martin Mar-all*, August, 1667 (Downes, p. 28); and may have played Ariel in the Davenant-Dryden version of *The Tempest*, November, 1667.

In 1667 Moll played Celania in a revival of Davenant's *The Rivals* and sang "My Lodging It Is on the Cold Ground" so charmingly that, as Downes said (p. 24), "not long after, it Rais'd her from her Bed on the Cold Ground, to a Bed Royal." On January 11, 1668, Pepys heard that Moll had become mistress to King Charles, who had given her a ring worth £600 and was furnishing a house for her in Suffolk Street. She was still an actress: on February 6, 1668, she played Gatty in Etherege's *She Wou'd If She Cou'd* (Downes, p. 29). By May 31 Pepys learned that she had left the stage and that Mrs. Gosnell had come back "in her room." On December 21, 1668, Pepys saw her in a box at the theatre exchanging amorous glances with the King. She returned to the boards only once, to sing as "The River Thames" in Crowne's *Calisto*, at court, February, 1675.

Her daughter, Lady Mary Tudor, was born October 16, 1673, and was married on August 18, 1687, to Edward, Viscount Radcliffe, later second Earl of Derwentwater. Lady Mary was married three times, lived a scandalous life, and died at Paris on November 5, 1726.

On December 4, 1686, James Paisible, "of St. James, Westm^r, Gent, Bach^r, abt 30, & Mrs. Mary Davis of the same, Sp^r, abt 25" took out a marriage license (*Marriage Allegations, Vicar-General*, ed. G. T. Armytage [1890]). Although Moll must have falsified her age (she was surely in her early thirties), there can be no doubt of her identity. Her husband-to-be, James Paisible, French flutist and composer (1636–1722) came to England about 1674 (W. J. Lawrence, *The Musical Antiquary* [1910], II, 58). The news of the marriage was received with mockery by the court wits and libelers. On May 12/22, 1687, Etherege (p. 206) wrote from Ratisbon, "Let me know how Mrs. Hughes has disposed of herself; Mrs. Davis has given a proof of the great passion she always had for music, and Monsieur Peasible has another (guess) bass to thrum than that he played so well upon." In "The Session of the Ladies. 1688," Moll, the "natural Mother" of Lady Mary Tudor, is refused Apollo's favor because "she an old Frenchman had got by the back." In "Satyr on Bent——g &c. 1688/9" ("A Choyce Collection," p. 301), we are told:

> Davis was looking out too for a Hero,
> Weary already of her Pypeing Lero.
> O Peaceable! thy own sad Farewell set,
> And make words to it of thy want of Wit:
> A Fidlers Name alone is Vile We know,
> Must thou then be a Pimp, & Cuckold too?

Nevertheless, there is no evidence that the marriage was unhappy. The Paisibles seem to have made several trips to France, and on January 31, 1698, a license to remain in England was granted to "James Paisible and Mary his Wife" (*CSPD*, 1698), presumably necessary because they had taken a trip to France since the Act of 1697 "to prevent correspondence with the late King James" (*HMC, House of Lords MSS*, V, 203–6). Paisible died in April or May, 1722.

DIXON, MRS. (Duke's Company, 1670–71). Genest (I, 111) conjectures that Mrs. Dixon was the daughter of James Dixon, a member of the original Duke's Company, and that she married Anthony Leigh, the comedian. This is no more than a double guess. Possibly the notion that she became Elinor Leigh is based on the fact that Mrs. Dixon disappeared from the stage just as Mrs. Leigh appeared. Mrs. Dixon played Melvissa, a dominating wife, in E. Howard's *The Womens Conquest*, ca. November, 1670; Orinda, a second lead, in Settle's *Cambyses*, ca. January, 1671; Petilla (Mrs. Foppering) in E. Howard's *The Six Days Adventure*, ca. March, 1671; Betty, a small role, in Revet's *The Town-Shifts*, March, 1671; and Julia, a second lead, in Crowne's *The History of Charles the Eighth*, November, 1671.

EASTLAND, MRS. (King's Company, 1663–70). Although Downes give Mrs. Eastland as one of Killigrew's seven original actresses and her name appears on the Lord Chamberlain's list of "Women Comoedians" for autumn, 1663, it appears in no dramatis personae until 1669 and is missing from the four livery warrants (1666–69). She may have been an occasional player rather than a regular hireling. She played the small parts of Cydnon, an attendant, in Dryden's *Tyrannick Love*, June, 1669, and Halyma, a slave, in Dryden's *Conquest of Granada*, December, 1670–January, 1671. "Edward Eastland, Comoedian," who may have been her husband, seems to have joined the King's Company about 1672. On March 14, 1673, Thomas Humphryes petitioned against him for a debt of "£8 or thereabouts" (LC 5, 189, p. 152). He played the small part of Garbato in Duffett's *The Amorous Old Woman*, March, 1674. On January 5, 1678, Daniel Meades petitioned against him for a debt of £9 10*s*. (LC 5, 191, p. 7).

EVANS, MRS. (Duke's Company, 1678). So far as we know, Mrs. Evans played only the very small role of Manto in Dryden and Lee's *Oedipus*, ca. November, 1678.

FARLEY, ELIZABETH (King's Company, 1660–65). Mrs. Farley was usually called Mrs. Weaver and was so listed by Downes with Killigrew's seven original actresses and by Flecknoe for the role of Erminia in his *Erminia*, 1661. Presumably she was briefly a mistress to King Charles II, ca.

1660 (Pepys, January 11, 1668). Thereafter she formed a liaison with one James Weaver, of Gray's Inn, which soon ended; on January 14, 1662, Weaver petitioned for leave to sue her on a bond for £30 (LC 5, 184, p. 41), although she was then passing as his wife. In the autumn of 1662 a rather confused situation arose. Evidently Secretary Henry Bennet had written a letter to Killigrew in Mrs. Weaver's behalf. In Killigrew's absence Sir Robert Howard replied, asserting that the King and Bennet had been misinformed, that some three weeks earlier Mrs. Weaver had "brought in all her parts," declaring her intention of leaving the stage. Since then she had been discovered to be "shamefully" with child, i.e., the marriage with Weaver had been proved false (*CSPD*, 1664–65).

A petition against her by Henry Dobson (undated but by its position in the Entry Book ca. October, 1662) states that "one Eliz: Farley hath gone by the name of Eliz: Weaver wife to a gent of Grayes Inne to defraud her creditors and now being discovered that she is none of his wife altho she hath had a child by him and having no other shift for the defrauding of her said creditors but merely being sworne one of his Maties servants"—she persisted in refusing to pay her just debts. The petitioner begged leave to "take his course at law" for a debt of £11 11s. 6d. (LC 5, 184, p. 77).

Evidently she left the stage only briefly. On her return she continued to call herself Mrs. Weaver. On June 3, 1663, Robert Kerby petitioned against her (LC 5, 185, p. 39). On August 24, 1663, Robert Toplady was ordered under arrest for attaching the goods of "Eliz: Weaver one of His Maties Comedians" (LC 5, 185, p. 68). Her name, as Farley, appears in the Lord Chamberlain's list of players for the autumn of 1663. David Little and Miles Lovett petitioned against her on March 1 and 3, 1664 (LC 5, 185, pp. 135–36). In November, 1664, Thomas Killigrew cast her ("Wèvar") for the role of Serulina in his *Thomaso* (Van Lennep, p. 805). On February 28, 1665, George Langford and Henry Rook filed separate petitions against her (LC 5, 186, pp. 54, 56). About this time she was cast as Silvania in William Killigrew's *The Seege of Urbin* (Bodleian Library, Rawlinson MS. Poet. 29).

In April, 1665, she had an important part (probably Alibech) in Dryden's *The Indian Emperour* (Pepys, January 15, 1667). On May 19, 1665, Francis Poyntz petitioned against her for a debt of £20, and on May 24 Mrs. Anne Hame was granted leave to sue her for an unspecified amount (LC 5, 186, pp. 68, 70). Mrs. Weaver was listed in the livery warrant for June 30, 1666, but in none thereafter.

It is possible that Mrs. Farley returned to the stage from time to time under her proper name. A "Mrs. Farlowe" played Martha in Wycherley's *Love in a Wood*, ca. March, 1671; a "Mrs. F." played Theocrine in Chamberlayne's *Wits Led by the Nose*, ca. July, 1677; "Mrs. Farlee" played Eudoria in Leanerd's *The Rambling Justice*, March, 1678, and a whore in D'Urfey's *Trick for Trick*, March, 1678; and "Mrs. Farlo" played Luce in E. Howard's *The Man of Newmarket*, ca. March, 1678. Of course, this could be a different woman, as could the "Mrs. Farley" referred to in a verse epistle, "The First Letter from B. to Mr. E." ca. 1670 (*Rochester's Poems on Several Occasions*, ed. James Thorpe [1950], p. 77). If the subject of these verses was the original Mrs. Farley, the first line, "Dreaming last night on Mrs. Farley" (with erotic results) suggests that after leaving the stage she became a professional *fille de joie*.

FORD, MRS. (Duke's Company, 1671). Mrs. Ford seems to have played only the small part of the First Lady in E. Howard's *The Six Days Adventure*, ca. March, 1671.

FRIER, PEG (Duke's Company, 1661). According to Ryan (I, 77–78) Mrs. Frier (later Mrs. Vandervelt) had been "a celebrated actress in the reign of Charles II." In a three-act farce, Molloy's *The Half-Pay Officer*, January 11, 1720, a compilation from several old plays, she played a role that she was supposed to have first played more than fifty years earlier, an Old Widow in Davenant's *Love and Honour*, revived in October, 1661. Although in 1720 she was eighty-five years old, she danced a jig at the end of the play "with the nimbleness and vivacity of five-and-twenty, laughing at the surprise of the audience, and receiving unbounded applause." According to Genest (III, 42) she acted also Mrs. Amlet in a revival of Vanbrugh's *The Confederacy* on March 28, 1720, her final appearance on the stage.

It is likely that Mrs. Frier was the "Pegg" who played Nell, a waiting maid in Parkhurst's translation of Ruggles' *Ignoramus*, at court, November 1, 1662 (Hotson, p. 214).

GIBBS, MRS. (Duke's Company, 1676–78). Mrs. Gibbs, possibly a younger sister of Anne Shadwell, played a succession of minor roles: Henrietta in Otway's *Don Carlos*, June, 1676; Mrs. Essence and the epilogue in Rawlins' *Tom Essence*, ca. August, 1676; Beatrice, a maid servant, in Ravenscroft's *The Wrangling Lovers*, ca. September, 1676; Arbella, the second lead, in D'Urfey's *Madam Fickle*, November, 1676; Clara in Otway's *The Cheats of Scapin*, ca. December, 1676; Iras, an attendant, in Sedley's *Antony and Cleopatra*, February, 1677; Clarina in Behn's *The Counterfeit Bridegroom*, ca. September, 1677; Maundy, a waiting woman, in Behn's *Sir Patient Fancy*, January, 1678; Chloe, a maid servant, in Shadwell's *Timon of Athens*, ca. January, 1678; Victoria, the second lead, in Otway's *Friendship in Fashion*, April, 1678; and Flora, a waiting woman, in Leanerd's *The Counterfeits*, May, 1678.

GILLO, MRS. (Duke's Company, 1675–77). Mrs. Gillo was an undistinguished player of small parts: Ardella, a maid, in Otway's *Alcibiades*, September, 1675; Garcia, a page, a breeches part, in Otway's *Don Carlos*, June, 1676; Jacinta, a maid, in Ravenscroft's *The Wrangling Lovers*, ca. September, 1676; Lucetta, a jilting wench, in Behn's *The Rover*, March, 1677; and Cleone, a confidante, in Pordage's *The Siege of Babylon*, ca. September, 1677. Probably Mrs. Gillo was the wife of an obscure actor, Thomas Gillo, who was with the Duke's Company from 1674 to 1687.

GOSNELL, WINIFRED (?) (Duke's Company, 1663–?). Mrs. Gosnell was the younger of two impoverished but well connected sisters who were trained to sing and dance. She was Mrs. Pepys's personal maid from December 5 to 9, 1662.

On May 28, 1663, Pepys was surprised to see her in *Hamlet* at the Duke's Theatre, probably as an attendant lady. She "neither spoke, danced, nor sung," but she looked very pretty. The next day Pepys saw her as Pyramena in Stapylton's *The Slighted Maid*, a role created by Mrs. Betterton. According to Pepys she "did it very well." She sang a song, "Ah, love is a delicate ting" (*sic*) in Act II of Davenant's *The Playhouse to be Let*, ca. August, 1663 (the only appearance of her name in the quartos). On September 10, 1664, Pepys saw her in Davenant's *The Rivals*, probably as Celania, a role later played by Moll Davis. We hear no more of Mrs. Gosnell until July 28, 1668, when Pepys saw her in Stapylton's *The Slighted Maid* and remarked that she "is become very homely, and sings meanly, I think, to what I thought she did." On June 21, 1669, he saw her in a revival of *The Tempest* and wrote, "but it is ill done by Gosnell, in lieu of Moll Davis," who had just left the stage. Thereafter Pepys closed his diary, and Mrs. Gosnell disappeared.

It is quite possible that she remained for years with the Duke's Company as an occasional singer and understudy. Sybil Rosenfeld has discovered a petition to the Lord Chamberlain, written between 1689 and 1697, in which "Winifred Gosnold" stated that she had "belonged to their Ma^ts Playe[ours] ever since it was a Company, and spent her youth in their service by Acting there . . . now they have hired other singers and Discharged her." ("Unpublished Stage Documents," *Theatre Notebook*, Vol. II [April–June, 1957].)

GWYN, ELLEN (King's Company, 1664–71). Born February 2, 1650, Nell Gwyn was "brought up in a bawdy-house to fill strong waters to the guests" (Pepys, October 26, 1667). In her early adolescence she was an orange girl in the Theatre Royal and presumably mistress of Charles Hart, leading actor of the company. She became an actress at the age of fourteen. In November, 1664, Thomas Killigrew cast "Nelle" for the small part of Paulina, a courtesan, in his *Thomaso*, ca. 1665 (Van Lennep, p. 805). "Mrs. Nell" was later cast for the role of a maid servant, Melina, a breeches

part, in Sir William Killigrew's *The Seege of Urbin*, ca. 1665
(Bodleian Library, Rawl. MS. Poet. 29). According to
Downes (p. 5) "Madam Gwin" played Panthea, the heroine,
in an early revival of Beaumont and Fletcher's *A King and
No King*, but it seems more likely that she appeared in a
later revival, between 1667 and 1670. Downes says also that
"Mrs. Ellen Gwin" played Cydaria in Dryden's *The Indian
Emperour*, ca. April, 1665. This is possible, yet when Pepys
saw her in that role on August 22, 1667, he implied that she
had only recently been "put to act the Emperour's daughter." The chances are that she played no important roles before the closing of the theatres in May, 1665.

Nell's name appears in all the livery warrants for the
women of the King's Company. After the reopening of the
theatres she played Lady Wealthy in a revival of J. Howard's
The English Monsieur (Pepys, December 8, 1666); Celia in
Fletcher's *The Humorous Lieutenant* (Pepys, January 23,
1667); probably the Second Constantia in Buckingham's *The
Chances*, February, 1667; Florimel, a breeches part, and the
epilogue in Dryden's *Secret Love*, February, 1667; the epilogue to a revival of Beaumont and Fletcher's *The Knight of
the Burning Pestle*, ca. March, 1667 (Thorn-Drury, p. 78):
probably Samira in a revival of Sir Robert Howard's *The
Surprisal* (Pepys, April 8, August 26, 1667); and Mirida in
J. Howard's *All Mistaken*, ca. May, 1667 (Pepys, December
28, 1667).

During part of the summer of 1667 Nell was temporarily
off the stage while she was mistress of Charles, Lord Buck-
hurst; she returned late in August when her lover deserted
her. She played Flora in a revival of Rhodes' *Flora's Vagaries*,
October, 1667 (Pepys, October 5, 1667); Bellario, a breeches
part, in a revival of Beaumont and Fletcher's *Philaster*, ca.
November, 1667 (Nicoll, p. 344; Settle's prologue to *Philaster*, 1695); Maria, the prologue (with Mrs. Knep), and the
epilogue in Sir Robert Howard's *The Duke of Lerma*, February, 1668; Angelo, the good angel, in Massinger and Dekker's
The Virgin Martyr, February, 1668 (J. H. Wilson, "Nell
Gwyn as an Angel," *Notes and Queries*, CXCIII [February
21, 1948], 71–72); possibly Olivia in Sedley's *The Mulberry*

Garden, May, 1668; Jacintha in Dryden's *An Evening's Love*, June, 1668. She was cast as Lysette, a waiting woman, in Flecknoe's *The Damoiselles a la Mode*, September, 1668 (4to, 1667); spoke the prologue and epilogue to Jonson's *Catiline*, December, 1668; danced in farces with Lacy between the acts of Phillips' *Horace*, January, 1669 (Evelyn, p. 734) probably played Pulcheria, a breeches part, in a revival of Shirley's *The Sisters*, ca. April, 1669 (Summers, *Essays in Petto* [1928], pp. 105–10); and played Valeria and the epilogue in Dryden's *Tyrannic Love*, June, 1669.

Some time after this Nell left the stage to become the mistress of King Charles II. Her first son by him, Charles, was born in May, 1670. She returned to the stage to play Almahide and speak the prologue to Dryden's *Conquest of Granada*, December, 1670–January, 1671. Thereafter she left the stage for good. For the details of her later life see Peter Cunningham, *The Story of Nell Gwyn* (1852); A. I. Dasent, *Nell Gwynne* (1924); and J. H. Wilson, *Nell Gwyn, Royal Mistress* (1952).

HALL, ELIZABETH (King's Company, 1664–67). Probably Mrs. Hall joined the company some time in 1664. In November, 1664, a "Bette" was cast for the role of Kecka, a servant, in Thomas Killigrew's *Thomaso* (Van Lennep, p. 805); and somewhat later a "Mrs. Bettie" was cast for the role of Clara, a maid, in William Killigrew's *The Seege of Urbin*, 1665 (Bodleian Library, Rawl. MS. Poet. 29), although the role was later cut out of the play. On January 23, 1667, after Pepys had been behind the scenes at the Theatre Royal, he wrote, "We also saw Mrs. Hall, which is my little Roman-nose black girl [i.e., brunette] that is mighty pretty: she is usually called Betty."

Mrs. Hall's full name appeared in the livery warrant for June 30, 1666. On March 30, 1667, at the Duke's Theatre, Pepys saw "Knipp and Betty [Hall] of the King's house" in the audience. On December 19, 1668, at the Theatre Royal, Pepys sat next to "Betty Hall, that did belong to the house, and was Sir Philip Howard's mistress; a mighty pretty wench." "Did belong" is to be taken to mean "used to belong."

In "Satyr on Both Whigs and Toryes. 1683" (p. 243), a reference to the various "Baggages" who were kept by the numerous Howard brothers includes "Phil's Player." Presumably this was Betty Hall.

HOLDEN, MRS. (Duke's Company, 1661–?). Listed by Downes as one of Davenant's original actresses, Mrs. Holden either left the stage very soon or was of so little consequence that she played no important roles. Summers (Downes, p. 175) asserts that she was the daughter of John Holden, "the friend and publisher of Sir William Davenant." Her only claim to fame is the fact that, according to Downes (p. 22) she played "Count Paris's Wife" (Lady Montague?) in a revival of *Romeo and Juliet,* ca. 1662, and

> There being a Fight and Scuffle in this Play, between the House of Capulet, and House of Paris; Mrs. Holden Acting his Wife, enter'd in a Hurry, Crying, O my Dear Count! She Inadvertently left out, O, in the pronuntiation of the Word Count! giving it a Vehement Accent, put the House into such a Laughter, that London Bridge at low-water was silence to it.

A stage direction in D'Urfey's *The Injured Princess,* ca. March, 1682, "Act II. *Enter behind Cymbeline, Queen, a Purse, Pisano, Doctor and Guards, Mrs. Holten, Sue,*" troubles Summers (Downes, p. 176) because the play was presented by the King's Company, while "Mrs. Holten" and "Sue" (Percival), he asserts, were members of the Duke's Company. Of course there is no certainty that this was the original Mrs. Holden. Susanna Percival started her theatrical career at the Theatre Royal, appearing there first as Welsh Winifred in D'Urfey's *Sir Barnaby Whigg,* ca. September, 1681.

HUGHES, MARGARET (King's Company, 1668–69; Duke's Company, 1676–77). Although Downes listed Mrs. Hughes as one of Killigrew's first actresses, there is no trace of her in dramatic records until 1668. At the King's Theatre,

on May 7, 1668, Pepys "did kiss the pretty woman newly
come, called Pegg, that was Sir Charles Sidley's mistress."
This was assuredly Mrs. Hughes (see J. H. Wilson, "Pepys
and Peg Hughes," *Notes and Queries*, N.S. III [October,
1956], 428–29).

Probably Mrs. Hughes played Theodocia in Dryden's *An
Evening's Love*, June, 1668 (Downes, p. 8); and certainly
Panura in Fletcher's *The Island Princess*, November, 1668;
probably Angellina in Shirley's *The Sisters*, 1669 (Summers,
Essays in Petto [1928], pp. 103–10), and Desdemona in the
version of *Othello* seen by Pepys on February 6, 1669
(Downes, p. 7); and certainly St. Catherine in Dryden's
Tyrannic Love, June, 1669. "Mrs. Hues" was listed in the
livery warrant for October 2, 1669. In 1669 or early 1670
she left the stage to become Prince Rupert's mistress (date
erroneously given as 1666 by Grammont [II, 101]).

In June, 1671, "Mr. Hues, Peg Hues' brother," was killed
by one of the King's servants "upon a dispute whether Mrs.
Nelly [Gwyn] or she was the handsomer now att Windsor"
(*HMC, Rutland Papers*, II, 7). William Hughes was a minor
member of the King's Company in 1669–70 (LC 5, 62, p.
107); on January 13, 1670, one Mary Hunt petitioned for
leave to sue "Wm Hughes Comoedian" for a debt of £80
(LC 5, 188, p. 199).

Mrs. Hughes gave birth to a daughter, Ruperta, in 1673.
Three years later she joined the Duke's Company and played
Mirva in Settle's *Ibrahim*, March, 1676; Mrs. Monylove, a
breeches part, in Rawlins' *Tom Essence*, ca. August, 1676;
Octavia in Ravenscroft's *The Wrangling Lovers*, ca. September, 1676; Gerana in Settle's *Pastor Fido*, ca. December,
1676; Charmion in Sedley's *Antony and Cleopatra*, February,
1677; Valeria in Behn's *The Rover*, ca. March, 1677; Leonora
in Porter's *The French Conjurer*, ca. March, 1677; and Cordelia in D'Urfey's *A Fond Husband*, May, 1677. Thereafter
she left the stage for good. At his death in 1682 Prince
Rupert left Margaret and Ruperta about £6,000 apiece
(Eliot Warburton, *Prince Rupert and the Cavaliers* [1849], III,
560). He is said to have bought for Margaret the house of
Sir Nicholas Crispe, near Hammersmith, worth some

£25,000 (James Granger, *Biographical History of Englana* [1779], IV, 190).

Mrs. Hughes, a pretty, round-faced woman, had black hair and eyes. She was versatile and attractive, but never a major actress. She is referred to slightingly in a number of contemporary lampoons. According to Tom Brown (II, 241–45) she gambled away the estate left by her lover. Presumably she spent her old age dependent upon her daughter, who married Emmanuel Scroope Howe (*Suffolk Correspondence*, ed. J. W. Croker [1824] I, 39–40). She died on October 1, 1719, and on October 15 was buried at Lee, in Kent.

JAMES, ELIZABETH (King's Company, 1669–76). Listed by Downes as one who "came into the Company some few Years after" 1660, she did not actually join the company until about 1669. Her first role was a minor singing part, as Damilcar in Dryden's *Tyrannic Love*, June, 1669 (Downes, p. 10). Thereafter she played Isabella in Dryden's *Conquest of Granada*, December, 1670–January, 1671; Isabella, a waiting woman, in Wycherley's *Love in a Wood*, ca. March, 1671; and Alleria in Corye's *The Generous Enemies*, ca. July, 1671. On August 7, 1671, one Mrs. Corney was given leave to sue "Mrs. James Comoedian" (later "Mrs. Elizabeth James") for debt; on August 25 the permission was withdrawn (LC 5, 14, pp. 57, 60).

Mrs. James continued to play secondary roles: Amalthea in Dryden's *Marriage A-la-Mode*, ca. April, 1672; Sophronia in Dryden's *The Assignation*, ca. November, 1672; Julia in Dryden's *Amboyna*, ca. May, 1673; Bianca in a revival of *Othello*, 1674 (4to, 1687); Arabella in Duffett's *The Amorous Old Woman*, March, 1674; Alithea in Wycherley's *The Country Wife*, January, 1675; Aurania in Fane's *Love in the Dark*, May, 1675; and finally Julia in Lee's *Gloriana*, January, 1676.

Alleria in Corye's *The Generous Enemies* (Act I, scene 2) was described as "Young, Fair, witty, modest, tall, slender, and a thousand other things." Presumably Mrs. James fitted this description in 1671. The author of "Lampoons" (ca. 1678) took a coarser view of her:

Pride that ill natur'd distemper of the minde
Keeps Rich women honest, but makes poore ones kind
Like a damn'd daub'd Picture upon the Ale house Wall
So James is ill painted, and Expos'd to all
   A Virgin as shee'l vow and sweare
   Poore Girl she forgetts the Couch at the Beare.

(In Shadwell's *The Miser,* 1672 [Act I, scene 1]), Hazard remarks that Mrs. Cheatly, a bawd, has promised to bring a young lady "to a Ball at the Bear at Charing-Cross, where you know there is a very convenient Couch.")

In his "The Playhouse. A Satyr," 1685, Robert Gould, speaking of an actress' ability to "glide into some Keeping Coxcomb's Heart" and "Jilt Him of his Patrimonial lands," offered as a case in point, "Think of Ned Bush—then think of Mistress James." Her mercenary quality is further suggested by Tom Brown (II, 243–45) when he represents Peg Hughes defending herself against Nell Gwyn's accusation of folly by asserting that she had not, like "Madam Ja——es, or Mrs. Kn——ght of Drury Lane," yielded her favors for gain.

JENNINGS, MRS. (Duke's Company, 1661–72). Downes listed Mrs. Jennings among Davenant's original eight actresses. She achieved no fame, and her name is attached to only a few roles. She played Rosabella in Parkhurst's translation of Ruggles' *Ignoramus,* November, 1662 (Hotson, p. 214); Ariana in Etherege's *She Wou'd If She Cou'd,* February, 1668; Princess Galatea in Behn's *The Forc'd Marriage,* ca. December, 1670; Phedima in Settle's *Cambyses,* ca. January, 1671; and Philadelphia in Boyle's *Mr. Anthony,* ca. March, 1672. Shortly thereafter she was one of three actresses who, wrote Downes (p. 35), "by force of Love were Erept the Stage."

JOHNSON, MRS. (Duke's Company, 1669–73). According to Downes (p. 31) Mrs. Johnson, famous for her dancing, was one of several who joined the company "About the Year 1670." Her first known role was as Betty, a naïve young girl, in Caryll's *Sir Salomon,* ca. 1669. Thereafter she played

Statyra, a Persian Princess, in E. Howard's *The Women's Conquest*, ca. November, 1670; probably Theodosia in Shadwell's *The Humorists*, ca. December, 1670 (in his Preface Shadwell said the play was sustained "by her kindness . . . who for four days together, beautified it with the most excellent Dancing that ever has been seen upon the Stage"); Morena in Settle's *The Empress of Morocco*, July, 1671; Honour Muchland, a breeches part, in Payne's *The Morning Ramble*, November, 1672; and Carolina in Shadwell's *Epsom Wells*, December, 1672. In a note to this play Downes (p. 33) wrote, "Mrs. Johnson in this Comedy, Dancing a Jigg so Charming well, Loves power in a little time after Coerc'd her to dance more Charming, elsewhere." However, she created one more role, Ismena in Arrowsmith's *The Reformation*, September, 1673, before dancing to the tunes of love.

On December 11, 1677, it was reported that the Earl of Peterborough had sent challenges to Lord Deincourt and Sir George Hewett "for having broken the windowes of one Mrs. Johnson, a lady of pleasure under his Lordship's protection, but his Majesty being informed of it made all friends" (*HMC, Rutland Papers*, II, 42; *HMC Seventh Report*, p. 469). According to the author of "Lampoons," the actress passed through the hands of more than one keeper:

> From Duke and from Lord pritty Johnson is fled
> Thus kindly embraceing her Godfery she said,
> If plenty of money my dearest had more
> I should not be Counted so Arrant a Whore
> If thou would'st maintaine me I'de not goe astray
> Nor ever receive more rings from Tho: Gray.

At least she left pleasant memories with her patrons. On February 16/26, 1688, Etherege (p. 328) wrote to the Earl of Middleton, "Not to affect to be le chevalier à bonne fortune the best adventure I have had here has been with a comedian no less handsome and no less kind in Dutchland than Mrs. Johnson was in England."

JORDAN, MRS. (United Company, 1688–90). Mrs. Jordan, whose name appears also as Jordain, Jordon, Jorden, and Jourden, made her first known appearance in the small role of Celia in D'Urfey's *A Fool's Preferment*, ca. April, 1688. She then played Mrs. Chrisante in Behn's *The Widow Ranter*, ca. November, 1689; Antramont in Lee's *The Massacre of Paris*, November, 1689; Armena, an attendant, in Powell's *The Treacherous Brothers*, February, 1690; Laura, a coquette, in Crowne's *The English Frier*, March, 1690; and Elvira, the juvenile lead, in Shadwell's *The Amorous Bigotte*, spring, 1690.

KNAPPER, MRS. (Duke's Company, 1676–77). Although Downes (p. 35) says that Mrs. Knapper (otherwise Napper or Napier) joined the company about 1674, her first known role was as Betty, a maid servant, a breeches part, in Rawlins' *Tom Essence*, ca. August, 1676. She seems to have played only small parts: Sylvia, an attendant, in D'Urfey's *Madam Fickle*, November, 1676; Celia, a confidante, in Settle's *Pastor Fido*, ca. December, 1676; and Betty, a maid servant, in D'Urfey's *A Fond Husband*, May, 1677. She was mildly successful as a singer.

KNEP, MARY (King's Company, 1664–78). Listed by Downes as one of Killigrew's original actresses, Mrs. Knep was not named in the Lord Chamberlain's list for autumn, 1663, unless she was then Mary Man and was later married to Mr. Knep, an "ill, melancholy, jealous-looking fellow . . . a kind of jockey" (Pepys, December 8, 1665; December 11, 1668). In November, 1664, she was cast by Thomas Killigrew as Lucetta ("Knep") in his *Thomaso*, ca. 1665 (Van Lennep, p. 805). Her name appears in all four livery warrants, 1666–69.

Primarily a singer and dancer, Mrs. Knep developed into a first-rate actress. She played the Widow in Beaumont and Fletcher's *The Scornful Lady* (Pepys, December 27, 1666); Guiomar in Fletcher's *The Custom of the Country* (Pepys, January 2, 1667); Alibech in a revival of Dryden's *The Indian Emperour* (Pepys, January 15, 1667); sang in Fletcher's *The Humorous Lieutenant* (Pepys, January 23, 1667); danced in Suckling's *The Goblins* (Pepys, January 24, 1667); sang in Buckingham's *The Chances* (Pepys, February 5, 1667); played Asteria in Dryden's *Secret Love*, February, 1667;

danced and sang in Heywood's *The Troubles of Queen Elizabeth* (Pepys, August 17, 1667); played in an unknown drama, *The Northern Castle* (Pepys, September, 14, 1667); played Otrante in a revival of Rhodes's *Flora's Vagaries* (Pepys, October 5, 1667; 4to, 1670); and Sevina in Boyle's *The Black Prince*, October, 1667.

Although Mrs. Knep was arrested on February 12 and again on April 23, 1668, for "misdemeanors" at the Theatre Royal (LC 5, 186, pp. 200, 218), her offenses and punishments must have been slight. With Nell Gwyn she spoke the prologue to Sir Robert Howard's *Duke of Lerma*, February, 1668. She played Aminta in Fletcher's *The Sea Voyage* (Pepys, March 25, 1668); possibly Elspeth in a revival of J. Howard's *The English Monsieur* (Pepys, April 7, 1668); sang, and possibly played Emilia, in a revival of Sir Robert Howard's *The Surprisal* (Pepys, April 17, 1668); played in a revival of Massinger's *The Virgin Martyr* (Pepys, May 7, 1668); played Beatrice, a waiting maid, in Dryden's *An Evening's Love*, June, 1668; was Epicœne in *Epicœne; or, The Silent Woman* (Pepys, September 19, 1668; Downes, p. 4); doubled in the roles of Nakar and Felicia in Dryden's *Tyrannic Love*, June, 1669 (Downes, p. 10; 4to, 1670); and perhaps played Paulina in a revival of Shirley's *The Sisters* ca. 1669 (Summers, *Essays in Petto* [1928], pp. 103–10).

After Pepys closes his diary, our information about Mrs. Knep is less detailed. She played Antonio in Joyner's *The Roman Empress*, August, 1670; Lady Flippant in Wycherley's *Love in a Wood*, ca. March, 1671; Hippolita in Dryden's *The Assignation*, ca. November, 1672; Leonella and the epilogue in Duffett's *The Spanish Rogue*, ca. March, 1673; Aglave, a priestess, in Lee's *Sophonisba*, April, 1675; Lady Fidget and the epilogue in Wycherley's *The Country Wife*, January, 1675; Prince Nicholas, a breeches part, in Duffett's *Psyche Debauch'd*, May, 1675; Eliza in Wycherley's *The Plain Dealer*, December, 1676; Barbara and the epilogue in Leanerd's *The Country Innocence*, ca. March, 1677; and Dorothy in D'Urfey's *Trick for Trick*, ca. March, 1678.

Although Mrs. Knep allowed Pepys a great many liberties, there is no evidence that she was ever his mistress. He had several opportunities "to be bold" with her, and once found her alone at Mrs. Pierce's house, "on a pallet in the dark." Apparently she rebuffed him; when he next saw her (May 30, 1668) he wrote, "Here I was freed from a fear that Knepp was angry or might take advantage to declare the essay that je did the other day, quand je was con her."

KNIGHT, FRANCES MARIA (King's, United, Drury Lane, second United, and New Lincoln's Inn Fields companies, 1676–1719). Mrs. Knight, the actress, has sometimes been confused with Mary Knight, the singer and former mistress of Charles II (Wiley, p. 337; Nicoll, Index and p. 359). Surprisingly little is known about Frances Maria Knight, yet she had a long and successful, if not distinguished, stage career. If she was at least fourteen when she made her debut with the King's Company as Lettice, a maid servant, in Wycherley's *The Plain Dealer*, December, 1676 (Genest, I, 161), she must have been born not later than 1662.

After her second recorded role, the small part of Queen Leonora in Ravenscroft's *King Edgar and Alfreda*, ca. October, 1677, Mrs. Knight disappeared from the theatre for seven years. Presumably the Mrs. Knight who played Angeline, a virtuous young girl, in Southerne's *The Disappointment*, April, 1684, is the same actress. In the list of the royal comedians constituted by James II on January 12, 1688, her name appears as "Francis Mariaknight" (Nicoll, p. 332).

For some years after her reappearance Mrs. Knight played mainly supporting roles, overshadowed, no doubt, by more experienced actresses. She created the roles of Aglaura, an Amazon, in D'Urfey's *A Commonwealth of Women*, ca. August, 1685; Teresia in Shadwell's *The Squire of Alsatia*, May, 1688; Mrs. Spruce, a cheating wife, in Carlile's *The Fortune-Hunters*, March, 1689; the Queen of Navarre in Lee's *The Massacre of Paris*, November, 1689; Madam Surelove in Behn's *The Widow Ranter*, ca. November, 1689; Dorothea, the lead, in Mountfort's *The Successful Strangers*, ca. December, 1689; the prologue to Powell's *The Treacherous Brothers*, February, 1690; the epilogue to Settle's *Distress'd*

Innocence, November, 1690; the epilogue to Powell's *Alphonso,* December, 1690; Volante in Southerne's *Sir Anthony Love,* December, 1690; Miss Jenny, a hoyden, in D'Urfey's *Love for Money,* ca. December, 1690; Mrs. Raison, a breeches part, in Mountfort's *Greenwich Park,* April, 1691; Teresia, a foolish girl, in Shadwell's *The Volunteers,* December, 1692; Mrs. Squeamish in D'Urfey's *The Richmond Heiress,* ca. February, 1693; Widow Lacy and the epilogue in Powell's *A Very Good Wife,* March, 1693; Lovewitt in Wright's *The Female Vertuosos,* April, 1693; Julia, a virtuous wife, in Southerne's *The Fatal Marriage,* February, 1694; Hermione, an Indian Princess, and the prologue in Settle's *The Ambitious Slave,* March, 1694; Dorothea in D'Urfey's *Don Quixote,* Part I, and the Duchess, Part II, ca. May, 1694; and Arabella, a breeches part, in Ravenscroft's *The Canterbury Guests,* September, 1694.

In 1695 the defection of Mrs. Leigh, Mrs. Barry, and Mrs. Bracegirdle to Betterton's new company left Mrs. Verbruggen (Mountfort) as the chief comic actress of the Drury Lane Company and Mrs. Knight as the chief tragic actress. Mrs Knight seems to have been particularly successful in villainess roles. She played Catalina, the villainess, in Gould's *The Rival Sisters,* ca. October, 1695; Widow Lackitt in Southerne's *Oroonoko,* November, 1695; Elvira, the villainess, in Trotter's *Agnes de Castro,* November, 1695; Queen Thermusa, the villainess, in Horden's *Neglected Virtue,* ca. December, 1695; Princess Arethusa, the heroine, in Settle's *Philaster,* ca. December, 1695; Belira, a passionate mistress, in Manley's *The Lost Lover,* ca. March, 1696; Pandora, the villainess, in Norton's *Pausanias,* ca. April, 1696; Bonduca in Powell's *Bonduca,* ca. May, 1696; Sheker Para, the villainess, in Pix's *Ibrahim,* ca. June, 1696; possibly Elenor in Pix's *The Spanish Wives,* ca. September, 1696 (Genest, II, 82); Lady Barter and the epilogue in Scott's *The Mock-Marriage,* October, 1696; Leonora in Cibber's *Woman's Wit,* ca. December, 1696; wicked Mirtilla in Behn's *The Younger Brother,* ca. December, 1696; Olympia in Drake's *The Sham-Lawyer,* May, 1697; wicked Lady Loveall in W. M.'s *The Female Wits,* 1697; Berengaria, a tragic mother, in *The Fatal*

Discovery (Anon.), ca. February, 1698, Althea, the heroine, in Gildon's *Phaeton*, March, 1698; Cesonia in Crowne's *Caligula*, ca. March, 1698; Angelica, the heroine, in D'Urfey's *The Campaigners*, ca. June, 1698; Clytemnestra in Boyer's *Achilles*, ca. December, 1699; Queen Elizabeth in Cibber's *King Richard III*, February, 1700; Astrea in Burnaby's *The Reform'd Wife*, ca. March, 1700; Lesbia, the lead, and the epilogue in Trotter's *Love at a Loss*, November, 1700; Elvira in Cibber's *Love Makes a Man*, December, 1700; and Lydia in D'Urfey's *The Bath*, ca. July, 1701.

By this time younger women, particularly Jane Rogers and Anne Oldfield, were challenging Mrs. Knight's supremacy. She continued to play leads in revivals, but, as time went on, created fewer and fewer major roles. She created Vileta, a waiting woman, in Cibber's *She Wou'd and She Wou'd Not* November, 1702; Probleme, a nurse, in D'Urfey's *The Old Mode and the New*, March, 1703; Florinda in Estcourt's *The Fair Example*, April, 1703; Mrs. Haughty, a passionate mistress, in Wilkinson's *Vice Reclaim'd*, June, 1703; the Princess Dowager, a villainess, in G. B.'s *Love the Leveller*, January, 1704; Queen Elizabeth in Banks's *The Albion Queens*, March, 1704; Abenede in Taverner's *The Faithful Bride of Granada*, ca. May, 1704; and Lady Easy in Cibber's *The Careless Husband*, December, 1704.

Although Mrs. Knight was still on the stage in 1705 and 1706 (she had a benefit on March 27, 1706), she created no new roles and may have temporarily retired after the season of 1705–6. If so, she returned after only a year to play Gertrude in a revival of *Hamlet*, the first play by the new United Company, January 15, 1708 (Genest, II, 395). Thereafter she played with some consistency in a number of revivals, stepping into several of the roles vacated when Mrs. Barry retired. She created Lady Fancy in Taverner's *The Maid the Mistress*, June, 1708; Cornelia in Dennis' *Appius and Virginia*, February, 1709; Ordelia in Hill's *Elfrid*, January, 1710; Lady Megro in Centlivre's *A Bickerstaff's Burying*, March, 1710; Lady Outside in *Injur'd Love* (Anon.), April, 1711; the Common-Council-Man's Wife in Settle's *The City*

Ramble, August, 1711; Cephisa, a confidante, in Philips' *The Distrest Mother*, March, 1712; Mrs. Bloodmore, a mother part, in C. Shadwell's *The Humours of the Army*, January, 1713; Empress Livia in *Cinna's Conspiracy* (Anon.), February, 1713; and Clytemnestra in Johnson's *The Victim*, January, 1714.

In December, 1714, Mrs. Knight was one of the "deserters" who joined Rich's company at the New Theatre in Lincoln's Inn Fields (Fitzgerald, I, 388). There she created Lady Thinwit in Molloy's *The Perplex'd Couple*, February, 1715; Lady Upstart in Taverner's *The Artful Husband*, February, 1717; Miranda in Sir Thomas Moore's *The Faithful Couple*, December, 1717; and Mrs. Wishit, a rich widow, in Taverner's *'Tis Well if It Takes*, February, 1719. After this her name appears no more.

Mrs. Knight's personal reputation was unsavory. The anonymous author of *A Letter to A. H. Esq.: Concerning the Stage* (1698) (Augustan Reprint No. 3 [1946], p. 12), protesting against the usual practice of condemning the stage because of the private characters of the players, said, "if we should see Mr. Powel acting a Brave, Generous and Honest Part; or Mrs. Knight, a very Modest and Chaste one, it ought not to give us Offence; because we are not to consider what they are off the Stage, but whom they represent." Tom Brown (II, 243–45) represented Peg Hughes as insisting that she had never sold her favors for gain, like "Madam Ja——es, or Mrs. Kn——ght of Drury Lane."

LEE, *MARY*, nee *ALDRIDGE*, later *LADY SLINGSBY* (Duke's Company, 1670–85). Because the spelling of the names was frequently interchanged, Mary Lee is often confused with the comic actress Elinor Leigh. The two joined the company at about the same time, in 1670 or 1671 (Downes, p. 31). Mary Lee was originally Mrs. Aldridge, but she almost immediately became Mrs. Lee, probably, as Summers suggests (Downes, p. 204), by marrying an insignificant actor named John Lee, who disappeared from the stage after 1677 and probably died about that time. Mrs. Lee's second

husband may have been Sir Charles Slingsby, Bart., of
Bifrons in Patrixbourne, near Canterbury (G. E. Cokayne,
Complete Baronetage, 1900–1906, *s.v.* Slingsby).

Mrs. Lee's strength was in romantic and tragic roles. She
was very popular in breeches. Her first known appearance
was as Doranthe in E. Howard's *The Womens Conquest*, ca.
November, 1670, which was followed by another small part,
Olinda, in Behn's *The Forc'd Marriage*, ca. December, 1670.
She played thereafter Eugenia, the second lead, in E.
Howard's *The Six Days Adventure*, ca. March, 1671; Leticia,
the lead, in Revet's *The Town-Shifts*, March, 1671; Princess
Mariamne in Settle's *The Empress of Morocco*, July, 1671;
Emilia in Arrowsmith's *The Reformation*, September, 1673;
Nigrello (Chlotilda), a breeches part, and the epilogue in
Settle's *Love and Revenge*, November, 1674; Amavanga, a
warrior, a breeches part, and a joint epilogue with Smith in
Settle's *The Conquest of China*, May, 1675; Queen Deidamia
and the epilogue in Otway's *Alcibiades*, September, 1675,
Christina, the lead, in Crowne's *The Country Wit*, January;
1676; Roxalana in Settle's *Ibrahim*, March, 1676; the Queen
of Spain in Otway's *Don Carlos*, June, 1676; Madam Fickle,
a breeches part, and the epilogue in D'Urfey's *Madam
Fickle*, November, 1676; Corsica, a wicked shepherdess, in
Settle's *Pastor Fido*, ca. December, 1676; Queen Berenice in
Otway's *Titus and Berenice*, December, 1676, and the epi-
logue to the afterpiece, *The Cheats of Scapin;* Cleopatra in
Sedley's *Antony and Cleopatra*, February, 1677; Circe in C.
Davenant's *Circe*, May, 1677; Astatius, a breeches part, and
the prologue in *The Constant Nymph* (Anon.), ca. July, 1677;
Roxana in Pordage's *The Siege of Babylon*, ca. September,
1677; Queen Isabella, the villainess, in Behn's *Abdelazar*, ca.
September, 1677; Elvira, a breeches part, in Leanerd's *The
Counterfeits*, May, 1678; Eurydice in Dryden and Lee's
Oedipus, ca. November, 1678; Cassandra in Banks's *The
Destruction of Troy*, November, 1678; Laura Lucretia, the
lead, in Behn's *The Feign'd Curtezans*, ca. March, 1679;
Cressida in Dryden's *Troilus and Cressida*, ca. April, 1679;
Bellamira, the lead, in Lee's *Caesar Borgia*, September, 1679;
Princess Arviola in Tate's *The Loyal General*, ca. December,

1679; Queen Margaret in Crowne's *The Misery of Civil War*, ca. March, 1680; and Julia, a breeches part, in Maidwell's *The Loving Enemies*, ca. March, 1680.

As Lady Slingsby she played Sempronia in Lee's *Lucius Junius Brutus*, December, 1680; Regan in Tate's *King Lear*, ca. March, 1681; Marguerite in Lee's *The Princess of Cleve*, ca. September, 1681; Lucia Well-bred and the prologue in *Mr. Turbulent* (Anon.), January, 1682; Tarpeia, a breeches part, and the epilogue in *Romulus and Hersilia* (Anon.), August, 1682; the Queen Mother in Dryden and Lee's *The Duke of Guise*, November, 1682; Lady Noble in Ravenscroft's *Dame Dobson*, June, 1683; Calpurnia in *Julius Caesar*, ca. 1684; and Clarinda in D'Urfey's *A Commonwealth of Women*, ca. August, 1685. According to Davies (III, 116) she also played Gertrude in *Hamlet*, probably succeeding Mrs. Shadwell in that role.

It is possible that Lady Slingsby left the stage because she was losing a bitter competition with the younger and more capable actress, Elizabeth Barry. She survived nearly ten years in retirement and was buried March 1, 1694, at St. Pancras, Middlesex (G. E. Cokayne, *Complete Baronetage*, 1900–1906, *s.v.* Slingsby). Making due allowance for the extravagant language of dramatic description, she must have been very attractive. In the role of Bellamira in Lee's *Caesar Borgia* (Act I, scene 1), she is described as having

> . . . such a skin full of alluring flesh!
> Ah, such a ruddy, moist, and pouting lip;
> Such Dimples, and such Eyes, such melting Eyes,
> Blacker than Sloes, and yet they sparkl'd fire.

Lady Slingsby seems to have paid her debts and lived respectably. Her only brush with authority came in August, 1682. Because it was thought that the epilogue to *Romulus and Hersilia* "spoken by the Lady Slingsby and written by Mrs. Behn . . . reflected on the D. of Monmouth," the Lord Chamberlain ordered both into custody "to answer that affront for the same" (*Curtis's Protestant Mercury*, August 12–16, 1682; LC 5, 191, p. 100). We may presume the two ladies were released after a scolding.

The libelers found little to charge against Lady Slingsby

In "Satyr on both Whigs and Toryes. 1683" (p. 244) we are told that Sir Gilbert Gerrard "Made love to Slingsby, when she plaid the Queen." This is neither defamatory nor specific, considering the large number of queenly roles she played. The scurrilous author of "Satyr on the Players" (p. 290) was almost as vague when he wrote,

> Imprimis, Slingsby has ye fatall Curse,
> To have a Lady's Honour, with a Players purse
> Tho' now she is so plaguy haughty grown,
> Yet Gad my Lady, I a time have known
> When a dull Whiggish Poet wou'd go down.

LEGRANDE, MRS. (Duke's Company, 1677–78). Mrs. Legrande is known to have played three very small roles: Eugenia in Behn's *The Counterfeit Bridegroom*, ca. September, 1677; Hesione in Pordage's *The Siege of Babylon*, ca. September, 1677; Phrinias, a whore, in Shadwell's *Timon of Athens*, ca. January, 1678.

LEIGH, ELINOR (Duke's, United, Lincoln's Inn Fields companies, 1672–1709). According to Downes (p. 31), "About the Year 1670, Mrs. Aldridge, after Mrs. Lee, also Mrs. Leigh Wife of Mr. Antony Leigh, Mr. Crosby, Mrs. Johnson, were entertained at the Duke's House." Genest (I, 111) conjectures that Mrs. Leigh might have been originally Mrs. Dixon (q.v.), daughter of James Dixon, an early member of the Duke's Company. Mrs. Dixon appeared about 1670 and her last recorded performance was in November, 1671. Mrs. Leigh's first recorded performance was as Betty Trickmore in Ravenscroft's *The Citizen Turn'd Gentleman*, July, 1672. Her husband, the comedian Anthony Leigh, first appeared with the Duke's Company as Pacheco in Arrowsmith's *The Reformation*, September, 1673. He had been a free-lance actor for some time; on December 27, 1671, he was ordered arrested with four other men for acting "stage playes in & about the Citty of London without Lycence from Mr Killegrew or ye Lady Davenant" (LC 5, 14, p. 96).

After appearing as Beatrice, a comic maid, in Ravenscroft's *The Careless Lovers*, March, 1673, Mrs. Leigh deserted the theatre for three years, probably because of the birth of her son Michael, who made his first appearance on the stage seventeen years later as "Young Leigh" in Shadwell's *The Amorous Bigotte*, spring, 1690. Mrs. Leigh reappeared as Isabella, a witty maid, in Crowne's *The Country Wit*, January, 1676. Thereafter she played Lady Woodvile in Etherege's *The Man of Mode*, March, 1676 (Downes, p. 36); Moretta in Behn's *The Rover*, March, 1677; and Scintilla in Porter's *The French Conjurer*, ca. March, 1677. Another three years' absence may be accounted for by the birth of Rachel (whom I take to be Mrs. Leigh's daughter) who appeared briefly on the stage as Judy in Southerne's *The Maid's Last Prayer*, January, 1693, and possibly as Vesuvia, a courtesan, in Dilke's *The Lovers' Luck*, December, 1695.

Mrs. Leigh returned to the stage in 1680 and played Paulina, a rich widow, in Maidwell's *The Loving Enemies*, ca. March, 1680; Mrs. Dashit in Behn's *The Revenge*, ca. June, 1680; Tournon, a bawd, in Lee's *The Princess of Cleve*, ca. September, 1681; Engine, a maid servant, and the epilogue with others in Ravenscroft's *The London Cuckolds*, November, 1681; Mrs. Closet in Behn's *The City Heiress*, March, 1682; Mrs. Prudence, a maid servant, in Ravenscroft's *Dame Dobson*, June, 1683; Clara, a maid servant, in Southerne's *The Disappointment*, April, 1684; and the Aunt in Crowne's *Sir Courtly Nice*, May, 1685. Another long absence may be accounted for by the birth of Francis Leigh, who became an actor about 1702 (Genest, II, 647).

Mrs. Leigh returned again to play Lady Sly in Carlile's *The Fortune Hunters*, March, 1689; Johayma in Dryden's *Don Sebastian*, November, 1689; Lady Pinch-gut in Crowne's *The English Frier*, March, 1690; Lady Maggot in Shadwell's *The Scowrers*, ca. December, 1690; Oyley in D'Urfey's *Love for Money*, ca. December, 1690; Queen Rhadegonda in Brady's *The Rape*, February, 1692; Mrs. Hackwell in Shadwell's *The Volunteers*, ca. November, 1692; and Lady Clare in *The Merry Devil of Edmonton*, 1692 (Genest, II, 15).

Anthony Leigh died in December, 1692. Mrs. Leigh continued on the stage, with her previous salary of 20*s.* a week raised to 30*s.* (Nicoll, p. 378). She played Mrs. Siam in

Southerne's *The Maid's Last Prayer*, January, 1693; Mar-
malette, an old waiting woman, in D'Urfey's *The Richmond
Heiress*, ca. February, 1693; Mrs. Sneaksby in Powell's *A
Very Good Wife*, March, 1693; Lucy, a maid servant, in
Congreve's *The Old Bachelor*, March, 1693; Lady Meanwell
in Wright's *The Female Vertuosos*, April, 1693; Lady Plyant
in Congreve's *The Double Dealer*, October, 1693; the Nurse
in Southerne's *The Fatal Marriage*, February, 1694; Rosalin
in Settle's *The Ambitious Slave*, March, 1694; and Teresa
Pancha (with "a long lean wither'd Wallnut coloured Face")
in D'Urfey's *Don Quixote*, Parts I and II, ca. May, 1694.

The next year Mrs. Leigh joined the group of players
under Betterton who set up a new company in Lincoln's Inn
Fields. In their first play, Congreve's *Love for Love*, April,
1695, she played the Nurse. Thereafter she played Plackett,
a waiting woman, in Granville's *The She-Gallants*, ca. December, 1695; Betty in Dogget's *The Country-Wake*, ca. April,
1696; Beldam in "Ariadne's" *She Ventures and He Wins*, ca.
September, 1696; the Doctor's Wife in Ravenscroft's *The
Anatomist*, November, 1696; Secreta, an essence seller, in
Dilke's *The City Lady*, January, 1697; Grossiere, a waiting
woman, in D'Urfey's *Intrigues at Versailles*, ca. February,
1697; Lady Beauclair in Pix's *The Innocent Mistress*, ca.
June, 1697; Lady Temptyouth in Pix's *The Deceiver Deceived*, ca. December, 1697; Sweetny, a boarding-house
keeper, in Dilke's *The Pretenders*, ca. March, 1698; Phenissa,
an attendant, in Dennis' *Rinaldo and Armida*, ca. November,
1698; Lady Wishfort in Congreve's *The Way of the World*,
March, 1700; the Hostess in Betterton's *Henry IV*, ca. April,
1700; Lady Autumn in Burnaby's *The Ladies Visiting-Day*,
ca. January, 1701; Sophia, the Empress, in Pix's *The Czar of
Muscovy*, ca. March, 1701; Lady Rakelove, "an Amorous
Old Woman," in Charles Johnson's *The Gentleman-Cully*,
ca. December, 1701; Adrastus, High Priest, in *The Fickle
Shepherdess* (Anon.), "Play'd all by Women," ca. March,
1703; Dromia in Burnaby's *Love Betray'd*, March, 1703;
Chloris in Boyle's *As You Find It*, April, 1703; Widow Bellmont, a country gentlewoman, in Pix's *The Different Widows*,
ca. November, 1703; Marama, an "antiquated Beauty," in

Trapp's *Abra-Mulé*, January, 1704; Lady Stale, an amorous old widow, in Rowe's *The Biter*, December, 1704; and Peeper, a waiting woman, in Centlivre's *The Platonick Lady*, November, 1706.

Probably Mrs. Leigh retired some time in 1707. The fact that a petition signed by a number of actors in 1709 contains the name of "Eli Leigh" (Fitzgerald, I, 273) suggests that she may have been a member of the second United Company. On the other hand this may have been her daughter-in-law (perhaps Elizabeth), the wife of Francis Leigh (Genest, II, 382). Mrs. Leigh usually spelled her first name "Ellenor" (Montague Summers, *Shadwell* [1927], I, ccxxxv). She has been confused with the Elizabeth Leigh who in April, 1687, sued Elkanah Settle for payment for the scenario of a play (Hotson, pp. 274–76). This Mrs. Leigh seems to have been an actress of drolls, performing in the booth of her mother, Mrs. Mynn, at Bartholomew and Southwark fairs.

According to Cibber, Elinor Leigh

had a very droll way of dressing the pretty Foibles of super-annuated Beauties. She had in her self a good deal of Humour, and knew how to infuse it into the affected Mothers, Aunts, and modest stale Maids that had miss'd their Market; of this sort were the Modish Mother in the *Chances*, affecting to be politely commode for her own Daughter; the Coquette Prude of an Aunt in *Sir Courtly Nice*, who prides herself in being chaste and cruel at Fifty; and the languishing Lady Wishfort in *The Way of the World:* In all these, with many others, she was extremely entertaining, and painted in a lively manner the blind Side of Nature.

Her private life was irreproachable.

LILBORNE, MRS. (Duke's Company, 1670). Mrs. Lilborne is known to have played only one very small role, that of Cydane, an Amazon ambassadress, in E. Howard's *The Womens Conquest*, ca. November, 1670.

LONG, JANE (Duke's Company, 1661–73). According to Downes, Mrs. Long was one of Davenant's original actresses. She played small roles at first: Jane, a maid servant, in Cowley's *Cutter of Coleman Street*, December, 1661; Flora in

Tuke's *The Adventures of Five Hours*, January, 1663 (Downes, p. 23); Diacelia in Stapylton's *The Slighted Maid*, February, 1663; Brianella, a lady in waiting, in Stapylton's *The Step-Mother*, ca. November, 1663; The Widow and the epilogue in Etherege's *The Comical Revenge*, March, 1664 (Downes, p. 25); Leucippe, a maid servant, in Davenant's *The Rivals*, spring, 1664; the Queen of France in Boyle's *Henry the Fifth*, August, 1664 (Downes [p. 24] assigns this role to Mrs. Betterton, who probably played it after Mrs. Long retired); and Zarma, a waiting woman, in Boyle's *Mustapha*, April, 1665.

After the reopening of the theatres in November, 1666, Mrs. Long played more important parts. As Dulcino in Shirley's *The Grateful Servant*, ca. 1667, "the first time she appear'd in Man's Habit" (Downes, p. 27), she was a success. Probably she played Hippolito, a breeches part, in Davenant and Dryden's *The Tempest*, November, 1667. In a lost play by Betterton, *The Woman Made a Justice*, she acted "the Justice . . . charmingly" (Downes, p. 30); and as Mrs. Brittle, in Betterton's *The Amorous Widow*, ca. 1670, "She Perform'd . . . so well that none Equall'd her but Mrs. Bracegirdle" (Downes, p. 30).

Her other known roles were Mandana, the Amazon Queen, and the epilogue in E. Howard's *The Womens Conquest*, ca. November, 1670; Prince Osiris, a breeches part, in Settle's *Cambyses*, ca. January, 1671; Crispina in E. Howard's *The Six Days Adventure*, ca. March, 1671; Fickle in Revet's *The Town-shifts*, March, 1671; Princess Pauline, a breeches part, and the epilogue (with Angel) in Crowne's *Juliana*, August, 1671; Betty in Boyle's *Mr. Anthony*, ca. March, 1672; Betty Rash in Payne's *The Morning Ramble*, November, 1672; and Lady Macduff in Davenant's operatic *Macbeth*, ca. February, 1673.

Sometime in 1673 she left the stage to become the mistress of George Porter, a Gentleman of the Privy Chamber to the Queen. Baroness d'Aulnoy (*Memoirs of the Court of England in 1675*, trans. Mrs. W. H. Arthur [1913]), presents her as a character in her semifictitious narrative (pp. 233–40). A reproduction of her portrait by Lely (facing p. 234) shows a small, slender, dark woman with a long face—no beauty. Porter is represented as saying that she was "sweet and amiable." The liaison lasted some years. On December 17, 1677, Henry Savile wrote to the Earl of Rochester that George Porter "surfeits of everything hee sees but Mrs. Long and his sonn Nobbs which he can never have enough on" (*The Rochester-Savile Letters*, ed. J. H. Wilson [1941], p. 52).

In a "Dialogue by Ld Rochester," ca. 1676 (British Museum, Harleian MS. 6914, p. 4) King Charles is made to say:

> When on Portsmouths lap I lay my head
> And Knight dos sing her bawdy song
> I envy not George Porters bedd
> Nor the delights of Madam Long.

The author of "Lampoons" dismisses her with a vicious sneer,

> Malicious Witch Long have a damn'd stinking breath
> Which to Bastard in Wombe does give sudden death.

MACKAREL, BETTY (King's Company, 1674). Mrs. Mackarel, "Orange Betty," a regular orange girl in the Theatre Royal, was so famed for her impudence and promiscuity that her name became a byword. Robert Gould pictures the wits in the pit as

> . . . hot at repartee with Orange Betty,
> Who tho not blest with halfe a grain of sense,
> To leaven her whole lump of impudence,
> Aided with that she allways is too hard
> For the vain things & beats them from their guard.

And from the prologue to D'Urfey's *A Commonwealth of Women*, ca. August, 1685, we learn that "The Censuring Spark . . . whispers Politicks with Orange Betty."

Montague Summers (*Shakespearean Adaptations* [1922], p. 261) points out two allusions to her in John Phillips' *History of Don Quixote* (1687 [pp. 184, 412]), one to her impudence, the other to her height ("the gyantess Betty-Makarela"). Her promiscuity is vouched for in "To Mr. Julian" (*Poems on Affairs of State* [1704], III, 143), by the passage "May Betty Mackrel cease to be a whore," and in "The Session of the Ladies. 1688," where she is called "Betty

Mackrell a favourite to the blind God," and marginally identified as "Tom [Sir Thomas] Armstrongs mistress." She must have been a statuesque beauty. On September 9/19, 1686, Etherege (p. 103), in a letter to a friend, described a German lady of distinction as "very like, and full as handsome as, Mrs. Betty Mackerel."

Her only known appearance on the stage was in Duffett's *The Mock-Tempest*, November, 1674, a burlesque of Shadwell's operatic version of *The Tempest*. The towering Mrs. Mackarel played the role of Ariel, a breeches part, and spoke the introduction with Haines.

MAN, MARY (King's Company, 1663). Mrs. Man's name appears only in the list of "Women's Comoedians" for the autumn of 1663.

MARSHALL, ANNE, afterward *QUIN* (King's and Duke's companies, 1661–82). The two Marshall sisters, Anne and Rebecca, were said to be the daughters of a Presbyter (Pepys, October 26, 1667) or at least "educated by godly parents" (Fane, p. 352). Downes lists Anne among the earliest members of the King's Company. Although in his casts of early revivals of old plays (ca. 1661), Downes (p. 3) lists "Mrs. Anne Marshall" only for the role of Margarita in *Rule a Wife and Have a Wife*, he gives (pp. 3–6) "Mrs. Marshall"—assuredly Anne—the roles of the Lady in Beaumont and Fletcher's *The Scornful Lady*, Edith in Fletcher's *Rollo*, Celia in Fletcher's *The Humorous Lieutenant*, Evadne in Beaumont and Fletcher's *The Maid's Tragedy*, and Celia in Jonson's *Volpone*. Flecknoe cast her as Cyrena ("Win Marshall"), a breeches part, in his then unacted *Erminia*, 4to, 1661. She played Mrs. Double-Diligence in Wilson's *The Cheats*, ca. March, 1663 (Nahm, p. 62). Both Anne and Rebecca appear in the Lord Chamberlain's list of "Actors or Comoedians," autumn, 1663. Anne played a leading role, probably Zempoalla, in Dryden and Howard's *The Indian Queen*, January, 1664 (Pepys, February 1, 1664), and was cast for the role of Angelica Bianca in Thomas Killigrew's *Thomaso*, November, 1664 (Van Lennep, p. 805). She was cast also as Celestina ("Mrs. Anne Martiall"), a breeches part, in William Killigrew's *The Seege of Urbin*, ca. 1665 (Bodleian Library, Rawl. MS. Poet. 29), and no doubt played Almeria in Dryden's *The Indian Emperour*, ca. April, 1665 (Downes, p. 9).

Probably Anne married some time after the threatres were closed by the Plague in June, 1665. Her husband may have been the Peter Gwyn or Quyn who was ordered arrested for acting without a warrant, January 28, 1668 (LC 5, 186, p. 193), and was no doubt the same "Mr. Quin" who was leading Rebecca Marshall (q.v.) home from the theatre on February 5, 1667, when she was assaulted by a ruffian (SP 29, 191, p. 31). Although we know from Pepys (October 26, 1667, and June 27, 1668) that Anne returned to the stage after playing was resumed in late November, 1666, her full name, as Anne Marshall, never appears after 1665, and only one Mrs. Marshall, evidently Rebecca, is listed in the Lord Chamberlain's records and in the dramatis personae of plays (See J. H. Wilson, "The Marshall Sisters and Anne Quin," *Notes and Queries*, N.S. IV [March, 1957], 104–6).

Early in 1667 Anne returned to the stage as Mrs. Quin and played the secondary role of Candiope in Dryden's *Secret Love*, late February, 1667. Finding herself treated as a newcomer, she quarreled with the management and appealed to the Lord Chamberlain, who, on May 4, 1667, ordered her private dressing room and all her old parts restored to her (LC 5, 138, p. 376). She and Rebecca were cast for the leads ("The Two Marshalls") by Flecknoe in his then unacted *The Damoiselles a la Mode*, 4to, May, 1667. She was listed as Mrs. Quin in the livery warrants for July 22, 1667, and February 8, 1668. As Mrs. Quin she played Alizia Pierce in Boyle's *The Black Prince*, October, 1667, and Aurelia in Dryden's *An Evening's Love*, June, 1668. She left the stage some time in 1668.

In 1677 Anne Quin joined the Duke's Company, playing Angelica Bianca in Behn's *The Rover*, March, 1677 (an alteration of Killigrew's *Thomaso* in which she had played the same character); Astrea ("Mrs. Wynn") in *The Constant Nymph* (Anon.), ca. July, 1677; Thalestris in Pordage's *The Siege of*

Babylon, ca. September, 1677; Lady Knowell and the epilogue in Behn's *Sir Patient Fancy*, January, 1678; Lady Squeamish in Otway's *Friendship in Fashion*, April, 1678; the epilogue to Banks's *The Destruction of Troy*, November, 1678; Queen Elizabeth in Banks's *The Unhappy Favorite*, ca. September, 1681; and Sunamira in Southerne's *The Loyal Brother*, February, 1682.

A miniature of Anne Quin was reproduced by Montague Summers in *The Restoration Theatre* (1934), p. 88, and an engraving of her speaking the epilogue to *Sir Patient Fancy* (miscalled by the engraver "Mrs. Ellen Guyn") is in his edition of Aphra Behn's *Works* (1915), IV, 115. Anne seems to have been a handsome woman with an oval face, dark hair and eyes, and a small mouth.

MARSHALL, REBECCA (King's Company, 1663–77; Duke's Company, 1677). Rebecca, younger sister of Anne Marshall (q.v.), joined the King's Company about 1663. Her name appears in the Lord Chamberlain's list of "Women Comoedians," autumn, 1663, but there is no evidence that she played any important roles until after November, 1666. She was certainly on the stage before that. Early in 1665 she petitioned the King for protection from one Mark Trevor, who had affronted her "as well upon the Stage as of[f]" (SP 29, 142, p. 160), and on April 3, 1665, Pepys, in the pit of the Duke's Theatre, was pleased that "pretty witty Nell [Gwyn], at the King's House, and the younger Marshall sat next us."

Only one Mrs. Marshall, presumably Rebecca, appears in the livery warrants for 1666–69. On December 7, 1666, Pepys saw part of *The Maid's Tragedy* and singled out for praise "the younger Marshall, who is become a pretty good actor"—probably in the role of Evadne, formerly played by her sister. On February 8, 1667, Rebecca petitioned the King against Sir Hugh Middleton, who had hired a ruffian to assault her (SP 29, 191, p. 21). From the evidence in her petition she must have played in Buckingham's *The Chances* —possibly the First Constantia—on February 5. On May 24, 1667, and again on January 24, 1668, Pepys praised

Rebecca as the Queen in Dryden's *Secret Love*, February, 1667. On August 24, 1667, Pepys was pleased "with Beck Marshall" in a revival of Shirley's *The Cardinal*. At the Duke's Theatre, on September 11, 1667, he sat beside "Beck Marshall, who is very handsome near at hand." On October 26, 1667, Pepys heard of a quarrel in which Nell Gwyn accused Rebecca variously of being "a whore to three or four, though a Presbyter's praying daughter," and of being "kept by [Henry] Guy an excise man" (Fane, p. 352). Pepys' belief that the Marshall sisters were daughters of Stephen Marshall, a famous divine, has since been proved erroneous (J. L. Chester, *Registers of Westminster Abbey* [1869], p. 149).

In May, 1667, Flecknoe cast "The Two Marshalls" for the leading roles in his then unacted *The Damoiselles à la Mode*, 4to, 1668. Rebecca played Plantagenet in Boyle's *The Black Prince*, October, 1667; Dorothea in Massinger's *The Virgin Martyr* (Pepys, February 27, 1668); and succeeded her sister as Aurelia in Dryden's *An Evening's Love*, June, 1668, after Anne left the stage.

Rebecca's other known roles were: Quisara in Fletcher's *The Island Princess*, November, 1668; Berenice in Dryden's *Tyrannic Love*, June, 1669; Empress Fulvia in Joyner's *The Roman Empress*, August, 1670; Calpurnia in *Julius Caesar*, ca. 1670; Lyndaraxa in Dryden's *Conquest of Granada*, December, 1670–January, 1671; Jaccinta in Corye's *The Generous Enemies*, ca. July, 1671; Doralice, a breeches part, and the epilogue in Dryden's *Marriage A-la-Mode*, ca. April, 1672; the prologue, in breeches, to Killigrew's *The Parson's Wedding*, and the prologue and epilogue to Beaumont and Fletcher's *Philaster*, both played "all by women," spring, 1672 (Thorn-Drury, pp. 3, 18, 19); Lucretia in Dryden's *The Assignation*, ca. November, 1672; Ysabinda in Dryden's *Amboyna*, ca. May, 1673; Poppea in Lee's *Nero*, May, 1674; Nourmahal in Dryden's *Aurenge-Zebe*, November, 1675; Gloriana in Lee's *Gloriana*, January, 1676; Spaconia in Beaumont and Fletcher's *A King and No King*, 1676 (4to, 1676); Queen Berenice in Crowne's *The Destruction of Jerusalem*, January, 1677, plus the epilogue to Part II; Roxana in Lee's *The Rival Queens*, March, 1677; and Lady Lovely in

Leanerd's *The Country Innocence*, ca. March, 1677. After that play she joined her sister at the Duke's Theatre, created the role of Maria in D'Urfey's *A Fond Husband*, May, 1677, and then retired.

On January 16, 1668, Hannah Johnson petitioned against Rebecca, probably for debt (LC 5, 186, p. 192). On April 7, 1668, Pepys heard of an affair between Hart and the Countess of Castlemaine, with Beck Marshall acting as go-between. On November 5, 1669, Mary Meggs, fruit woman at the Theatre Royal, was arrested for "abuseing" Rebecca (LC 5, 187, p. 175); and on May 18, 1672, Richard Uttings petitioned against her for a debt of £7 9s. 6d. (LC 5, 189, p. 27).

A liaison between Rebecca and the famous fop, Sir George Hewett, is suggested by a passage in "Satyr on both Whigs and Toryes. 1683," in which Hewett is represented as a fool

> With whom as much our Satyr strives in Vain
> As Love, to wound his heart, since Marshal's Reign.

For the possibility that Rebecca had a daughter see "Lampoons":

> Proud Curtizan Marshall tis time to give o're
> Since now your Daughter, shee is turn'd whore
> But be not discourag'd it was in Cambridge shee fell
> And her London Maidenhead you have still to sell.

Rebecca must have been above average height, well qualified to play queenly roles. Probably she had black hair and eyes. In Dryden's *Secret Love* (Act V, scene 1) we are told to

> Behold how night sits lovely on her Eye-brows
> While day breaks from her Eyes!

and in Lee's *Nero* (Act I, scene 2) we learn that "Her quick black eye does wander with desire," while in the chase, "Her long black locks, on her fair shoulders flow."

MERCHANT, MRS. (King's Company, 1678). Mrs. Merchant played Lucilla, a waiting maid, in D'Urfey's *Trick for Trick*, ca. March, 1678, and Petulant Easy, a leading role, in Leanerd's *The Rambling Justice*, March, 1678 (a "young" actors production).

MILES, MRS. (United Company, 1689). Mrs. Miles' name is listed in only one minor role, "A Niece to Don Pedro," in Mountfort's *The Successful Strangers*, ca. December, 1689.

MITCHELL, KATHERINE (King's Company, 1661–63). Listed as a member of the King's Company in the autumn of 1663, Mrs. Mitchell was probably on the stage in 1660 or 1661. When Flecknoe printed his then unacted *Erminia* (1661) he cast "Mrs. Michel" as Althea, a waiting woman. There is no evidence that she ever played the role, but she must have been on the stage at the time. Nothing is heard of her after 1663, unless she became Katherine Corey (q.v.).

MOUNTFORT, MRS. See Percival, Susanna.

MOYLE, MRS. (King's Company, 1681–82). Mrs. Moyle played the supporting role of Millicent in D'Urfey's *Sir Barnaby Whigg*, ca. September, 1681. Probably she also spoke the epilogue "By a New Actress." On July 18, 1682, she delivered an epilogue at Oxford (Wiley, p. 122).

NANNY, MISS (United Company, 1685). We know this young lady only by her nickname. She played Clita in D'Urfey's *A Commonwealth of Women*, ca. August, 1685, and spoke an epilogue beginning,

> How silly 'tis for one, not yet Thirteen,
> To hope her first Essay should please you Men.

Possibly it was Miss Nanny who played Pipeau, a youth, in a revival of Fletcher's *Rollo* in 1685 (4to, late 1685). The name in the dramatis personae is "Miss Cockye, the little girl." "Cocky" is a term of endearment rather than a nickname.

NAPIER or *NAPPER, MRS.* See Knapper, Mrs.

NEPP, MRS. See Knep, Mary.

NORRIS, MRS. (Duke's Company, 1661–83). Listed by Downes as one of Davenant's eight original actresses, Mrs. Norris was probably the wife of Henry Norris, a minor actor with the Duke's Company. According to Chetwood (p. 197), she was the mother of Henry Norris (born 1665), known as "Jubilee Dickey" because of his performance in Farquhar's *The Constant Couple*, 1699.

Mrs. Norris was a useful actress, good at "humours" characters: old ladies, mothers, nurses, and the like. She played Polla, a shrew, in Parkhurst's translation of Ruggles' *Ignoramus*, November, 1662 (Hotson, p. 214); the Countess of La Marr in Boyle's *Henry the Fifth*, August, 1664; Mitza, a servant, in Boyle's *Mustapha*, April, 1665; Lady Dupe in Dryden's *Sir Martin Mar-all*, August, 1667; Goody Fells, a landlady, in Revet's *The Town-Shifts*, March, 1671; Goody Winifred in Boyle's *Mr. Anthony*, ca. March, 1672; the Witch in Payne's *The Fatal Jealousy*, August, 1672; Breedwell, a whore, in Ravenscroft's *The Careless Lovers*, March, 1673; the Nurse in Arrowsmith's *The Reformation*, September, 1673; Cariola in a revival of Webster's *The Duchess of Malfi*, ca. 1673 (4to, 1678); Goody Rash in Crowne's *The Country Wit*, January, 1676; Callis, a governess, in Behn's *The Rover*, March, 1677; Sabina, a servant, in Porter's *The French Conjurer*, ca. March, 1677; the governess in D'Urfey's *A Fond Husband*, May, 1677; Lilla, the mother, in *The Constant Nymph* (Anon.), ca. July, 1677; old Lady Santloe in Behn's *The Counterfeit Bridegroom*, ca. September, 1677; Comet in D'Urfey's *Squire Oldsapp*, ca. June, 1678; Philippa, a servant, in Behn's *The Feign'd Curtezans*, ca. March, 1679; Tissick in D'Urfey's *The Virtuous Wife*, ca. September, 1679; Nuarcha in Maidwell's *The Loving Enemies*, ca. March, 1680; Mrs. Dunwell, a bawd, in Behn's *The Revenge*, ca. June, 1680; Petronella Eleanora, a bawd, in Behn's *The Rover*, Part II, ca. April, 1681.

In April, 1681, Mrs. Norris was dismissed from the company for quarreling with one of her colleagues. She appealed to the Lord Chamberlain, who, on May 7, wrote to Betterton:

I did yesterday signifie unto you that Mrs. Norris should be received into yor Company againe And this is to Explayne that Order That it is His Maties pleasure she reconcile herselfe unto her adversary and submit herselfe to ye rules and Government of ye

Company & upon this condicon she is to be admitted as formerly
[LC 5, 144, p. 114].

Readmitted, Mrs. Norris played the Aunt in Ravenscroft's *The London Cuckolds*, November, 1681; Mrs. Turbulent in *Mr. Turbulent* (Anon.), January, 1682; Mrs. Clacket
in Behn's *The City Heiress*, March, 1682; and Chloris, a
servant, in Otway's *The Atheist*, ca. July, 1683. After this
her name disappears from dramatic records.

Two Mrs. Norrises are listed in the dramatis personae of
Behn's *The Rover*, Part II, ca. April, 1681. Probably the one
who played Lucia, "a Girl," a breeches part, was Mrs. Norris'
daughter. She appeared only once. In "Satyr on the Players"
(p. 294) is this passage:

> Then *Norris* & her Daughter, pleasant are,
> One's very Young, ye other desperate fair
> A very equal well-proportion'd Pair.
> The Girl's of Use, faith as ye matter goes,
> For she must F——k to get her Father Cloths.

In a variant of this in British Museum, Harleian MS. 7317,
page 101, the fifth line reads, "Yet Mall's of use, faith as the
matter goes." Possibly the daughter's name was Mary.

If the father in question was indeed Henry Norris the
actor, there may have been some truth in the obscene charge.
Henry Norris was a hireling with a very small list of minor
parts to his credit. Some notion of his economic situation may
be gleaned from the fact that on September 15, 1671, "John
Beard, Butcher," was forced to petition against him for the
small debt of £3 18s. (LC 5, 14, p. 69).

NORTON, MRS. (Duke's Company, 1662–70). Mrs. Norton
is not mentioned by Downes, yet according to Pepys (December 27, 1662) she was the "fine wench" who replaced Mrs.
Davenport as Roxalana in *The Siege of Rhodes* and played
the role "rather better in all respects for person, voice and
judgment than the first Roxalana." Since Mrs. Davenport
left the stage in January, 1662, and Pepys first saw Mrs.
Norton on December 1, 1662, she must have joined the company at some time between those two dates.

Her name appears in no dramatis personae, yet she remained a member of the company for eight years. On July 2, 1666, Pepys met her at Peg Pen's house and described her as "a fine woman, indifferent handsome, good body and hand, and good mien, and pretends to sing, but do it not excellently." In 1670 she left the company under unpleasant circumstances. On December 5, 1670, the Lord Chamberlain issued a warrant to "take into Custody the body of Mrs Norton late one of his Maties Comoedians & to bring her before mee to answer unto such things as shall be then & there objected agt her" (LC 5, 188, p. 61).

OSBORN, MARGARET (Duke's and United companies, 1672–91). Mrs. Osborn, an undistinguished player of small parts, seems to have begun her career at the Duke's Theatre as Flora, a waiting woman, in Payne's *The Fatal Jealousy*, August, 1672. Thereafter she played Lady Turnup in Payne's *The Morning Ramble*, November, 1672; Mrs. Clappam, a whore, in Ravenscroft's *The Careless Lovers*, March, 1673; Lelia, a confidante, in Arrowsmith's *The Reformation*, September, 1673; an Old Lady in a revival of *The Duchess of Malfi*, ca. 1673 (4to, 1678); the Queen in Settle's *Love and Revenge*, November, 1674; Luce, a rich widow, in Rawlins' *Tom Essence*, ca. August, 1676; Widow Landwell in Behn's *The Counterfeit Bridegroom*, ca. September, 1677; and Elvira, a waiting woman, in Behn's *Abdelazar*, ca. September, 1677.

Late in 1677 Mrs. Osborn journeyed to Ireland where she spent two years or so at the Dublin Theatre (W. S. Clark, *The Early Irish Stage* [1955], p. 82). On her return to the Duke's Company she played Florella, a waiting woman, in Otway's *The Orphan*, ca. March, 1680; Jacinta in Behn's *The False Count*, November, 1681; Jane, a waiting woman, in Ravenscroft's *The London Cuckolds*, November, 1681; Mrs. Sly, an Anabaptist, in *Mr. Turbulent* (Anon.), January, 1682; Hellen, a waiting woman, in Ravenscroft's *Dame Dobson*, June, 1683; Mrs. Furnish in Otway's *The Atheist*, ca. July, 1683; and Ariadne, an Amazon, in D'Urfey's *A Commonwealth of Women*, ca. August, 1685.

Mrs. Osborn's name ("Margrett Osborne") was included

in a list of comedians constituted by James II in 1688 (Nicoll, p. 332). She created the roles of Grycia, an old governess, in Shadwell's *The Amorous Bigotte*, spring, 1690; Abigail, a housekeeper, in Shadwell's *The Scowrers*, ca. December, 1690; Tearshift in D'Urfey's *Love for Money*, ca. December, 1690; and Lady Hazard in Mountfort's *Greenwich Park*, April, 1691.

The author of "Satyr on the Players" dismissed Mrs. Osborn with contempt:

> But Osborn moves in a Religious Strain
> She'l F——k and Pray, and Pray, and F——k again
> Sure now her F——king, Praying Dayes are o're
> Who'd have an Ugly, Old, yet Zealous Whore?

PERCIVAL, SUSANNA, afterward *MOUNTFORT*, afterward *VERBRUGGEN* (King's, United, and Drury Lane companies, 1681–1703). If she gave her correct age at the time of her first marriage, Mrs. Percival was born in 1667. Although her father, Thomas Percival, was a minor actor with the Duke's Company (ca. 1675–93), Susanna enlisted first with the King's Company, perhaps because at that time there was more opportunity for a young actress in the Theatre Royal. Her first appearance, at the age of fourteen, was in the small role of Welsh Winifred in D'Urfey's *Sir Barnaby Whigg*, ca. September, 1681. She played also an attendant in D'Urfey's *The Injured Princess*, ca. March, 1682.

With the United Company she played a double role, Mrs. Jenkins, a breeches part, and Mrs. Susan, a country girl, in Ravenscroft's *Dame Dobson*, June, 1683; Phillis, a maid, in Otway's *The Atheist*, ca. July, 1683; Juliana, a cast mistress, in Southerne's *The Disappointment*, April, 1684; Prudentia in Tate's *A Duke and No Duke*, November, 1684; Constance Holdup in a revival of Brome's *The Northern Lass*, ca. 1684; Gertrude in Tate's *Cuckolds-Haven*, ca. June, 1685; Julietta, an Amazon, in D'Urfey's *A Commonwealth of Women*, ca. August, 1685; Matilda in Fletcher's *Rollo*, 1685; Lucia in D'Urfey's *The Banditti*, February, 1686; and Nell, the lead, and the epilogue with Jevon in Jevon's *The Devil of a Wife*, March, 1686.

On July 2, 1686, she married William Mountfort, a rising young actor (Borgman, p. 24). The young couple played together often thereafter, and both were highly successful as comedians. Mrs. Mountfort played Bellamante in Behn's *The Emperor in the Moon*, ca. March, 1687; Panura in Tate's *The Island Princess*, April, 1687; Diana in Behn's *The Lucky Chance*, ca. December, 1687; Isabella and the epilogue in Shadwell's *The Squire of Alsatia*, May, 1688; and Maria in Carlile's *The Fortune Hunters*, March, 1689. It is likely that Mrs. Mountfort's first daughter, also named Susanna, was born some time in 1688.

Mrs. Mountfort continued to grow in stature as a comic actress, playing madcap Gertrude and the epilogue in Shadwell's *Bury Fair*, ca. April, 1689; Morayma and the epilogue with Mountfort in Dryden's *Don Sebastian*, November, 1689; Feliciana in Mountfort's *The Successful Strangers*, ca. December, 1689; Phaedra and the epilogue in Dryden's *Amphitryon*, October, 1690; Lucia, a breeches part, in Southerne's *Sir Anthony Love*, December, 1690; Florella, a breeches part, and the epilogue in Mountfort's *Greenwich Park*, April, 1691: and Mrs. Witwoud in Southerne's *The Wives Excuse*, December, 1691. Her career was interrupted on March 22, 1692, by the birth of a second daughter, who died eight days later (Borgman, p. 171). Some months later Mrs. Mountfort returned to the stage, playing Eugenia in Shadwell's *The Volunteers*, ca. November, 1692.

On December 10, 1692, William Mountfort died as the result of a wound inflicted the night before by Captain Richard Hill, abetted by Lord Mohun. Captain Hill, insanely in love with Anne Bracegirdle and jealous of Mountfort, ran the actor through in the street before Mountfort could draw his sword. Left a widow with one child and another coming, Mrs. Mountfort continued on the stage, playing Lady Susan Malepert, an old woman, in Southerne's *The Maid's Last Prayer*, January, 1693; Belinda in Congreve's *The Old Bachelor*, March, 1693; Annabella, a breeches part, in Powell's *A Very Good Wife*, March, 1693; and Catchat and the epilogue in Wright's *The Female Vertuosos*, April, 1693. Her third daughter, Mary, was baptized April 27, 1693.

Mrs. Mountfort's troubles were not ended. On September 10, 1693, her father was arrested for clipping coins; on October 17 he was condemned to death. Mrs. Mountfort's petition to the Queen for mercy was granted, possibly as a reward for withdrawing her petition against Lord Mohun, who had been exonerated of complicity in her husband's murder (Narcissus Luttrell, *A Brief Relation of State Affairs* [6 vols., 1857], III, 207, October 19, 1693). Percival's sentence was commuted to transportation. He died in Portsmouth on his way to the convict ship.

Apparently Mrs. Mountfort played on steadily, her last performance for 1693 being Lady Froth and the epilogue in Congreve's *The Double-Dealer*, October, 1693. She was still young (only twenty-six) and handsome; on January 31, 1694, she married another rising young actor, John Verbruggen (Borgman, p. 173). Thereafter she appeared with her usual success, delivering the epilogue to Southerne's *The Fatal Marriage*, February, 1694, and playing Dalinda and the epilogue in Dryden's *Love Triumphant*, March, 1694; Mary the Buxom, the epilogue to Part II with Underhill, and the epilogue to Part III, in D'Urfey's *Don Quixote*, May, 1694, and November, 1695; and Hillaria, a breeches part, in Ravenscroft's *The Canterbury Guests*, September, 1694.

Although the Verbruggens seem to have planned to join Betterton's seceding troupe, which started playing at Lincoln's Inn Fields in April, 1695, the Lord Chamberlain ordered them to remain with the Drury Lane Company (Nicoll, pp. 338–39). Verbruggen was allowed to join the new company in January, 1697; Mrs. Verbruggen continued with the Drury Lane Company. Cibber (I, 200), submits that the Betterton company refused to give her a full share. Her known roles at Drury Lane were Ansilva, a wicked maid, in Gould's *The Rival Sisters*, ca. October, 1695; Charlotte Welldon, a breeches part, and the epilogue in Southerne's *Oroonoko*, November, 1695; the epilogue "in Men's Cloaths" to Trotter's *Agnes de Castro*, November, 1695; Narcissa in Cibber's *Love's Last Shift*, January, 1696; Olivia in Manley's

The Lost Lover, ca. March, 1696; Demetria and the epilogue in Norton's *Pausanias*, ca. April, 1696; Achmet, the chief eunuch, a breeches part, in Pix's *Ibrahim*, ca. June, 1696; the Governor's Lady and the epilogue in Pix's *The Spanish Wives*, ca. September, 1696; Clarinda, a breeches part, in Scott's *The Mock-Marriage*, October, 1696; Berinthia and the prologue for the third day in Vanbrugh's *The Relapse*, December, 1696; Olivia, a breeches part, in Behn's *The Younger Brother*, ca. December, 1696; the Nurse in Vanbrugh's *Aesop*, ca. December, 1696; Jacintha in Settle's *The World in the Moon*, June, 1697; Marsilia (a caricature of Mrs. Manley) in W. M.'s *The Female Wits*, 1697; Celia in a revival of *The Humourous Lieutenant*, 1697 (Genest, II, 112); Margaretta in *The Fatal Discovery* (Anon.), ca. February, 1698; Mme la Marquise in D'Urfey's *The Campaigners*, ca. June, 1698; Margaret, the shrew, in a revival of Lacy's *Sauny the Scot*, ca. 1698 (Genest, II, 139); Letitia in Pinkethman's *Love without Interest*, ca. April, 1699; Lady Lurewell in Farquhar's *The Constant Couple*, November, 1699; Lucia in Baker's *The Humour of the Age*, ca. February, 1700; Lady Dainty in Burnaby's *The Reform'd Wife*, ca. March, 1700; Louisa in Cibber's *Love Makes a Man*, December, 1700; Lady Lurewell again in Farquhar's *Sir Harry Wildair*, ca. April, 1701; Miranda, "a Gay Coquet," in Trotter's *Love at a Loss*, ca. April, 1701; Gilian Homebred in D'Urfey's *The Bath*, ca. July, 1701; Lady Brumpton in Steele's *The Funeral*, ca. December, 1701; Lady Cringe in Burnaby's *The Modish Husband*, ca. January, 1702; whimsical Bisarre in Farquhar's *The Inconstant*, ca. February, 1702; Hypolita in Cibber's *She Wou'd and She Wou'd Not*, November, 1702; Hillaria in Baker's *Tunbridge-Walks*, January, 1703; and Mrs. Whimsey in Estcourt's *The Fair Example*, April, 1703.

According to Cibber (I, 306), the Drury Lane Company acted at Bath in the summer of 1703, and Mrs. Verbruggen, "by reason of her last Sickness (of which she some few Months after dy'd) was left in London." Davies (III, 395) reports that "This admirable comic actress died in child-bed, 1703." The two statements are not irreconcilable. Genest (II, 401) lists a performance on April 26, 1708, "for the bt

of a young orphan child of the late Mr. & Mrs. Verbruggen."
Verbruggen died in 1707. Mrs. Verbruggen's older daughter,
Susanna Mountfort, was on the stage from about 1703 to
1718, apparently successful as a comic actress. After some
unhappy love affairs, including one with Barton Booth, she
went insane and died.

Anthony Aston (II, 313) describes Mrs. Verbruggen as "a
fine, fair Woman, plump, full-featur'd; her face of a fine,
smooth Oval, full of beautiful, well-dispos'd Moles on it, and
on her Neck and Breast." Testimonies to her excellence as
a comedienne are numerous. Cibber (I, 165) wrote that she
was "Mistress of more variety of Humour than I ever knew
in any one Woman Actress," and devoted some of his most
eloquent pages to an analysis of her performance as Melantha
in Dryden's *Marriage A-la-Mode*. In his Preface to *The Female Wits* (4to, 1704), the anonymous author wrote sorrow-
fully of Mrs. Verbruggen as one "whose Loss we must ever
regret, as the Chief Actress in her Kind, who never had anyone that exceeded her." In *A Comparison between the Two
Stages*, 1702 (Wells, p. 106), she is called "a Miracle" in contrast to Mrs. Rogers and Mrs. Oldfield, who were "meer
Rubbish that ought to be swept off the Stage with the Filth
and Dust."

Although the author of "A Satyr on the Players" insists
that in her youth Susanna was so debauched that she grew "in
Lewdness faster than in Age," she seems to have been a virtuous wife. On March 8/18, 1688, Etherege (p. 337) wrote
consolingly to his friend Jephson, who had evidently at-
tempted the actress's virtue: "Mrs. Percivall had only her
youth and a maidenhead to recommend her, wch makes me
thinke you do not take it to heart that Mrs. Mumford
[Mountfort] is so discreet."

PETTY, MRS. (Duke's and United companies, 1676–83).
According to John Aubrey (*Brief Lives*, ed. Andrew Clark
[2 vols., 1898], II, 143), Mrs. Petty was the illegitimate
daughter of the famous virtuoso, Sir William Petty: "He
has a naturall daughter that much resembles him, no legitimate child so much, that acts at the Duke's play-house, who

hath had a child by ——— about 1679. She is [1680] about 21." If Mrs. Petty was born in 1659, she would have been seventeen when she played her first known role, Dorinda, a young nymph, in Settle's *Pastor Fido*, ca. December, 1676. Probably she was much younger. Settle confessed in his Epistle Dedicatory that the character of Dorinda "was made up new to fit it for the person design'd to Act it," and the play has several references to Dorinda's extreme youth. Six years later, in the epilogue to Behn's *Like Father, like Son*, March, 1682, the comedian Jevon says:

> Here Mistris Petty, Hah! she's grown a very Woman,
> Thou'st got me Child, better me than no Man.

After her first appearance Mrs. Petty seems to have left the stage for five years, perhaps being kept by the unknown by whom she had a child in 1679. She returned to the Duke's Theatre to play Clara in Behn's *The False Count*, November, 1681; Peggy, a young wife, and the epilogue with others in Ravenscroft's *The London Cuckolds*, November, 1681; Philipa, a breeches part, in D'Urfey's *The Royalist*, January, 1682; Lady Diana Talbot in Banks's *Vertue Betray'd*, April, 1682; and Lady Rich (described as "a great Beauty, a delicate Brown") in Ravenscroft's *Dame Dobson*, June, 1683.

The author of "A Satyr on the Players," complained:

> What is't, a Pox makes Petty seem to be
> Of so demure, pretended Modesty
> When 'tis apparent she'l in private prove
> As Impudent, as any Punk of Love?
> Strangers she fears, so cares not much to roam
> While she can have a Sharers pr——k at home.

PRATT, MRS. (King's Company, 1671). Mrs. Pratt played the role of Sophia, a mother, in Corye's *The Generous Enemies*, ca. July, 1671.

PRICE, MRS. (Duke's and United Companies, 1678–86). Mrs. Price played only minor or secondary roles: Lucretia in Behn's *Sir Patient Fancy*, January, 1678; Camilla in Otway's *Friendship in Fashion*, April, 1678; Violante in Leanerd's *The Counterfeits*, May, 1678; Christina, the second lead, in

D'Urfey's *Squire Oldsapp*, ca. June, 1678; Helena in Banks's *The Destruction of Troy*, November, 1678; Adorna, the second lead, in Lee's *Caesar Borgia*, September, 1679; Edraste, a breeches part, in Tate's *The Loyal General*, ca. December, 1679; Sylvia in Otway's *The Souldiers Fortune*, March, 1680; Diana, the second lead, in Behn's *The Revenge*, ca. June, 1680; and Pricilla in *Mr. Turbulent* (Anon.), January, 1682.

With the union of the two companies Mrs. Price disappeared for a time, returning to play even smaller parts: Winifred in Tate's *Cuckolds-Haven*, ca. June, 1685; Hippolita, an Amazon, in D'Urfey's *A Commonwealth of Women*, ca. August, 1685; and Jane, a maid servant, in Jevon's *The Devil of a Wife*, March, 1686.

As Sylvia in Otway's *The Souldiers Fortune*, Mrs. Price was particularly described by Sir Jolly (Act IV, scene 1): "Light Brown Hair, her face oval and Roman, quick sparkling Eyes, plump pregnant ruby lips, with a Mole on her Breast, and the perfect likeness of a Heart-Cherry on her left Knee."

QUIN, MRS. See Marshall, Anne.

REEVES, ANNE. (King's Company, 1670–72). Although Downes says that Mrs. Reeves was one of those who joined the King's Company "some few Years after" 1660, her first known role was the tiny part of Esperanza in Dryden's *Conquest of Granada*, December, 1670–January, 1671, and there is no record of her on the stage before that date. Not long after her first appearance contemporary gossip identified her as Dryden's mistress, and his favor is supposed to have helped her to the few small roles she played. In Buckingham's *The Rehearsal*, December, 1671, there is a coarse allusion to the liaison of Bayes (Dryden) and Amaryllis (Mrs. Reeves) (see Buckingham's *Works* [1705], I, p. 2). If Mrs. Reeves was indeed Dryden's mistress, he does not seem to have been overly generous. On January 9, 1672, Elizabeth Bracy petitioned against "Mʳˢ Anne Reeves Comoedian" for a debt of £4 10*s.* for clothes (LC 5, 14, p. 132).

Dressed in man's clothes, Mrs. Reeves spoke the epilogue

to a revival of Dryden's *Secret Love*, "acted all by women," in the spring of 1672 (Thorn-Drury, p. 2). She played Philotis, a witty waiting woman, in Dryden's *Marriage A-la-Mode*, ca. April, 1672, and Ascanio, a page, a breeches part, in Dryden's *The Assignation*, ca. November, 1672. Thereafter she disappeared. According to the gossips she entered a foreign nunnery (see Rochester's *A Session of the Poets*, ca. 1676; the prologue to *Everyman Out of his Humour* [July, 1675], in Duffett's *New Poems* [1676], p. 73; and the epilogue to Otway's *Don Carlos*, June, 1676).

Writing in *The Gentleman's Magazine* in February, 1745 (XV, 99), a garrulous old gentleman asserted, "I remember plain John Dryden (before he paid his court with success to the great) in one uniform cloathing of Norwich drugget. I have eat tarts with him and Madam Reeve at the Mulberry-Garden, when our author advanced to a sword, and chadreux wig. . . . " Mr. Clifford Leech believes the writer of this letter to have been Dryden's friend, the dramatist Thomas Southerne (*Notes and Queries*, CLXIV [June 10, 1933], 401–3).

The "Mr. Reeve" mentioned by Downes (p. 2) as one of four who were "Bred up from Boys" in the King's Company and who later played a role in a revival of Jonson's *Catiline*, December, 1668, may have been Anne's brother.

ROCH, MRS. (King's Company, 1676). The prologue to Lee's *Gloriana*, January, 1676, was spoken by "Mrs. Roch"; she seems to have been impressed into service for this occasion only. Probably this was "Madam Le Roch" (or La Roche-Guilhen), a French singer and composer attached to the King's Company (Nicoll, p. 355).

RUSSELL, JANE (King's Company, 1663). Mrs. Russell's name appears only in the list of "Women Comoedians" for the autumn of 1663.

RUTTER, MARGARET (King's Company, 1661–77). Although Downes asserts that Mrs. Rutter was one of those who "came into the Company some few Years after" 1660, she was cast by Flecknoe as the Duchess of Missena in his then unacted *Erminia* (8vo, 1661); therefore she must have been one of the earliest members of the company. In early revivals of old plays (ca. 1661) she is listed by Downes for the roles of Dame Plyant in Jonson's *The Alchemist*, Martha in Beaumont and Fletcher's *The Scornful Lady*, the Lady in Fletcher's *The Elder Brother*, and Emilia in *Othello*. Probably she was the "Mrs. Marg^t^" who played Mrs. Mopus in Wilson's *The Cheats*, March, 1663 (Nahm, p. 62). Her name appears in the Lord Chamberlain's list of actors, autumn, 1663. She was named also in all four of the Lord Chamberlain's livery warrants, 1666–69.

Mrs. Rutter played Olinda ("tall, and fair, and bonny") in Dryden's *Secret Love*, February, 1667. On December 4, 1667, John Humphreyes petitioned against her for a debt of £9 (LC 5, 186, p. 186). Flecknoe cast her as "Isabella, a Witty Damoiselle" in his then unacted *The Damoiselles à la Mode*, September, 1668 (4to, 1667). She played Mrs. Crossbite in Wycherley's *Love in a Wood*, ca. March, 1671. On July 1, 1671, Humphrey Weld petitioned against her for a debt of £200 (LC 5, 14, p. 30). She played Emilia in a revival of *Othello*, 1674 (4to, 1687); Old Lady Squeamish in Wycherley's *The Country Wife*, January, 1675; Princess Wou'hamore in Duffett's *Psyche Debauch'd*, ca. May, 1675; Lady Malory in Leanerd's *The Country Innocence*, ca. March, 1677; and Alicia in Ravenscroft's *King Edgar and Alfreda*, ca. October, 1677.

A quatrain in "The Session of the Poets. To the Tune of Cook-Lawrel" (ca. 1665, Dryden's *Miscellany Poems* [1716], Part II, p. 91) suggests that Mrs. Rutter's morals were not above reproach:

> Humorous Weeden came in a pet,
>   And for the Laurel began to splutter;
> But Apollo chid him, and bid him first get
>   A Muse not so common as Mrs. Rutter.

SAUNDERSON, MARY. See Betterton, Mary.

SEYMOUR, MRS. (Duke's Company, 1677–79). Mrs. Seymour played several very minor roles: Parisatis in Pordage's *The Siege of Babylon*, ca. September, 1677; Thais, a whore, in Shadwell's *Timon of Athens*, ca. January, 1678; Lettice, a maid servant, in Otway's *Friendship in Fashion*, April, 1678; Lucinda in D'Urfey's *Squire Oldsapp*, ca. June, 1678; Sabina, a confidante, in Behn's *The Feign'd Curtezans*, ca. March, 1679; and Lidia in D'Urfey's *The Virtuous Wife*, ca. September, 1679.

SHADWELL, ANNE, nee *GIBBS* (Duke's Company, 1661–81). According to Downes "Mrs. Ann Gibbs" was one of Davenant's original actresses. She was the daughter of Thomas Gibbs, Norwich proctor and public notary. Between 1663 and 1667 she married the dramatist, Thomas Shadwell (see A. S. Borgman, *Thomas Shadwell* [1928]).

As Mrs. Gibbs she played Olivia in *Twelfth Night*, 1661 (Downes, p. 23); Mrs. Lucia in Cowley's *Cutter of Coleman Street*, December, 1661 (Downes, p. 25); Gertrude in *Hamlet*, ca. 1662, probably succeeding Hester Davenport (Downes, p. 21; 4to, 1683); and Decio (Ericina), a breeches part, and the epilogue in Stapylton's *The Slighted Maid*, February, 1663.

As Mrs. Shadwell she played Heraclia (succeeding Mrs. Betterton) in Davenant's *The Rivals*, ca. 1664 (4to, 1668); Cleora, an attendant, in Boyle's *Mustapha*, April, 1665 (4to., 1668); Lady Cockwood in Etherege's *She Wou'd If She Cou'd*, February, 1668 (Downes, p. 29); Emilia in Shadwell's *The Sullen Lovers*, May, 1668 (Downes, p. 29); Clarina ("a pretty, black-ey'd rogue") in E. Howard's *The Womens Conquest*, ca. November, 1670; Celinda, a second lead, in E. Howard's *The Six Days Adventure*, ca. March, 1671; Joanna, a breeches part, in Crowne's *Juliana*, August, 1671; Irene in Crowne's *History of Charles the Eighth*, November, 1671; Caelia, the lead, in Payne's *The Fatal Jealousy*, August, 1672; Rose, a breeches part, in Payne's *The Morning Ramble*, November, 1672; Lucia in Shadwell's *Epsom Wells*, December, 1672 ("Mrs. Gibbs" [Downes, p. 23]); and Julia in a revival of *The Duchess of Malfi*, ca. 1673 (4to, 1678).

Mrs. Shadwell seems to have left the stage for two or three years at about this time. Her next roles were: the Duchess of Eboli in Otway's *Don Carlos*, June, 1676; Melissa, a

coquette, in Shadwell's *Timon of Athens*, ca. January, 1678;
Lucinda in Maidwell's *The Loving Enemies*, ca. March, 1680;
and Goneril in Tate's *King Lear*, ca. March, 1681.

Shadwell died November 19, 1692. His widow was still
living in 1709 (Fitzgerald, I, 271). She seems to have been a
competent actress and an exemplary wife and mother. The
only mention of her in contemporary lampoons is an ill-
natured slur at possible youthful follies in "A Satyr on the
Players":

> . . . antiquated Shadwell swears in Rage,
> She knows not what's the Lewdness of ye Stage:
> And I believe her, now her days are past,
> Who'd tempt a Wretch, that on meer force is Chast?
> Yet in her Youth, none was a greater Whore
> Her Lumpish Husband Og can tell you more.

SLADE, ELIZABETH (King's Company, 1668–75). Mrs.
Slade has been given undue eminence by an often quoted
reminiscent poem in *The Gentleman's Magazine* (XV [Febru-
ary, 1745], 99) which ended with the lines:

> . . . and think again
> Of Hart, of Mohun, and all the female train,
> Coxe, Marshall, Dryden's Reeve,
> Bet. Slade, and Charles's reign.

To this the editor added notes on the ladies mentioned, describing Betty Slade as "The sly servant-maid actress of
those days," as if she had been famous.

As a matter of fact, Mrs. Slade played few roles and none
of importance. She played Camilla, a waiting woman, in
Dryden's *An Evening's Love*, June, 1668; Lucy, Dapperwit's
wench, in Wycherley's *Love in a Wood*, ca. March, 1671;
Beliza, a singing waiting woman, in Dryden's *Marriage A-la-
Mode*, ca. April, 1672; and Melinda, a supporting role, in
Fane's *Love in the Dark*, May, 1675.

On November 25, 1675, for an unknown reason, the Lord
Chamberlain sent Killigrew the following order: "These are
to require you not to suffer Elizabeth Slade to Act at His

Maties Theatre or to receive any allowances or proffitts thence untill you receive further order from mee" (LC 5, 141, p. 294). No further order is recorded.

SLAUGHTER, MRS. (Duke's Company, 1671). According to Downes (p. 35) Mrs. Slaughter was one of those who joined the Duke's Company about 1673. However, she has only one role to her credit, that of Cornelia, the exiled Queen of Cyprus, in Crowne's *History of Charles the Eighth*, November, 1671. Summers (Downes, p. 222) agrees with Genest that in all probability she became Mrs. Osborn (q.v.) by marriage. If so, it is surprising indeed that Downes would have remembered her only by her maiden name.

SLINGSBY, LADY. See Lee, Mary.

SPENCER, MRS. (Duke's Company, 1673–75). Mrs. Spencer spoke the epilogue to Pordage's *Herod and Mariamne*, October, 1673, and created the role of Vangona, a breeches part, in Settle's *The Conquest of China*, May, 1675.

TWYFORD, MRS. (Duke's and United companies, 1676–86). Downes (p. 35) lists Mrs. Twyford (or Twiford) among those who joined the Duke's Company around 1673. Her first known role was Emilia in Etherege's *The Man of Mode*, March, 1676 (Downes, p. 36). She played, next, Princess Osmida in C. Davenant's *Circe*, May, 1677 (Downes, p. 36). After this she seems to have left the stage for some years. She joined the United Company to play Aurelia in D'Urfey's *The Royalist*, January, 1682; Beatrice, a servant, in Ravenscroft's *Dame Dobson*, June, 1683; Flametta in Tate's *A Duke and No Duke*, November, 1684; Mildred in Tate's *Cuckolds-Haven*, ca. June, 1685; Menalippe, an Amazon, in D'Urfey's *A Commonwealth of Women*, ca. August, 1685; Christina in D'Urfey's *The Banditti*, February, 1686; and Lettice, a maid, in Jevon's *The Devil of a Wife*, March, 1686.

Mrs. Twyford was an undistinguished performer of secondary roles. She attracted the attention of the author of "A Satyr on the Players," who wrote:

> Once Twyford had som modesty but she
> Her Husband being close in Custody
> Wou'd be unkind to let him famish there
> So F——ks for Guineas, to provide him Fare.

Collier quotes (as he put it) three stanzas from "a ballad in my possession thus entitled—'A new ballad, shewing how one Tim Twyford, a player of the King's Company was carried to the Marshalsea for money he owed to his laundress, and what he did there.' 1674":

> Beware, ye players all, beware
>   Of poor Tim Twyford's fate,
> And learn to live upon your share,
>   Although it be not great.
>
> For players, too, must pay their debts,
>   Or in cold prison lie,
> At which each proud stage-strutter frets,
>   And some do almost cry.
>
> No longer can they strut and huff,
>   Though once they could do so,
> And smooth or rough, they get enough
>   To pay the debt they owe.

Collier's forgeries are so numerous that one hesitates to accept this ballad as genuine. Moreover there are no records of a Timothy Twyford on the Restoration stage. On the other hand, Collier seems never to have seen "A Satyr on the Players" and knew of Mrs. Twyford only as an actress with the Duke's Company. The dates, too, fit well enough. If Twyford had been a very minor actor imprisoned for debt in 1673 or 1674, his wife, deprived of his support, might well have chosen a theatrical career right after her husband went to prison. That she would still be contributing to his maintenance ten years later is surprising but not unlikely.

Coincidentally, we must point out that a Timothy Twyford was a rather unsuccessful publisher with a shop "within the Inner-Temple-Gate" in the early years of the Restoration. He published Stapylton's *The Step-Mother* in 1664.

UPHILL, SUSANNA (King's Company, 1669–75). Although Downes listed her as one of Killigrew's original ac-

tresses, there is no record of Mrs. Uphill as a player until
1669, when she played the very small role of Erotion, an
attendant, in Dryden's *Tyrannick Love*, June, 1669. The fact
that her name does not appear in the livery warrant for
October 2, 1669, suggests that she may have been still on
probation. Her next role was the small part of Livia, a waiting woman, in Corye's *The Generous Enemies*, ca. July, 1671.
Thereafter she played Artemis in Dryden's *Marriage A-la-
Mode*, ca. April, 1672; Rosella in Duffett's *The Spanish
Rogue*, March, 1673; Syllana ("Mrs. Uptiel") in Lee's *Nero*,
May, 1674; Parhelia in Fane's *Love in the Dark*, May, 1675;
and Zayda in Dryden's *Aurenge-Zebe*, November, 1675. Of
these only Rosella and Parhelia were major roles.

Mrs. Uphill seems to have been both popular and promis-
cuous. Fane (p. 362) repeats a contemporary quip: "Sr Oliver
Butler sade to Sr Tho: Stiles betweene you and I neighbour
Mrs Uphil is with child." According to a newsletter dated
August 30, 1675 (*HMC*, *Seventh Report*, p. 465), "Mrs. Up-
hill, the player" had come into the Duke's Theatre, masked.
One Mr. Scrope (younger brother of Sir Carr Scrope, or
Scroope) "would have entertained discourse with her, which
Sir T[homas] Armstrong would not suffer, so a ring was made
wherin they fought." Scrope was killed. This may be the
event referred to by Robert Gould. Discussing the arts of
the actress backstage, he wrote:

> But talking of their shifts I morn my freind,
> I mourn thy sad, unjust, disastrous end.
> Here 'twas thou didst resign thy worthy breath,
> And fell the victim of a suddain death;
> The shame the guilt the horrour & disgrace,
> Light on the Punk, the murdrer & the place.

Mrs. Uphill seems to have left the stage to become Sir
Robert Howard's mistress. In *A Seasonable Argument To
Persuade All the Grand Juries in England To Petition for a
New Parliament* (1677), we are told that Sir Robert has had
"many great Places and Boons . . . but his W—— Uphill
spends all and now refuses to marry him," and in a discussion
of the Howard brothers and their mistresses in "Satyr on
both Whigs and Toryes. 1683," the phrase, "Sr Pos's comon

Jade," seems to refer to Mrs. Uphill. Sir Robert was the original of Shadwell's Sir Positive At-all in *The Sullen Lovers*, 1668.

Sir Robert Howard, who had been a widower since September, 1676, probably married, as his third wife, Mary Uphill, who may have been a kinswoman of the actress. For discussions of this and the identity of "his W—— Uphill" see *Notes and Queries*, CLXXXVII (December, 1944), 281; *Notes and Queries*, CLXXXVIII (November, 1945), 61; and *Notes and Queries*, CXCII (July and October, 1947), 314, 445.

VERBRUGGEN, MRS. See Percival, Susanna.

VERJUICE, MRS. (King's Company). Although mentioned by Downes as one of those who joined the King's Company some few years after its organization, Mrs. Verjuice has left no record of her existence.

VINCENT, MRS. (King's Company, 1677). Mrs. Vincent seems to have played only Aurelia, the lead, in Ravenscroft's farce, *Scaramouche*, May, 1677.

WEAVER, Mrs. See Farley, Elizabeth.

WILLIAMS, MRS. (Duke's Company, 1663). Mrs. Williams, evidently one of Davenant's earliest actresses, played the supporting roles of Leandra in Stapylton's *The Slighted Maid*, February, 1663, and Pontia, the stepmother, in Stapylton's *The Step-Mother*, ca. November, 1663.

WISEMAN, MRS. (Duke's Company). According to Downes (p. 26) the part of Roxalana in Boyle's *Mustapha*, April, 1665, was originally played by Mrs. Davenport, later by Mrs. Betterton, "and then [perhaps after Mrs. Betterton's retirement] by one Mrs. Wiseman." Nothing else is known about this lady. Genest (II, 258) suggests that she might have been Jane Wiseman, author of *Antiochus the Great*, 1702.

WRIGHT, MRS. (Duke's Company, 1670). Mrs. Wright was only briefly on the stage, playing the tiny part of Renone, an Amazon ambassadress in E. Howard's *The Womens Conquest*, ca. November, 1670, and the supporting role of Aminta in Behn's *The Forc'd Marriage*, ca. December, 1670. It is likely that she was the Mrs. Wright referred to by Etherege (p. 117) when he wrote on November 11/21, 1686, of a comedienne in a troupe newly arrived at Ratisbon as being "as handsome at least as the Fair Maid of the West which you have seen at Newmarket and makes as much noise in this little town, and gives as much jealousies to the ladies as ever Mrs. Wright or Mrs. Johnson did in London."

The "Henry Wright Comoedian" who was petitioned against on February 25, 1678, for a debt of £4 by Eliz. Colbelt may have been Mrs. Wright's husband (LC 5, 191, p. 10).

WYATT, MRS. (King's Company, 1675). Mrs. Wyatt's name is attached to only one role, Mrs. Squeamish in Wycherley's *The Country Wife*, January, 1675.

WYN, MRS. See Marshall, Anne.

YATES, MRS. (King's Company, 1666–67). On September 9, 1667, Killigrew told Pepys that he now had "the best musick in England . . . that is two Italians and Mrs. Yates," who "is come to sing the Italian manner as well as ever he heard any." Mrs. Yates is listed in the livery warrant for June 30, 1666, but in no dramatis personae. Probably she was a singer only.

YOUCKNEY, ELIZABETH (King's Company, 1669–70). "Mrs. Yackley" is listed in the livery warrant for October 2, 1669. "Mrs. Yockney" played a small part (perhaps Francescina) in a revival of Shirley's *The Sisters* in 1669 (Montague Summers, *Essays in Petto* [1928], pp. 103–10). On November 3, 1670, Henry New petitioned against "Mrs. Elisabeth Youckney Comoedian" for a debt of £30 (LC 5, 188, p. 45). Nothing more is known about this undistinguished actress. One William Youckney or Yockney seems to have been a Court Musician in Ordinary from about 1662 to 1672 (LC 5, 137, p. 277; LC 5, 140, p. 78).

Appendix B. Records Frequently Cited

I. John Downes, *Roscius Anglicanus* (1708), ed. Montague Summers (1928).

   A. Pp. 2–3: "His Majesty's Company of Comedians" (ca. October, 1660–April, 1663):

WOMEN

Mrs. Corey	Note, these following
Mrs. Ann Marshall	came into the Company
Mrs. Eastland	some few Years after.
Mrs. Weaver	Mrs. Boutel
Mrs. Uphill	Mrs. Ellin Gwyn
Mrs. Knep	Mrs. James
Mrs. Hughs	Mrs. Rebecca Marshall
	Mrs. Rutter
	Mrs. Verjuice
	Mrs. Reeves

The Company being thus Compleat, they open'd the New Theatre in Drury-Lane, on Thursday in Easter Week, being the 8th, Day of April 1663, with the Humorous Lieutenant.

   B. P. 20: The Company formed "to serve his Royal Highness the Duke of York" (ca. October, 1660–spring, 1662):

Sir William Davenant's Women Actresses were,
   Note, These Four being his Principal Actresses, he Boarded them at his own House.

Mrs. Davenport	Mrs. Davies
Mrs. Saunderson	Mrs. Long
Mrs. Ann Gibbs	Mrs. Holden
Mrs. Norris	Mrs. Jennings

II. E. S. De Beer, "A List of the Department of the Lord Chamberlain of the Household, Autumn, 1663," *Bulletin of the Institute of Historical Research*, XIX (November 1941), 13–24.
A. P. 24: "Actors or Comoedians":

WOMEN COMOEDIANS [King's Company]

Mrs. Jane Russell	Mrs. Mary Man
Mrs. Anne Marshall	Mrs. Katherine Mitchell
Mrs. Rebecka Marshall	Mrs. Margaret Rutter
Mrs. Eliz: Farley	Mrs. Eastland

III. Livery warrants in the Lord Chamberlain's Records, Public Record Office, London.
A. June 30, 1666:

A warrant to provide and deliver to Mrs. Weaver Mrs. Marshall Mrs. Rutter Mrs. Yates Mrs. Nepp Mrs. Dalton Ellen Gwyn Eliz: Hall ffrancis Davenport and Anne Child Women Comoedians in his Maties Theatre Royall unto each of them foure yards of bastard scarlet cloath and one quarter of a yard of velvett for their liveryes for this present yeare 1666. [LC 5, 138, p. 71].

B. July 22, 1667: Similar warrant to

Mrs. Quin Mrs. Marshall Mrs. Corey Mrs. Rutter Mrs. Gwyn Mrs. Nepe Mrs. Francis Davenport Mrs. Elizabeth Davenport Mrs. Jaine Davenport [LC 5, 62, p. 1].

C. February 8, 667/8 (July 22 crossed out): Similar warrant to

Mrs. Quinn   Mrs. Cory
~~Mrs. Weaver~~ Mrs. Marshall Mrs. Rutter ~~Mrs. Yates~~ Mrs. Nep ~~Mrs. Dalton~~ Ellen Gwyn ~~Elizabeth Hall~~ ffrancis Davenport [in margin "Elizabeth & Jane"] & ~~Anne Child~~ [LC 5, 138, p. 271].

D. October 2, 1669: Similar warrant to

Mrs. Marshall Mrs. Cory Mrs. Ellen Guynn Mrs. Kneepe Mrs. Rutter Mrs. Hues Mrs. Davenport and Mrs. Yackley [LC 5, 62, p. 107].

References

ASTON, ANTHONY. "A Brief Supplement," in Colley Cibber's *Apology for the Life of Mr. Colley Cibber*, ed. R. W. LOWE, II, 297–318. 1889.

BORGMAN, A. S. *The Life and Death of William Mountfort*. 1935.

BROWN, THOMAS. *The Works of Mr. Thomas Brown*. 4 vols. 1720.

CHETWOOD, W. R. *A General History of the Stage*. 1749.

"Choyce Collection, A." Manuscript in the Ohio State University Library, Columbus, Ohio.

CIBBER, COLLEY. *An Apology for the Life of Mr. Colley Cibber*, ed. R. W. LOWE. 2 vols. 1889.

COLLIER, JOHN PAYNE. "History of the British Stage." Manuscript in the Harvard College Library, Cambridge, Mass.

CSPD. *Calendars of State Papers Domestic*.

CURLL, EDMUND. *Betterton's History of the English Stage*. 1741.

DAVIES, THOMAS. *Dramatic Miscellanies*. 3 vols. 1784.

DOWNES, JOHN. *Roscius Anglicanus; or, An Historical Review of the Stage* (1708), ed. MONTAGUE SUMMERS. 1928.

ETHEREGE, SIR GEORGE. *The Letterbook of Sir George Etherege*, ed. SYBIL ROSENFELD. 1928.

EVELYN, JOHN. *The Diary and Correspondence of John Evelyn*, ed. WILLIAM BRAY. n.d.

FANE, SIR FRANCIS. "Commonplace Book." Manuscript in the Shakespeare Memorial Library, Stratford-on-Avon.

FITZGERALD, PERCY. *A New History of the English Stage*. 2 vols. 1882.

GENEST, JOHN. *Some Account of the English Stage*. 10 vols. 1832.

GILDON, CHARLES. *The Life of Mr. Thomas Betterton.* 1710.

GOULD, ROBERT. "The Playhouse. A Satyr." British Museum Additional MS. 30, 492.

GRAMMONT. *Memoirs of Count Grammont,* by ANTHONY HAMILTON, ed. GORDON GOODWIN. 2 vols. 1903.

HMC. Appendices to the Reports of the Royal Commission on Historical Manuscripts.

HOTSON, LESLIE. *The Commonwealth and Restoration Stage.* 1928.

"Lampoons." Ca. 1678. Harvard MS. Eng. 636 F., Harvard College Library, Cambridge, Mass.

LC. Lord Chamberlain's Records, Public Record Office, London.

MALONE, EDMUND. *The Plays and Poems of Shakespeare,* Vol. I. 1730.

NAHM, H. C. (ed.). *John Wilson's "The Cheats."* 1935.

NICOLL, ALLARDYCE. *A History of Restoration Drama: 1660–1700.* 4th ed. 1952.

OLDYS, WILLIAM. Manuscript notes to Gerard Langbaine, *An Account of the English Dramatick Poets.* 1691. British Museum.

PEPYS, SAMUEL. *The Diary of Samuel Pepys,* ed. HENRY B. WHEATLEY. 6 vols. 1893.

RYAN, RICHARD. *Dramatic Table Talk.* 3 vols. 1825.

"Satyr on both Whigs and Toryes. 1683." British Museum, Harleian MS. 7319.

"Satyr on the Players, A." Ca. 1684. British Museum, Harleian MS. 7319.

"Session of the Ladies, The. 1688." British Museum, Harleian MS. 7317.

SP. State Papers. Public Record Office, London.

THORN-DRURY, G. (ed.). *Covent Garden Drollery* (1672). 1929.

VAN LENNEP, WILLIAM. "Thomas Killigrew Prepares His Plays for Production," in *Joseph Quincy Adams: Memorial Studies,* ed. JAMES G. MCMANAWAY *et al.,* pp. 803–8. 1948.

WELLS, STARING B. (ed.). *A Comparison between the Two Stages.* 1942.

WILEY, AUTREY NELL. *Rare Prologues and Epilogues: 1642–1700.* 1940.

WOOD, ANTHONY. *The Life and Times of Anthony Wood,* ed. ANDREW H. CLARK, 5 vols. 1891–1900.

Index

PRINTED IN U.S.A.